Dumbfounded

Dumbfounded

A memoir

Matt Rothschild

 Crown Publishers / New York

Published in the United States by Crown Publishers, an imprint of the Crown
Publishing Group, a division of Random House, Inc., New York.
www.crownpublishing.com

CROWN and the Crown colophon are registered trademarks of
Random House, Inc.

Library of Congress Cataloging-in-Publication Data
Rothschild, Matt.
Dumbfounded: a memoir / Matt Rothschild.
1. Rothschild, Matt.   2. Rothschild, Matt—Family.   3. Rothschild, Matt—
Childhood and youth.   4. Jews—New York (State)—New York—Biography.
5. Grandparent and child.   I. Title.
F128.9.J5R68   2008
974.7'10049240092—dc22
[B]   2008002947

ISBN 978-0-307-40542-5

Printed in the United States of America

Design by Lauren Dong

10 9 8 7 6 5 4 3 2 1

First Edition

For my grandparents. It's just a book. Relax.

acknowledgments

So this is the part of the acknowledgments page where I'd thank all of the cool fellowships I haven't earned. I'd thank the Guggenheim and the NEA and the Mr. and Mrs. Somebody-or-Other. I really can't be bitter about not having earned anything since I haven't applied for anything. By the time this book arrives in paperback I will have applied and then I'll update this paragraph.

This is the part where I'd thank all of the editors of the various magazines—large and small, I'm no snob—who have supported my career by giving me jobs and publishing my work. Well, there is none, so I can't thank them. I'm optimistic, though. So if you're at a major magazine and you read this, please know that I'm available for hire. I'll be very thankful and acknowledge you if you do.

Which leaves everyone else. Let's see if I can't ostracize myself further from my friends . . .

Chronologically, I need to thank the Gordons first. They showed me what a family is *supposed* to look like and invited me into their lives, even giving me a couple of jobs here and there.

In terms of this book and of my writing in general, I'd like to thank Rebecca first. It was she who took the original draft of this book and a red pen and started asking the questions that led me to keep writing after I'd been so discouraged. And then she stuck by me through this whole process. Honestly, she's read this book like forty-five thousand times and still laughs and returns my phone calls.

I am also deeply indebted to my Friday-night writing group—Fran, Bettie, Doug, Kevin, LaRita, Ashley, Kathleen, and Valerie—whose support and interest have proven invaluable and inspiring.

Then to my wonderful agent, Daniel Lazar at Writers House, who, although he'd never admit it, never saw this day happening in a million years when we met at JQY in 2002. It was Dan who busted my ass in the beginning and whose tireless spirit and enthusiasm made the process bearable until . . .

Until February 21, 2007, when the wonderful Heather ran into Allison's office and told her to put down whatever rubbish she had been reading and handed her my chapters. And finally to Allison, who, on February 28, 2007, picked me out of a lineup and said, "Yes, he'll do." She took a chance on me and rewarded my efforts with substantially more than the "bag of Doritos" I said I'd sell my work for. The rest, as they say, is history that will hopefully be studied by scholars for hundreds of years at Yale.

I'll tell you the truth, but only this once and only because it's you. I don't always make the best first impressions, and I don't want to start our friendship off on the wrong foot. You've read these author's notes before, but mine is different. It's special. I'm not going to feed you that same old baloney about how memory is imperfect and we're all ships passing in the night and perception is reality. No. The truth is that while everything in this book happened, it didn't always happen the way I say it did. You see, I've changed things. I had to do it. Sometimes I changed names or descriptions of people and places. Big deal. But . . . sometimes I altered chronology, created composite characters or places, made people look foolish when they weren't so foolish, made people look good when they were fools, compressed events, and—I know you'll love this one—said things happened in one place when they really happened somewhere else. Okay, so maybe that is a big deal. But I want you to know I had my reasons. There was the obvious reason (to protect people's privacy) but other times I changed things because—God help me—I thought it was the right thing to do. You should know that about me before going on. I always do the right thing in the end, and that's why I had to tell you all this before you read on. I can tell you this, though: Nothing I've changed really affects the truth of the story itself. So if it were me, and I were you, I would keep reading. Some of this stuff is damn funny and some of it's tragic. Just don't take the window dressing too literally.

contents

Dumbfounded

one

Why I Don't Believe in Santa Claus

My grandfather was a grand storyteller, but you could not count on him for accuracy. As far as he was concerned, it was the *point* of the story that mattered—that is, when he remembered the point he was trying to make. And when my grandmother, who hated cigars and had limited patience for my grandfather's story-telling, was out of the house, he'd light up a good Cuban, settle into his favorite leather chair, and launch into a tale so contrived it would make the Brothers Grimm blush.

"When I was a little boy in Paris . . ." he would begin.

"I thought it was Vienna."

"Don't interrupt, Matthew. Now. When I was a little boy in Vienna . . ."

My grandfather came to the United States sometime before World War II. He arrived from either France or Austria, wherever he felt like telling me at a given time. This was a man who knew five languages, and if he didn't like what you had to say in English, he began speaking another language. Then he would shake his head, wide-eyed and innocent, pretending he couldn't understand you. Rarely seen without a smile, my grandfather was always quick to tell a story—it was just the truth that gave him trouble.

Personally, I didn't care that his stories weren't always true. When he told a story, it was him and me, alone. My grandmother wasn't invited. She would just make fun of us, anyway. Now that I was seven years old—almost eight, really—this was the only time it didn't feel awkward to climb into his lap and play with his arm hair. I liked to make mountains by pulling on the hairs as I listened to him reinvent his childhood. My grandfather was a retired diplomat, and he often said, "World leaders could forget their differences, I'm sure, if they'd just listen to a few good stories." Presumably, the underlying moral of his tales would make them see the error of their ways while showing them how much they had in common. I didn't know what a diplomat was, but if they got to tell stories and have their pictures taken with famous people, the way my grandfather did, this is what I wanted to do as well. They also got expensive gifts from people, and I loved presents.

I devoured his stories voraciously. I thought that if I learned to tell stories the way my grandfather did, I might be as successful as he was. But despite all his success, I knew there was one leader his stories failed to work on: my grandmother.

"Listen here, snail eater," she'd say, materializing out of nowhere, shiny silver hair falling down to her chin, and pointing a well-manicured finger at my grandfather. "Maybe they're hot on having cigar butts litter the floors of Paris, but I don't want that shit in my house. Take it to the curb."

My grandfather would mumble about how it was really his house and everyone else was just a guest—after almost fifty years of marriage, my grandfather was still trying to assert his dominance over his castle, but he never did get it quite right. So, indignantly, he finished his story—cigar defiantly lit—from a bench in Central Park, across the street from our nineteen-room apartment. "Your house indeed," my grandmother would say, slamming the door behind us. My grandfather paid the rent, but we all knew who wore the pants in my family.

.   .   .   .

My grandfather was raised in a genteel, aristocratic Europe, where people politely disagreed over a friendly glass of absinthe. But my grandmother was born and raised in New York City, where every waking minute is a potential street fight. These two opposing figures stepped in to raise me after my own parents—who wished to remain children themselves—abandoned me when I was still a baby. My father disappeared altogether, never to be heard from again. And my mother, seeing her own parents' offer to raise me as an opportunity to reinvent herself as a party girl, hopped on a plane and flew to Europe without a backward glance. She called exactly four times a year—on birthdays and my grandparents' wedding anniversary— and did not visit New York again until I was ten years old.

My grandparents and I lived in Manhattan, on Fifth Avenue, the only Jews in our building. Jewish delicatessens and bakeries may punctuate every other block of New York City, but thirty years after my grandparents settled on the Upper East Side's Museum Mile— that glorious stretch of asphalt from 82nd Street to 105th—theirs was still the only Jewish name in the most exclusive building in the most exclusive neighborhood in one of the most exclusive cities in the world. "She threatened to tear someone's balls off, and they let her in," I heard people say behind my stylish, petite grandmother's back. But like so many half-truths, this, I learned, was an urban legend. The whole truth was far more typical of Old-Moneyed New York in the 1950s.

Old Money never allowed anti-Semitism to become advertised policy—it was just an unspoken rule. Review boards famously barred Greenbergs and Friedmans from inhabiting the same space as Rockefellers and Vanderbilts. Yet they compromised for my grandparents. Much later I would wonder what my grandparents compromised, in turn, to live within such gilded bigotry.

In order to live in this historic building, my grandparents must have jumped through some hoops, offered to play by someone else's rules, the most prominent of which was keep the Jewish thing quiet. For my grandfather this was no great compromise—he left religion when the world allowed Hitler to wipe out most of European Jewry. But my grandmother was a woman who thrived on being contrary. That's how I know it was my grandfather who pushed for his family to suck it up and live in that building. If his own family had lived among princes in Europe, why should they not live among them in America, too? My grandmother, the daughter of an affluent merchant, couldn't have cared less about living among those who sneered at her family's "new money," who blocked them from membership in every prestigious social club in New York City. But for my grandfather she agreed to live in a hotbed of Waspy prejudice. It was her way of telling him, "I love you."

When she made any kind of concession, however, she'd never let anyone forget it.

"Oh, no," my grandfather told our driver once, "this is the wrong car." It was late November—well after Labor Day—and we were on our way to dinner. The driver had pulled up in the white Rolls-Royce.

My grandmother, buttoning her coat, snorted. "Howard, shut the hell up. Just get in the car," she said, grabbing my hand.

"What will people think when they see us in the white?" he asked. My grandfather was always battling to earn some neighbor's respect, reassuring people they'd made the right decision letting *these* Jews in when they had rejected so many others. He had just as much, if not more, money than his neighbors did. He had finer clothes, better cars—he had everything they did, but still he was afraid of being seen as an outsider. He had massaged Old Money until it begrudgingly paid him attention, and he was determined not to make them regret it—but his wife often refused to cooperate.

"What do you expect him to do? Take the car back to the garage while Matthew and I just stand here?"

My grandfather was silent.

"It's bad enough that I have to live around a bunch of oil paintings in suits," she continued. I was seven years old when I realized she was referring to our neighbors, not actual paintings. "Now I have to freeze when there's a perfectly good heated car, just because it's after Labor Day."

I felt sorry for my grandfather, whose refined taste was obviously lost on my grandmother. She didn't understand the benefit of appearances. If she had her way, we would have sat at home eating

Kentucky Fried Chicken out of the bag instead of going to a fancy restaurant. She took off with great strides, dragging me toward the waiting car. "Oil paintings do not run our life!"

My grandfather knew she would leave him behind, so he huffed under his breath in French and got into the white car. And once we were on our way, she put her hand in his, and he squeezed it because—though he'd never admit it—he loved his wife even more than he loved his reputation.

.   .   .   .

My grandfather's preoccupation with the rules of our elitist surroundings was probably why our apartment was bare of the usual symbolism with which most Jewish people decorate their homes. There was no mezuzah to kiss upon entering the apartment, no "*shana tova*" cards on the fridge, no menorah to remind us of a miraculous history. All this makes me wonder now, if our neighbors didn't want us there, why was it so important for us to stay? Why did he care so much? My grandfather was something of a martyr in this way, which is great—in theory—but who wants to fight a cultural war in the elevator of an apartment building? Certainly not my grandmother. She stayed all those years on Fifth Avenue because of one proud Jewish characteristic: spite. For her, living on Museum Mile and raising hell was a constant reminder that she could not be ignored.

"Isn't my money just as good as theirs?" she'd ask whenever my grandfather would ask her to please behave in front of our neighbors.

"Sophie, it's *my* money," my grandfather would answer.

"What is this, the old country? What's yours is mine, and isn't my money good enough?"

It's strange to think my grandparents really believed that religion was the only thing separating us from our neighbors, because I wasn't told we were Jewish until I was in the second grade. And even then my grandparents only told me because I wanted to know why Santa never visited me but regularly made pilgrimages to all the other kids at school.

"Because you were bad," my grandmother explained. "Santa only visits good children."

Sarcasm was not something I understood. I was also more gullible than Hansel and Gretel then, and since I was often in trouble, I just nodded and took her word for it.

But my grandfather cleared his throat behind the *New York Times*.

"The cough drops are in the other room," my grandmother said, not looking up from her crossword puzzle.

He dropped the newspaper and glared at his wife.

My grandmother rolled her eyes and turned back to me. She sighed. "Matthew, Santa doesn't visit because we don't celebrate Christmas."

From what I heard, Christmas was an entire day devoted to presents, so why wouldn't we celebrate it? My friends said Santa brought them horses and toy cars and cashmere pea coats. I really wanted a horse like the one I saw on *Mister Ed,* and I thought this Santa might be just the man to provide it.

"We have Hanukkah," she said. "Don't be greedy."

Hanukkah? I thought. *I never get anything good on Hanukkah.*

"But why can't I have both?" I asked.

My grandmother was a woman who had an answer for every question. She looked at me and said, "Goddamn it, Matthew, ask your grandfather."

So I did. He put aside his newspaper, took off his glasses, and began explaining religion in a way that might appeal to a second-grader. "Christmas is the time when Christians celebrate the birth of Jesus. We don't celebrate Christmas because we're not Christian. We're *Jewish.*" He studied my face for a reaction.

I had no idea what he was talking about, so I nodded in agreement. He patted me on the head and returned to his newspaper. My grandmother, understanding that nothing had been accomplished, shook her head, and I walked back to my room, thinking, Who was Jesus? How was he related to Santa? Most important, where were my presents?

"This is all America's fault," I heard my grandfather say from the living room. "In France there is no Sandy Clause."

"In France," said my grandmother, "there are no Jews."

. . . .

I never knew any Jewish people in school, at least none who advertised it. My grandparents wanted me to have a well-rounded education, so they sent me to a school without religious affiliation. That was my grandmother's decision—my grandfather's only stipulation was that it be a school where the best families in New York sent their children. Since it was New York City in the 1980s, this basically meant I was a Jewish student receiving a Christian education from a secular school.

My first school was called the Briar Patch. Or the School of Happy Thoughts. Or something equally ridiculous. Like other schools on the Upper East Side, it created meaningless honors for the benefit of overeager parents who were petrified their kids wouldn't get accepted into the Ivy League universities. At my school the most prestigious of these honors was the much-coveted Student of the Month Award. It was supposed to go to one deserving student each month, but after the parents' organization threatened to cut their annual contribution to the endowment, Mr. Dennis ("Dennis the Menace" I heard some teachers call him), the headmaster, changed the rules. Now, instead of to one deserving student, the Student of the Month Award went to at least a dozen. This way all the students in the school got a shot, at least once a year, and all honorees were already on their way to the Ivies.

When my second-grade teacher placed my name on the long easel on December 1, it meant that it was finally my turn. This was big news. I was an only child, spoiled but craving more attention, and I was thrilled. After all, the lucky honoree got to wear a hat! And he or she was photographed! Sure the hat was made of construction paper—it looked more like a dunce cap than the Indian chief's hat it was intended to—but it would be *my* dunce cap. I would be the chief! Meanwhile, it goes without saying that if there were no obvious Jews at my school, there were certainly no Native Americans.

Student of the Month honorees were always announced on the first day of each month. Even so, I was surprised, ungroomed, and that day my unruly Jewfro was in rare form. My hair had a personality of its own, and after an exhaustive effort to fit the hat on, the teacher sighed. "Here," she said, handing me the cap. "Just hold it." Then I went down to Mr. Dennis's office to have my picture taken.

December was a particularly crowded time to be Student of the Month; there were at least twenty honorees in line for the photographs. Like sarcasm, standing in line was a concept I did not understand: My grandparents encouraged me to fight for my place at the movies and the ice-skating rink, so why was it any different at school? I once told my kindergarten teacher, "My grandfather says it's okay to arm wrestle for a place in line. He said it's better than pushing people out of the way like my grandmother does in department stores." When the teacher's face contorted in horror, I reassured her, "My grandmother says you have to muscle your way in because people on the Upper East Side will screw you however they can."

But that morning I was too excited to push in line, so I stood and fidgeted, anxiously awaiting my turn. I thought about how I would look in my picture and wondered if I would receive wallet-size prints for friends and family.

The other kids didn't seem as interested in their pictures, and their conversation focused on holiday plans.

"I hope Santa brings me a new horse this year. That last one hasn't won any competitions," said Colby Johnson, a girl from the third grade.

"Where are you spending Christmas this year, anyway?" asked her friend Margaret Vanderburg, who was always rubbing the fact that her father owned three planes in everybody's face.

"Barbados," said Colby with a tinge of pride. "We have a house there."

"Barbados?" Margaret pursed her lips and lifted her nose. "My mother says nobody's going to Barbados this year. That was *so* last year. We're taking *one* of our planes to Mustique."

Colby began to hyperventilate. "I hope we can still change our plans! Come over later and help me convince my mom."

Margaret placed her stubby, sausagelike fingers on Colby's arm. "You are so lucky you have me as your friend."

I kept my mouth shut and avoided eye contact. I worried that if the kids found out I didn't celebrate Christmas, they'd think I wasn't as good as they were. Not that anyone from the third grade would be caught dead talking to a second-grader. But what if someone *did* ask about my Christmas plans? I had none! What was I going to do—tell them about Hanukkah? I had done some asking around and already concluded that Hanukkah's piddly eight nights didn't matter when everyone else had one giant night, with eight reindeer pulling a fat man who brought them anything they wanted. Not that any of this Santa business made any real sense. Could deer even fly? Why would people have a tree in their house in the first place? Still, it was the principle of the matter, and, like my grandfather, I wanted to be liked.

Then, inside Mr. Dennis's office, I saw I would be photographed in front of a Christmas tree with lots of presents, and my heart sank.

"Say 'Ho! Ho! Ho!' " Mr. Dennis instructed a student.

I could have taken the picture and nobody would have known the difference—nobody but parents ever saw these pictures. But suddenly the Christmas tree was wrong. I didn't understand why I was so angry so abruptly, but I refused to cooperate.

"What do you mean, no?" asked Mr. Dennis.

"I'm not taking a picture in front of something I don't celebrate. I'm Jewish." Mr. Dennis locked his jaw, but he wasn't surprised. Though my second-grade teacher had not yet sent me to his office, I had visited Mr. Dennis in kindergarten and first grade because of "behavioral problems." These amounted to eye rolling and talking back—behavior I had seen my grandmother model. What neither my teachers nor Mr. Dennis ever realized was that there were patterns to my behavior.

I caused trouble when I felt threatened. And that almost always happened on holidays. For instance, in first grade, on Mother's Day, the teacher had us sit in a circle and, one by one, recite a favorite thing about our mothers. Well, what was I supposed to say? *My favorite thing about my mother is how she never calls or visits.* No thank you. I was so scared someone would figure out I didn't have a mother at home and laugh at me that I ran across to the art-supplies table and knocked it over. Pasta and rice and finger paints spilled all over the carpet. My teacher was so furious she sent me directly to Mr. Dennis. But Mr. Dennis didn't ask me any questions, either. Instead he stared at the space just above my head and recited some jargon about the school's high expectations. Because he was afraid of upsetting parents—they were potential donors, after all—he never bothered calling home to investigate. Now it was Christmas, and I was causing a scene all over again, but he still didn't get it.

"Matthew. Just say 'Ho! Ho! Ho!' and smile," he said, not smiling. "You want to be a good boy so Santa comes and visits you, right?"

"I don't care about your dumb Santa. I'm not Ho! Ho! Ho!—ing anything, and I already told you I'm not taking a picture in front of a tree I don't celebrate!"

"Fine," he said, snatching the hat out of my hands. "Then you can't be Student of the Month." I knew that he didn't want to make a scene and that if I apologized, all would be forgotten. I'd get my picture taken, and he'd be on to the next child. But I was really angry now.

"I don't want to be the dumb Student of the dumb Month!" I shouted. "It's not like you need me. You have twenty other jerks right here!" I ran out of the room, and Mr. Dennis screamed after me, "Rothschild, you'll never be Student of the Month again!"

I ran past the classrooms of my school and saw for the first time that each was decorated with Christmas propaganda. There were cardboard cutouts of Santa and those little dwarfs he carted around with him. Some classrooms had plastic dolls wearing sheets hanging around a barnyard. Christmas, Christmas, everywhere, but not a single present for me! When I finally returned to class, my teacher saw that I was crying. She quietly asked her teaching assistant to take over and pulled me aside.

"What's the matter?" she asked.

"Mr. . . . Dennis . . . took . . . He took my hat. . . ." I sobbed.

After calming down, I told her what had happened. I asked her to call my grandmother; I wanted to go home. I could have asked for my grandfather instead, but I was already scheming beneath my tears. I knew what would happen if my grandmother showed up, and I wanted revenge. "Oh, he did, did he?" I could hear my grandmother shouting through the receiver when my teacher called her. "I'll drop-kick his Santa-loving ass from here to Macy's."

When my grandmother showed up, I heard her long before I saw her.

"Where is he? Where's that son of a bitch?" she was shouting. "I'm going to call the United Jewish Appeal. I'm calling the Associated Press! Does he know I'm on the board of Hadassah?"

She was not, but she knew that her bluff would be taken seriously, and she was quickly ushered into Mr. Dennis's office. These were halls where children were encouraged to speak in a whisper, where "sucks" was a terrible word, and my grandmother's intrusion was not welcome. My teachers blushed and closed the door.

The PA system beeped. It was my grandmother, paging me, calling me down to Mr. Dennis's office. I could also hear Mr. Dennis in the background saying that it was his office, his intercom to use. Before the message ended, I heard my grandmother telling him to shut up.

"If you weren't so stupid, I—"

The intercom went dead, and the class stared at me in a mixture of curiosity and awe. I shrugged my shoulders.

True, she wasn't the type of grandmother who baked or knitted; she was the type who would bail you out of jail or take bartending jobs on the weekends for the free drinks—except she had married my grandfather and was relegated instead to a world of charity luncheons and teas. She lived for confrontations like these.

Walking into Mr. Dennis's office, I saw that the color had

drained from his face. My grandmother's face was red, as if she had sucked the color out of Mr. Dennis's. My grandfather sat chomping on a cigar. Since retiring, he often tagged along with my grandmother, entertained by a woman who could make attending the movies an adventure. Secretly, I know he envied my grandmother's problem-solving style: a cross between physical violence and public humiliation. Unlike my grandfather, she didn't care what people thought, and that was her not-so-secret weapon.

"Mr. Dennis has something he would like to say to you, Matthew," announced my grandmother, sitting down.

Mr. Dennis withered under her gaze and turned to me. "I'm sorry that it seemed I wasn't respecting your cultural beliefs. I never meant to insult your religion; I just thought you were fooling around."

"And?" said my grandmother.

"We should have had another scene for your picture."

"And?"

Mr. Dennis looked at her, his eyes pleading. "You can't be serious."

She raised an eyebrow. "One phone call," she said. "That's all it would take."

It was like watching a private conversation between Ronald Reagan and Mikhail Gorbachev. *My guns are bigger than your guns,* she was saying. Mr. Dennis was just another oil painting in a suit to her, and he would be knocked from his pretentious pedestal.

My grandfather's cigar sat poised on his lips.

"And . . ." Mr. Dennis sighed, lowering his voice. "There's no Santa Claus."

"Ho! Ho! Ho!" said my grandfather, lighting up the cigar.

It was like hearing that there is no such thing as the Tooth Fairy or Thanksgiving.

"But I've seen him," I said. "On the street ringing his bell, asking for money."

"No, Matthew," said Mr. Dennis, "those are men in costume. Santa is pretend."

I had been wondering how Santa could be both black and white and still be the same man.

"This will be our little secret," said Mr. Dennis. "Okay?"

"Okay," I said, wondering whom I would tell first. I thought of Chandler, a kid from my class who had bragged all about the great presents Santa was bringing him, and I imagined him crying over this news. A smile spread across my face.

"That'll do," said my grandmother. "Come on, Howard, let's take Matthew to lunch; it's almost his feeding time."

"Do I get my hat back?" I asked.

Mr. Dennis reached into a drawer for the hat and set it on his desk. I studied it, then looked at him.

"Well?" he asked.

"He wants you to put it on his head, moron," said my grandmother. "What, have you never seen a child before? Do they not grow them where you come from?"

Mr. Dennis turned red, and he attempted to secure the hat on my head.

As we were leaving, my grandfather said, "Why do we pay so much money for inadequate American education? This never would have happened in France."

"Yeah," said my grandmother, "it's much better in France, where they've replaced study hall with lessons on how to blow perfect smoke rings with your unfiltered cigarette."

My grandfather started to say something, but my grandmother cut him off.

"Get in the car, Howard; I have a menorah to dig out of storage."

And although I expected it—we were right in the middle of December, after all—I did not hear him complain once that the car was white.

China Girl

By the time I was born, my grandparents were both nearly seventy years old, had raised their two children, and were devoted to their own passions. My grandfather found his calling dozing in front of televised golf, and my grandmother committed herself to photography. Up until I was about eight years old, I can remember her taking off for weeks at a time every six months, traveling to exotic locations in Asia or Africa, and returning to Fifth Avenue with rolls of film. My grandfather was usually still napping on the sofa in the same position as she'd left him. I was sitting by his feet waiting for him to wake up and tell me some stories.

As a young newlywed in the 1940s, photography had been a hobby to fill her time while her husband was away on diplomatic missions, which he did regularly and often for months at a time. In those years my grandmother made a name for herself as a freelancer, receiving assignments from magazines like *Collier's Weekly*. But when my grandfather retired, my grandmother's trips did not end.

"Matthew, there's a whole world out there waiting to be explored," she told me before she made her last trip alone. Her eyes were blazing, and she reached out into midair as if there were something to be grabbed. "The world is more than just charity luncheons given by people who don't know anything about the people they're raising money for. They're all pretense and no depth. I want to be out there exploring, doing things, not just stagnating on the Upper

East Side." The way she spoke the name of our neighborhood came out like a sigh, as if she were disappointed to live here.

I didn't know what the word *stagnating* meant, but I did know that if I asked, my grandmother would lose her train of thought. So I pretended to understand until she was finished, and then I left her in the living room and went off in search of my grandfather. "Stagnating?" he said, rising from the sofa in his study. "Let's go look it up. How did you hear that word?"

"Something Grandma said about people on the Upper East Side."

The study was lined with bookshelves, and he had been walking toward the one containing his favorite leather-bound dictionary, but he stopped short. He turned and considered me for a moment before taking my hand and leading me over to a pair of chairs by the window.

"There's something you have to understand about your grandmother. She is the kind of woman who needs a lot of freedom. If she stays put for too long, she gets upset, like she's missing something."

"She said there's a whole world out there to explore."

My grandfather nodded in agreement.

"But hasn't she seen enough yet?" I complained. "She's always leaving and not asking us to go. It's like she doesn't love us."

"That's not true," he said. "Your grandmother needs her space. She always has, even when she was young."

A loner by nature, she had few close friends—mostly artists and writers—and hosted monthly cocktail parties for them. These were the times when my grandmother was the most animated. She thrived under lively debate, philosophical conversation, and receiving praise for her work. And there was one subject that aroused her interest more than any other: China.

Most of my grandmother's photos were taken in China. During the 1980s, a period marked in that country's history by social unrest, my grandmother made frequent visits. Over time her photographs documented men and women going about daily life—and suffering the indignity of seeing burning books or being arrested for speaking against the government. When I think of these pictures now, I find it hard to believe that the images were shot at random; I can hear my grandmother's voice directing each shot. *You there, when you beat your laundry against that rock, squint up at the sun. I really want you to look miserable, like, "Why is this happening to me?" miserable.*

As for the people in the photographs, I can almost read their minds: *Who the hell is this woman? Why won't she leave me alone?*

After what would become her last trip to China, when I was eight years old, my grandmother's photos showed recurring images of one woman in particular. She had long hair and looked like someone who would be more comfortable sipping a Coke at McDonald's than filling sandbags in Tiananmen Square. This woman appeared in picture after picture: There she was at the Great Wall, marveling at Chinese engineering. And there, again, walking through a field. And here—a stunning image of her frowning at a riot.

My grandmother wanted to exhibit these photographs for her friends in our apartment during one of her monthly cocktail parties, but she was worried that they clashed with the art and the antiques. So, in order to make our home look more like the headquarters for UNICEF, everyone—me, my grandfather, and our middle-aged Ethiopian butler, Atse—had to pitch in and help. As it was, we considered Atse a member of the family, and especially when there was work to do, my grandmother made it clear there was definitely no distinction between employer and employee.

"Howard, get the hell over here and roll up the carpets. Matthew, take this key and go lock up the booze."

"*You* gonna have a dry party?" asked Atse, who was locking up some of the smaller antiques in the study. He laughed. "I'd like to see that happen."

She smiled. "Oh, you think you're funny? I'll tell you what else would be funny: seeing you do some real work for once. What a joke that would be." She sighed. "For your information, I paid for the caterer to bring the alcohol. These people will drink us out of house and home otherwise."

"These must be her friends." Atse slapped my grandfather on the shoulder, and they shared a laugh together.

When we were done rolling up the carpets and hiding the

antiques, my grandmother supervised us as we stripped my grand-father's collection of paintings by impressionist greats off the walls. Gone were the two landscapes by Monet and the minor sunflower painting by van Gogh that hung in the never-used gallery off the main hallway, and in their place stood pictures of despondent women and their laundry. We had to rearrange the furniture in the gallery to accommodate what my grandmother called her "big surprise."

My grandmother's monthly cocktail parties were usually black tie, and this one was no different, so I was required to dress up. Depending on her mood, my grandmother either kept me upstairs with Atse, out of the way, or put me to work in the kitchen. Occasionally, like a liveried midget, I was allowed to bear a tray of hors d'oeuvres, but only if I really forced the issue. I loved watching how the adults conversed with one another so easily, and I longed for the days when I could be accepted into these conversations as an equal, not just as a walking tray of speared meatballs. Later, alone in my room upstairs, I would stand in front of the mirror and reenact the conversations I'd heard and emulate their sophistication.

But for the China Girl opening, my grandmother was especially anxious and asked me to stay off to the sidelines. I knew that this party was different—it had something to do with that surprise she'd mentioned—and it frustrated me to think I'd done all that furniture rearranging and then wasn't allowed to attend.

"I want to work with the caterers," I protested. Walking around serving appetizers was the easiest way to eavesdrop on the adult conversations without anyone's feeling awkward around me. If I stood too close without any real purpose, the grown-ups either changed the subject, stopped talking altogether, or asked me questions like, "What grade are you in now?" or "How old are you?"

I wasn't going to let my grandmother ruin my fun without a fight.

"You don't love me," I said, trying to make her feel guilty. "You always leave, and when you *are* here, you make me hide in the corner."

"Oh, stop," she said. "I do love you. I don't want to mess up the party. It's nothing personal."

My grandmother often delivered pronouncements like this because she spoke without thinking. The remarks weren't meant to hurt anyone's feelings, but she did understand that this happened, which is why she would follow a particularly cutting statement with, "It's nothing personal." I always imagined this was her way of telling you that while she recognized your flaws, she did not blame you for them. "This is how I am," she often said. "Take it or leave it." Sometimes I'd look over to my grandfather, who would nod, having already accepted his wife's peculiarities years before.

So I stood off in the main hall by the front door, pacing between the living room and the gallery, listening to guests ooh and aah over the Chinese woman and my grandmother's attention to line and balance. My grandmother floated from group to group, lapping up attention like a thirsty dog. Unlike the men and women from her double life, the Upper East Side charity circuit, these guests were all dressed in stylish black. The absence of feathers and sequins meant there was also an absence of pretension, and my grandmother was free to relax.

After several of the guests asked about the enigmatic figure from the photographs, my grandmother raised her voice.

"Now, now, I promised you all a surprise. I won't keep you waiting any longer."

The crowd parted, and the young woman from the photographs emerged in the center of the room. She was like Venus in a Botticelli painting. Where had she been waiting? I wondered. Had she always been there? How did I not notice?

The room was silent as the guests tried to figure this out. Had my grandmother brought back a live woman from China as a party favor?

"Sophie!" one white-haired gentleman finally exclaimed. "She's exquisite."

There were similar reactions by the other guests, though I couldn't really see; I was barely at waist level with most of the adults. But from all the commotion you would have thought Chairman Mao had come back to life as a cocktail waiter.

"Where can I get one?" someone joked.

"Uhm . . . China," I said, trying to force my way through the throng of people. I was as shocked as anyone else.

I could hear my grandfather's voice, with his distinctive French accent, through the crowd. He was explaining that the woman, Anh Hong, would be working for us. "Sophie fell in love with her, so I brought her back. You know how she is about anything exotic." I thought of Atse and wondered if the same thing had happened to him.

The party guests turned to Anh Hong with their questions:

How did she like America?

"Is *velly* nice!"

What did she think of Communism?

"Is *velly* bad! All the poor make me sad."

These men and women were an elite circle of artists and intellectuals, but many had never traveled to a non-Western country, and Anh Hong was too exotic for words. My grandmother, proud of her wondrous show-and-tell, strutted around, Anh Hong in tow. The party went until early the next morning; my grandmother was too excited to throw anyone out.

While her friends might have been fooled into thinking my grandmother had brought Anh Hong back for companionship, the next afternoon, after my grandmother woke up, she settled in to teach Anh Hong about her true role in our home.

"Anh Hong, could you fetch my slippers? . . . Anh Hong, would you iron my newspaper? . . . Anh Hong, could you bring me some of that nice food you Asians are so good at making?"

"Yes'm, missy," she would say to each request, but out of my grandmother's hearing range I heard Anh Hong complain to Atse, "What am I? A dog?"

"Arf! Arf!" he said, before cackling. "You one of us now, China Girl."

. . . .

What with cooking and cleaning and keeping my grandmother company, Anh Hong's schedule was packed. Walking past the living room, I often heard them conversing about Anh Hong's life back in China.

"How many generations of your husband's family did you have to live with?" asked my grandmother.

"Three," said Anh Hong, polishing the picture frames above the mantel. "Everyone in China live long life, so Anh Hong have to suffer."

My grandmother let out a deep sigh. "It's a good thing I rescued you."

"Yeah, rescue," said Anh Hong, moving on to clean another part of the room.

. . . .

After Anh Hong showed up, it seemed that my grandmother barely paid me any attention. She was always busy talking to Anh Hong. Jealous of the time they were spending together, I created my very own Chinese maid from reruns of *Fantasy Island*. I named him "Little Saigon," and though I knew that he didn't really exist, I also knew he would get people's attention.

"Don't you talk to Little Saigon," I said one night after dinner while Anh Hong and my grandmother were bonding and Atse and my grandfather were playing chess. "Or ask him to do anything. He won't listen."

"What is a Little Saigon?" my grandmother asked as Anh Hong rubbed her feet.

"He's my Chinese maid," I said.

My grandfather and Atse paused their game midmove and looked on. "He's finally cracked," Atse told my grandfather under his breath.

My grandmother thought this was hilarious. She laughed and slapped Anh Hong's arm.

"And how did we get him?" she asked

I was not able to fly off to China to procure him, like some people, so I explained that he found his way to me through a portal. My closet.

"Not the closet again," my grandfather groaned. "I'm calling an exorcist."

"I don't know what you're complaining about," said my grandmother. "This is all your fault. Ever since you gave him those damn C. S. Lewis books, he's been a mess. It's why we can't keep a nanny."

She was right. Ever since my grandfather showed me the books during one of our Saturday trips to the New York Public Library, I was petrified of my closet. This was the place, I was sure, that housed every dark spirit and psychopath in New York City. Each night before going to bed, I apologized to the demons living in close quarters among my school uniforms. I asked them to have mercy on my sleeping body. I was, they'd realize, much more useful alive than dead. Alive, I could continue to bring them sandwiches or candy bars.

Sometimes I was so afraid of the closet that I couldn't sleep. So I'd sneak into the adjoining bedroom where the nanny slept—when there was a nanny—and curl up on the floor beside the bed. Most of these women were so scary-looking that I thought for sure I'd be safe. But having a nanny in the house was becoming increasingly rare. The last one quit when she woke up in the middle of the night and stumbled over me on her way to the bathroom. Because of her trip to China and the ensuing party, my grandmother hadn't thought to call the staffing agency to hire a new one.

When I mentioned that Little Saigon was a midget like Tattoo, my grandmother asked, "Can I meet him?"

"Sophie, don't encourage this," said my grandfather. "Tell him to go outside and do something with a ball."

"So he has a little originality," said my grandmother. "It's not like he's strangling cats and leaving them under his bed." She turned back to me. "What does Little Saigon do all day?"

"Mostly he brings me things. Like my slippers or rice," I said.

"He have my job," Anh Hong said, laughing, but I could tell she didn't think it was funny. I could have sworn she scowled as she kneaded my grandmother's feet. Later I heard her complain to Atse in the kichen that everything she did could be done by an imaginary midget. The servants might have hung out with us in the living room, but if they complained, they did it in the privacy of the kitchen. They were careful not to complain too much in front of my grandparents, but they didn't even think twice about complaining in front of me.

"I gotta get outta here," she said as I stood at the counter dunking Oreos in milk. "This place is killing me."

He waved her off. "First ten years is the hardest."

.   .   .   .

After a few weeks, Anh Hong's accent disappeared and I learned that people called her Hong.

"In China," she said, "your last name goes first."

Contrary to what my grandmother had been led to believe, Hong had been born in Brooklyn, not China. When she wasn't mangling her speech to suit the Upper East Side, you could hear New York in her voice. "I married this bum, and he made me go to China. I told him, 'Listen, man, I'm not made to live with six generations of your family and wash out your grandmother's garters,' but he said, 'Oh, oh, I love you.' Whining little mama's boy."

Hong did not consider her position in our apartment permanent. For her it was a means to an end.

"Neither did I," Atse said, pushing the mop across the kitchen floor.

"Matthew," she told me, "your grandmother is going to introduce me to a rich man. Then I'm going back to that village in China and evict those old hags that looked down on me because I was American. Only she doesn't know it yet. For now I'm just a maid."

This was big news. I rarely found out anything before my grandmother. What would happen when *she* found out? She *always* found out. But still, being on the inside of a secret . . . it was intoxicating.

"Anh Hong," my grandmother called from the den.

"Sophie Rothschild," Hong hissed.

"Anh Hong?" she called again.

"God, what does she want now?" Hong slapped her hand on the kitchen table.

"Probably to make your grandma come to work, too," Atse said, rinsing the mop.

For an Upper East Side resident, my grandmother was exceptional in many ways: She had the mouth of a truck driver, and she didn't care if you were a maid or a millionaire. But in other ways, she was quite stereotypical.

"Where are my slipperrrrrrrs?"

Before pushing open the swinging kitchen door, Hong slipped back into character. "In your *velly* pretty closet, missy?" she called back, and then added quietly, "Where they always are."

.   .   .   .   .

Anh Hong had been working for my grandparents for several months when my grandmother's cousin Jacob came to dinner. An investment banker with Goldman Sachs, Jacob lived in London but was in New York on business.

My family must have taken God's proclamation to go forth and populate the earth literally, because I was accustomed to meeting new family members with alarming frequency. "Matthew," my grandmother might say, "this is your cousin Albert. His family lives in Canada." The next week I would meet someone else, who was also stopping on the way through New York. When asked if any of these cousins knew any other cousins, they usually laughed. "I didn't even know about Albert in Toronto. I should go visit him, too."

Normally, my grandmother did not encourage relatives to stay for meals or a sleepover, but for some unknown reason Jacob was an exception. He was in his fifties, white hairs punctuating his scalp, but when he saw Hong, his eyes glazed over like those of a child watching a Disney movie. He was quiet until Hong left the room.

"Sophie, how did you find such a beautiful creature?" he asked.

We had no animals in our apartment, so I assumed that Jacob was slightly delusional, like most of my grandmother's family, people who brought their own vodka and could forget which city they were in at least three times over dinner.

"No thank you, Little Saigon," I said glancing away from the dinner table. "I couldn't possibly have anything else to drink. I'm already a little tipsy."

Jacob looked at me. Then he looked at my grandfather. My grandfather looked down and sighed into his plate.

"I found her feeding some ducks by a pond," my grandmother said.

I rolled my eyes. In Hong's version she ran out of her way to get to the pond so that the "rich white lady" would see her.

"How you know she was rich?" Atse had asked, and Hong replied, "I recognize Chanel. She was the only woman in a Communist country with pink shoes." .

"She's been here for several months," my grandfather told Jacob. "She does a wonderful job."

Later that night Hong regaled Jacob with stories of the Chinese president—"*Velly* bad man, *velly* bad"—and told him she was a girl with simple needs. "I like soft bed of America—or Britain. That where you from, Mis'r Jacob? I always want to go!" My grandmother nodded as if she were privy to Hong's wish to meet a rich bachelor. My grandfather snored softly on the sofa. After a while, bored with being ignored while my grandmother and Jacob fawned over Hong, I went upstairs to watch television in my room and then went to bed.

The following morning at breakfast, Jacob strolled into the dining room with a serious expression. "Howard, Sophie, I've decided that Anh Hong and I should be married. That is"—he looked at Hong longingly—"if she'll have me."

"Oh, Mis'r Jacob, Mis'r Jacob," she said. "I do not know what to t'ink."

My grandfather and I sat dumbfounded.

Even my grandmother looked shocked, but she recovered quickly. "I'll tell you what to 't'ink,'" she said. "T'ink about who brought you here. T'ink about the time we spent together." She was staring at Hong, as close to being devastated as she could allow herself to look.

Hong looked at Jacob, then to my grandmother. "I am maid, missy. I make you bed, not keep you secrets."

My grandmother was grudgingly forced to accept that Hong was lost to her. She helped her pack her very few things and sent her off with Jacob.

After they were gone, she flopped down onto the sofa in the living room and groaned. "This," she said to my grandfather, "is why we don't have my family over."

My grandfather draped an arm over her shoulder. "She is better off. She'll be well taken care of."

"Yeah, it's nothing personal." I stuck my tongue out at her.

"My cousin Eddie married a hairdresser," said my grandfather.

"Oh, I don't care that she was a maid. If he wanted a gold digger, he could have asked me to introduce him to one. He didn't have to take *my* gold digger!"

Pretending I'd heard something funny, I laughed. "That's a good one, Little Saigon."

"Oh, shut up, Matthew," said my grandmother. "You've made your point. We all know that Anh Hong was a maid and bound to leave eventually."

I wondered if my grandmother had seen right through Hong's act the whole time.

.   .   .   .   .

With Hong gone, my grandmother was moping around our apartment. I was jealous all over again. If *I* left, she wouldn't think twice. Hong left and she was practically bereaved. My own neurosis then kicked into full swing. I found a pair of reading glasses, a legal pad and a pen, and I sought out my grandmother for psychoanalysis.

"What's the problem, Sophie?" I asked.

Normally she would have swatted me away, too engrossed in *Love Boat* reruns to play along, but she was in a pinch and needed to talk to someone.

"My friend is gone." She sighed. "And none of these other jokers knows how to use a wok, for chrissake." She raised her voice. "I mean,

how hard can it be? You put in some lousy oil and stir up some goddamn rice. Rice!"

"Calm down, woman," Atse said, waving the wok from the safety
of the dining room. "I'm from Ethiopia. Half my people don't know
what rice looks like."

"If you need some rice, Little Saigon can do that for you," I said.
My grandmother looked at me, confused. "What?"

"Little Saigon."

"Again with Little Saigon?" she asked.

"Didn't you ask to meet Little Saigon?" my grandfather teased
from a chair in the corner.

"That's enough, Howard," she snapped, and he laughed.

"If you want, he can be your new friend, since Anh Hong is gone,"
I said. "Little Saigon is a nice little man who can do all your chores.
He'll take you on walks around the apartment and tuck you in."

My grandmother's lips curved into a smile. "Is that what he does
for you? Maybe I should stick around for a while, then, so he can be
my friend, too."

"Or I could do it. I could be your friend, and I'm right upstairs.
You don't even have to go to China."

My grandmother shook her head and smiled, then put her arms
around me. "Thank you, Matthew." Uncomfortable with physical
displays, she did not hug me often, and I held on long after she did,
inhaling her perfume.

"That's enough," she said. "Let go."

Yawning from his chair, my grandfather reminded her that they
still had some applications to go over for the nanny position.

She jabbed me softly on the nose. "I don't think we need a nanny
anymore. I think we can manage this by ourselves for once."

My grandfather shot her a puzzled look, but I spoke for him.
"What about when you go away to take pictures? Or," I said, remembering something my grandfather had told me, "because you
need to be alone?"

"Let the Sierra Club pollute the magazines," she said. "I'm done.
Besides, I think this is where I need to be now."

All in the D's

My friend Elaine Kensington was my upstairs neighbor. We were both only children, both the same age, and after the Student of the Month fiasco my grandmother transferred me to Elaine's school, so she and I carpooled together. But that's where the similarities ended.

Elaine was everything that I was not. She was blond; I was redheaded. She was smooth; I was freckled and plagued with psoriasis. She was thin, and by eight years old I was already chubby. Elaine was chatty, refined, almost charming; I was silent and rarely wore matching socks. In short, she was like every other kid at my new school. These perfect kids always looked like they'd stepped out of a Ralph Lauren ad. After soccer or tennis, the other kids glowed. Me? Let me walk from the cafeteria to the swing set and I was a sweaty mess. Next to the other polished faces in the classroom or playground, I looked like a homeless kid. I was the hangnail on the manicured hand of the Upper East Side. I spent the better part of my days busy not making eye contact with anyone, and people at school often wondered why Elaine bothered to talk to me at all.

But Elaine didn't care about any of that. We had been around each other since birth; our two mothers had even grown up together. In that sexless way in which boys and girls can make such easy companions before the fifth grade, Elaine and I were inseparable. The adults around us teased that we'd get married one day, though I was already pretty sure I wanted none of that.

I knew that my grandparents had been married for something like a hundred years, but even in third grade I realized that that was uncommon. It seemed as if half my classmates came from broken homes and the other half's parents were in trial separation. I had been eavesdropping on a telephone conversation between my mother and my grandmother and learned that my mother was thinking of ending her fourth marriage. I had picked up the phone midconversation, but I knew something was up when I heard my mother's voice on the other end. She called only four times a year, and this wasn't anybody's birthday or anniversary.

"Jude, I recognize one needs practice to be good at this marriage thing," my grandmother was saying, "but can't you practice with the same person?"

"I don't know why I called," said my mother. "All you ever do is make jokes out of everything. You can't be serious about anything, can you?"

My mother started to cry. I wanted to reach out to her, to tell her that I still loved her. Now that she didn't have a husband anymore, she could come back to New York and live with us. We could finally be a family. It didn't matter if she didn't have a husband. But my grandmother took the conversation in another direction

"Sweetheart, I'm not a man. That crying doesn't work on me. You called because you're looking for approval, but you won't get that from me. If you want approval, ask for your father next time. He's good at that sort of thing. But I'll tell you, young lady, at your age you shouldn't still be looking for that from everyone. It's your life, do what you want. If you want to spend half in divorce court and the other half in a chapel, then do it."

"What did I ever do to you?" my mother asked, close to hysterics. "I try to make you love me, but you just can't, can you? You can never love anyone but yourself."

I wondered how she could say such a thing. My grandmother loved my grandfather and me. Maybe she just didn't love my mother?

My grandmother's voice rose. "Calling to tell me you want to get a divorce is how *you* show love? You don't know what love is. There's a little boy upstairs right now who's proof of that."

"Don't you bring him into this!" my mother said.

"And if I don't bring him up, will you?" My grandmother sighed. "You don't even ask to talk to him when you call."

"Why should I? So he can be disappointed in me like everyone else is? You've poisoned him against me as it is."

"Jude, you are thirty years old. I would like for you to call me when you finally grow up." My grandmother hung up the phone. I stood with the receiver in my hand, my mother still on the other line asking if anyone was there. I tried to gather up the courage to say that I was, to say that I wasn't disappointed in her, and to ask if my grandmother was wrong, if she did really love me, but I couldn't speak. My mother hung up, and then so did I.

Staring out my window directly onto Central Park and the Met, I wondered why I didn't speak up when I had the chance. What was I afraid of? That she loved her loveless marriage more than she loved me? Of being rejected again?

I tried to shake this doubt and get downstairs, where I was sure my grandmother was relaying the conversation to my grandfather, but by the time I found them in the study, the discussion was extinguished. My grandfather was watching my grandmother, who stood silently at the window looking at what I'd looked at upstairs. They didn't see me, and I backed out of the room and told Atse I was going up to Elaine's apartment.

.   .   .   .

"You know," Elaine said after I told her about the telephone call, "yours may not have wanted you around, but at least she didn't pretend she did. Not like the Heiress does." In the third grade, Elaine began calling her mother "the Heiress" behind her back—and sometimes to her face.

The Heiress had grown up in their apartment and had inherited it after her mother died and her father ran off with a younger woman. The apartment itself wasn't as large as ours—it was only one floor—but its formal décor made it seem imposing. With its scratchy fabrics and hand-plastered ceilings, it was hard to picture anyone actually living there.

"Ever since the Heiress bought herself the Tennis Player, everything is all about him. I'm here all by myself most of the time." The Tennis Player was Elaine's name for her stepfather.

"Elaine," I said, "you were a baby when they got married. How do you remember what things were like before?"

Elaine sniffed. "I can remember. She and my real father were married, and they were happy."

The Heiress had first eyed the Tennis Player at Wimbledon, and shortly after she began an intense campaign for his love. She already had a husband and a child, but no matter. If the Africans could dig up more diamonds, that Latin god in tight white shorts would come home with her. When the Tennis Player realized that the Heiress would not leave him alone, and that she would finance anything he wanted, he gave in. Elaine's father was removed from the Fifth Avenue apartment without much resistance—a cash settlement no doubt helped to ease the pain—and voilà! Elaine had a new daddy.

After school every day, Elaine arrived home to an apartment run by servants. She flipped on the TV to watch talk shows and picked up the *New York Post* to catch up on Page Six. "I want to see what the Heiress is up to." At my home I had a snack with my grandparents and talked about what I'd learned at school that day. When my grandfather began teaching me "things you should be learning in that fancy American school"—namely, about the stock-market pages in the newspaper and politics—my grandmother would rise and say she'd be in the other room "rotting my brain with television. Feel free to join me if you can break away from the *Encyclopaedia Britannica* over here."

Elaine watched R-rated movies like *Cujo* or *Rosemary's Baby*. Her ability to stomach these was another reason she and I were easy friends. Elaine was fearless and independent, a she-warrior in a prep-school pleated skirt of appropriate length. My grandparents never censored me, but I knew my limits. Stephen King scared the bejesus out of me, but luckily I knew that if Cujo or that devil's spawn copped an attitude, Elaine would kick some major ass.

Theirs—or Ms. Wood's.

My third-grade teacher, Ms. Wood, was a heavyset, efficient woman who (more or less) resembled Jabba the Hutt. Being no great looker myself, I might have sympathized, even overlooked this simple observation, if only she hadn't decided that gentle encouragement was no way to teach a child. "Stop making fun of her, you guys," I might have said to the kids on the playground. "She may be large and hideous. But she is our teacher, and she loves us!" This was sadly not the case, since Ms. Wood preferred the more effective method of tearing down our self-esteem.

A spinster teacher in need of electrolysis, Ms. Wood attacked every day with a score to settle, and I was an unfortunate, easy target. In a sea of perfectly uniformed children, I was the one child who dressed himself: shirt wrinkled and untucked, buttons in all the wrong holes. This was not my grandfather's choice, but my grandmother told him to lay off. "It's not you who has to go out in the getup," she said. "Let him dress himself. He'll learn."

"What will people think?" my grandfather complained.

"Who gives a shit what they think?" she snorted.

And faced with that kind of logic, what else could my grandfather say? He threw his hands up, recited a few sentences in what sounded like Spanish, shook his head a couple times, and left the room.

Apparently Ms. Wood shared my grandfather's opinion. In front of the entire class, she would regularly admonish, "Don't they dress you where you come from?"

I looked down at my white shirt. Was this some kind of trick question? I was dressed, after all.

"A whole lot better than they dress you," Elaine said.

The entire class fell silent. Ms. Wood huffed but turned back to the board and began writing some words for us to copy.

Later, in the car on the way home, Elaine asked, "Why do you let her talk to you like that?"

"She's the teacher," I said. "I can't yell at a teacher; my grandfather would kill me. He told me I'm stuck with her until the end of the year."

"Whatever," said Elaine. "We can buy her and sell her in a flea market."

I laughed. With a single sentence stolen from daytime television, Elaine was regularly capable of changing my entire mood.

She thought for a moment. "What you have to remember, Matthew," she said, patting my hand, "is that Ms. Wood is a terribly lonely and unhappy woman. She fits all of the characteristics of a manic-depressive."

I stared at her.

"I heard that on *Joan Rivers.* How did it sound?"

"Like you knew what you were talking about."

"I know it's true, too," said Elaine, "because the only time she ever smiles is when she's picking on you. Just let her talk to me like that and I'll tell you what'll happen." Rubbing her hands together, Elaine stared out the window. I lost her for a few daydreaming moments.

"Tell me!" I said, bouncing on the seat.

"First," Elaine said, grabbing my hand, "I'd tell her to shut her fat self up. Then I'd take a chain saw and cut off that giant mole from her face, and she'd probably bleed to death, and we would jump around her dead body!"

We laughed, the two of us on the floor of the car in hysterics until the chauffeur threatened to stop driving.

He's next, I mouthed at her, and she burst into more giggles.

Each day Ms. Wood blocked the doorway to her classroom, clipboard in hand, checking off attendance. "Still getting your clothes from the hamper, I see," she said when she saw me the next morning.

"Actually, yes," I said, smiling. We didn't normally retrieve my clothes from the hamper. But that morning Atse hadn't been able to find a clean uniform, so this one *had* been salvaged from the dirty clothes.

"I just don't understand your family," she said.

I could hear my grandmother's voice telling her to shut the hell up. I could hear Elaine say she was just a teacher—yet I only felt my own shame, forcing my eyes down. I wanted this woman's approval. I *needed* to make her like me, even at the expense of ignoring my grandmother's voice.

"I'll wear a new uniform tomorrow," I said.

"Promises, promises," she said. "Besides, you've got bigger fish to fry, young man." She ushered me into the classroom and closed the door. I sat down, worried.

Ms. Wood grabbed a paper from her desk and held it in front of the entire class. It was mine. I understood right away we had moved on from my appearance; Ms. Wood was about to attack my academic inferiorities: chiefly my inability to learn cursive.

I loved writing, don't get me wrong, but I was completely uninterested in switching from print to cursive. I saw nothing wrong with block printing, and I felt I should be able to write the way I wanted. Miss Wood, however, thought otherwise.

"Bad handwriting," she said, "is the mark of a future slob. Of no analytical style and a lifetime of messy rooms. Do you all want to have a sloppy, nonanalytical style?"

The class shook their heads. I stared at my untied shoes and made a mental note to ask my grandmother what "analytical style" meant.

Ms. Wood continued. "It seems one of our *friends* is having a problem with his handwriting. I don't think he'll make it to the fourth grade." She paused. The class was silent and afraid. Who was she talking about? everyone wondered. Everyone except for me. I already knew. "Matthew, I hope you're paying attention."

Of course I was; the woman had a voice that could cut through glass.

"Matthew? I'm talking about *you*."

The class burst out laughing. "We'll wave hello to you from the next grade," someone said. I looked at Elaine, hoping she would say something, that she would stick up for me. But she was staring ahead.

Ms. Wood slapped my assignment on my desk, marked with a giant red D. "Since he places more emphasis on wearing his breakfast than on practicing his *D*'s, perhaps Matthew won't mind staying with me another year." She towered above me, arms folded, lips protruding, the sweat on her mustache catching the light like a prism.

The class stared, and I turned as red as the incriminating D. Ms. Wood waddled up the aisle of miniature desks toward the blackboard.

"He doesn't even live with his own parents," said Andrew, a tanned blond boy with puffy cheeks that Ms. Wood loved to pinch every morning. "Freak of nature."

I knew for a fact that Andrew's nanny laid out his neatly pressed, monogrammed underwear every morning. I shot up. My chair fell over. The class went silent as I clenched my hands into fists. I might have been the third-grade doormat, but that was before someone brought my mother into it. I turned to Andrew. "Say that to my face."

I had no idea what I would do if he did.

Some boxing moves I saw on HBO, perhaps.

"At least his mother's not a whore like yours is, Andrew," said Elaine.

"Elaine!" scolded Ms. Wood. "Don't you ever use language like that in this classroom again! Learn to speak like a lady."

"Oh, whatever," she said, waving Ms. Wood off. "Everyone knows that his mother sleeps around." This may have been true, but judging by Andrew's reaction, it was definitely not common knowledge. Elaine had been eavesdropping on the Heiress's conversations again.

Andrew's mouth fell open, and I sat back down at my desk, wondering what had just happened. I didn't know what a whore was, but from the reaction it got, I figured it was a bad word—yet nothing happened. Elaine didn't go to the principal's office. Ms. Wood squawked a little, then turned around and started writing spelling words on the board. *What gives?* I thought about my grandparents and how my grandfather was always so soft-spoken but how my grandmother always got what she demanded. I looked over to

Elaine. She held me with her gaze, and I thought, *If she can do it, I can do it. I'm done being nice to these jerks.*

.   .   .   .

After school a girl from my class was walking with Andrew and a couple other third-graders. "Hey, Matty," she said, "are you going to get a haircut today?"

I pulled at my overgrown curls. "Yeah, but I want to make sure I don't go to the same place your mom goes, since she looks like your dad now."

Elaine patted me on the back. "Good one."

The girl pursed her lips and stalked off to her nanny.

"Whatever," said Elaine. "*Her* mother's a whore, too."

"Elaine, what's a whore?" I asked.

She looked at me for a couple seconds before answering, "Well, if you're too dumb to know, I'm not going to tell you," which I understood was code for "I don't know, but I saw it on *Joan Rivers,* too."

.   .   .   .

Even though I decided I wasn't taking any more crap from the kids at school, I still wanted Ms. Wood to finally like me. That night I thought of a new angle in my campaign to win her over. Since my handwriting could not improve drastically over the next twenty-four hours, I thought she might enjoy some humor. So I copied a few comics from *The New Yorker* onto my assignments.

"Now look what he's done, class," said Ms. Wood a couple mornings later, waving my paper. "He's buttoned his shirt correctly, but he's coloring all over his work. Very nice indeed," she said, dropping the assignment onto my desk. There was a giant red D plastered across the top of the paper, and she'd corrected the spelling in the cartoons. "Matthew, please see me after class."

At the end of the day, Ms. Wood asked me to stand by her desk as she scribbled on a piece of pale blue stationery.

"What's that?" I asked.

"A note home for your grandmother."

"Honestly, Ms. Wood." I tried to avoid staring at the slight beard growing on her chin. "There's no reason to bring my grandmother into this. We're both adults, right? Don't you see that I'm changing?"

This was a line from *General Hospital.* Elaine and I frequently watched. It seemed a good time to use it.

For a long moment, Ms. Wood just looked at me. "You're a mess," she said finally, and handed me the note. "Matthew, our students have always been of the very highest caliber, and we can't have you as the exception. Either you will shape up or you will be cut loose. Please have your grandmother sign this note."

At the end of every day, a line of chauffeured town cars parked outside the brownstone for pickup. Nannies stood next to drivers and waited for their perfect young masters and madams. When it was Elaine's turn to have her driver take us to and from school, her nanny would accompany him. I didn't have a nanny, so on the days when my driver picked us up, there wouldn't be anyone standing next to our car.

In the car Elaine badgered me about what happened.

"She gave me a note for my grandmother because I drew on the homework," I admitted.

"She's a nasty witch," said Elaine. I had to agree.

I sat in the backseat, ignoring the driver and looking through my book bag to find a graded handwriting assignment. "What's wrong with my D's?" I asked. "And look at her handwriting. My D's are a lot better than hers."

Suddenly Elaine had an idea. "What about the black holes?" she joked.

Back before we went to the same school—we couldn't have been more than six or seven years old—we were watching television in my apartment one summer afternoon when we came across a PBS documentary about black holes. The gist was, anything that went into a black hole never came out. I'm pretty sure there was more to the story line than that—like this phenomenon only happens in outer space—but that's all we took away from it.

In fact, we were so sure this rule applied to any dark area that we began feeding items indiscriminately into random dark spaces we discovered around our building—namely, the trash chute and the laundry chute. This was a fun way to pass a couple of days, until one of our building's maintenance workers caught us and told my grandparents.

"Black holes?" my grandmother said when I tried to explain the rationale behind my science experiment. "Howard, talk to your grandson."

"I knew a boy," he said, "who lost his name down a black hole. He was walking along the road and found this hole and shouted his name into the hole. It wasn't until he got home that he realized it was gone forever. His own mother—"

"Old man, what the hell are you talking about?" my grandmother interrupted.

"I was telling him about the little boy from Chelm who lost his name down a hole and how black holes are nothing to meddle with."

My grandmother cut him off again and grabbed my shoulders. "Listen, little man, you can't just go around taking people's welcome mats and newspapers and throwing them down the trash. That's called petty theft! It's stealing. You'll go to jail! Do you want to go to jail?"

I told her that I did not want to go to jail, and she said, "Good boy. Now go off and play something that doesn't involve breaking the law." She turned her attention to my grandfather. "Little boy from Chelm indeed. Where do you get this stuff?"

But now, sitting in the back of the car, looking at the handwriting assignment, I wasn't sure what to do. We were pulling up to the apartment building, and I panicked. I quickly stuffed the piece of paper under the driver's seat; the handwriting and its bad grade temporarily disappeared. Making a mental note to come back the next morning, retrieve the assignment, and trash it at school, I followed Elaine out of the car.

That still left the teacher's note, however. It required a signature or I would have shoved it under the seat, too.

Walking into the lobby, I asked Elaine if she thought anyone would find the assignment, and she waved my concerns aside. "Who looks under there, anyway? Relax."

I sighed and trudged along through the marbled lobby, and we got onto the elevator. My apartment came first, and as I stepped out of the car, Elaine said, "Come up later and I'll teach you how to sign your grandmother's name."

At home, Gloria, the maid who'd been working in our apartment since Hong had left the year before, took my backpack, and my grandmother stood at the foot of the stairs. When she saw the note in my hands, she rolled her eyes and held out her hand.

I slapped it. "High five!"

She frowned. "Give me the note, Einstein. Let's hear what that dumb broad has to say now." From the third day of school, Ms. Wood had nagged my grandmother with incessant notes and telephone calls—so she'd been pegged "that dumb broad."

I must have appeared shocked, because my grandmother said, "Don't look at me like that. Your teacher already called."

I stood next to her so that I could read it, too. "She says you don't follow the rules," my grandmother said, "and that you don't take much care of your appearance." She laughed. "I could have told her that."

"Maybe you should call her up and tell her I dress myself and that I don't have to follow her dumb rules, and then tell her she's a big fat mess." I said this hoping to make her laugh, and it worked.

She rubbed my head and mumbled something about a haircut. "Of course, you *could* make more of an effort to match your socks in the morning. Tell her you're proud of your appearance but you take more pride in your independence. She won't understand, but it'll shut her up for once."

Ms. Wood hadn't mentioned the handwriting assignment. The note was about my behavioral problems, not my grades, and this was a relief since it was acceptable to my grandmother for me to be rebellious or difficult, just so long as I wasn't stupid. My grandfather disagreed and tried to stress the importance of reputation, but my grandmother would get a dreamy look on her face and then tell me about all the trouble *she'd* been at school.

My plan regarding the handwriting assignment would have

worked out if I'd remembered to get the paper from under the seat the next morning. I remembered only when I was sitting with Elaine the following afternoon with another assignment to dispose of. "I'm telling you, nobody ever checks under these seats," Elaine whispered, and I stuffed that paper under the seat, too. I was nervous for about a week, but when nobody busted me for the assignments, I thought Elaine must be right: Nobody *did* check under the car seats. So a pattern was born. I would finish an assignment, decorating it with stick figures and witty comics, confident that my banter would wear Ms. Wood into accepting me. Sure, it hadn't worked thus far, but I figured if I kept at it, eventually she'd have to give in. She placed D's on all of them, and I hid them under the driver's seat. This all worked beautifully until the day it blew sky high.

I was sitting in my room watching television on Saturday when I heard the doorbell downstairs. I could hear Elaine's voice, and she came into my room carrying a small duffel bag. I thought she was spending the night. Since the Heiress was often gone, and sometimes with virtually no warning, it wasn't uncommon for Elaine to spend the night in my apartment.

"Look what I brought you," she said.

From the bag she retrieved a frumpy patterned dress and set it next to me. It took a minute for me to recognize where I'd seen it. I looked at the garish print and flowing prairie skirt and understood that this wasn't something my grandmother would own. This was something Ms. Wood would wear to school "Did you break into Ms. Wood's house?" I asked. I would not have been one bit surprised if that were the case.

"No, I found it in my maid's closet. I guess they shop at the same dollar store." She dug a pair of black pumps from her bag and set those on the bed next to the dress.

"Try them on," she said.

"Why?" I asked.

"So we can play school, duh."

Elaine and I did this regularly. I would be the teacher, and she would be me. I would yell like Ms. Wood, and she would show me what I could have said in response. I'm not sure if her intention was to toughen me up or to show me how to use my vocabulary to elicit a response. Either way it was entertaining, but I didn't possess the self-confidence to put into practice what she preached.

I felt awkward. Admittedly, I pretended to be my female teacher in these games, but I hadn't ever tried on a dress before. What if someone came in? What would anybody think?

"Go ahead," she urged. "What's the matter?"

I didn't want to explain that I felt weird doing this. That would ruin the game. Elaine would get mad, stomp off back home, and then I'd be watching television alone again. I threw the dress over my clothes and slipped my socked feet into the shoes. The dress was huge, but the shoes fit okay.

"How do I look?" I asked, and spun around. I sucked in my cheeks the way Ms. Wood did when she was thinking.

"Beautiful, Ms. Wood," she said.

"Good," I said. "Now, sit your lazy behind down so I can get to work. Don't you know that Ms. Wood has a lot to do today and that Matthew is going to keep her from getting it all done?"

"Yes, ma'am," said Elaine. "That's why I came to class today, so you could not do your work."

"Now, class," I said, fanning myself with a book, "I want to explain something to you, but first I have to make fun of Matthew because his socks don't match and his handwriting is bad."

"Shut up, Ms. Wood," said Elaine. "I'm not your patsy."

I paused. "My what?"

"I don't know. I heard it in a movie."

"Well, you most certainly are my patsy, and one more thing—"

I stopped, dumbfounded. My grandmother was at my bedroom door. She was holding a stack of wadded papers. I recognized them immediately. Fortunately, the sight of me in a dress threw her off.

"What the hell are you doing?" she asked. She looked surprised but not angry.

I glanced down at my dress. "Playing school."

My grandmother began stroking her chin. Clearly, there were

several ways she could take this conversation. "Matthew, what are you wearing?"

I could see that she didn't really want to ask this question but felt she had to.

"A dress," I said. *See,* I thought, *I knew people would think this was weird.* I looked at Elaine, but she refused to make eye contact. I was all on my own.

"And where did you get this dress?" asked my grandmother, looking at Elaine.

"I found it?"

My grandmother sighed. "So you've been wandering around the women's department at JC Penney? Do you expect me to believe you couldn't find a better dress than that?"

This was not exactly the reaction I was expecting, but at least it wasn't rage. I didn't know what JC Penney was, and I didn't care. I didn't want my grandmother to remember the papers in her hand. So I began dancing around in my dress to distract her.

"Have I taught you nothing about style?" she asked.

"We thought that it looked like Ms. Wood," I said.

Elaine stared at me like I was crazy, but I couldn't lie to my grandmother. The woman was psychic. She could see right through me.

"Are you telling me that you're pretending to be Ms. Wood?" My grandmother looked down at her own Chanel shoes and remembered the papers in her hand. "Oh! Matthew, what the hell are these?" she asked, waving them at me.

I tried distracting her again. "Hey, do you like the pattern of the dress?"

"No, I don't, and the driver found these under the seat of the car."

Elaine slid quietly past my grandmother out the door. I really was on my own.

"Did he say whose they were?" I asked, twirling the skirt.

"Matthew, how many third-graders named Matthew Rothschild live in this house and ride home from school in our car?"

Valid point. "He must have done those himself to get me in trouble!"

I wasn't making any sense, but I thought if she was unable to talk, I could escape punishment. "Maybe he needs more to do. He could wash the car, and maybe wax it. You don't want people to say that we don't take care of our—"

"I don't understand," she interrupted. "Why didn't you just show these to me?"

"I thought you would get mad every time you saw one. At least now you're just mad once. And besides, doctors have bad handwriting. So I can be a doctor. Do you want to be my first patient? I can run and get my doctor's bag in the other room."

I tried to run out of the room. But she yanked me back. "You don't have a doctor's bag in the other room, little man," she said, her voice rising.

My grandfather walked in and saw his wife holding me by the collar of my dress. His eyes widened. "Sophie? The boy's wearing a dress."

"I can see he's wearing a dress, Howard, but that's not the problem."

My grandfather stood silently, looking me up and down.

"Matthew decided to hide his homework assignments under the seat in the car rather than to show them to us."

"That's our problem?" he asked. "He's in a dress and *that's* our problem?"

She handed him the papers, but he was preoccupied with my outfit. He stood motionless. Of all the things my grandfather had seen in his life—genocide, dictators, and misbehaving presidents— it was clear this was something new.

"Will you forget about the dress and look at the damn papers?" said my grandmother. She clearly had her priorities straight: deception first, cross-dressing later.

He took the papers. I winced.

"These are pretty good," he said. He started to laugh. The wrinkles around his eyes softened. "Look at this one. Is this Moses?"

"Yes, and those are the Hebrews," I said. "Here he's leading them across the sea when he starts to get hungry for a fish and—"

"What are you doing, old man?" asked my grandmother, yanking the papers out of his hands. "You don't ask him to expound on his artistic achievement right now. Stuffing homework under the seat of a car is not behavior you're supposed to encourage."

"Quite right," he said, serious again. "Listen to your grandmother. Now, why are you wearing this dress?"

I told him that I was playing school and this was how my teacher dressed.

"But why are you pretending to be her?" he asked.

"You'd rather him be Ava Gardner?" said my grandmother.

From their reaction I understood that pretending to be my teacher so I could yell at Elaine, who was pretending to be me, was definitely something I should not advertise.

"I don't know," I said. "It was just a game."

"Scrabble is a game, Matthew," said my grandmother. "This is role-playing."

My grandfather patted me on the head and went off to his study, conveniently located downstairs and on the other side of the apartment. This wasn't something he wanted to discuss any further. My grandmother was merely perplexed as to why I'd dressed like some "dumb broad" in the first place. "Have some self-respect," she said. "The next time you want to wear a dress, come get me, and we'll find you something decent."

I walked over to the large mirror in the corner of my room and posed. I tried different positions and speculated on what might make Ms. Wood more attractive so she could finally get a husband. Did Ms. Wood feel as awkward every day as I did?

I had heard the other kids calling her fat or saying she was "just a teacher." But my grandparents had taught me that intelligence and the ability to treat everyone equally were the only things that mattered in life. My grandfather thought it was crass to say you were better than someone else because you were wealthier. My grandmother said, "If you do that, you're a prick."

I wondered if Ms. Wood knew that her students considered her inferior, that they made fun of her clothes behind her back. My grandfather said people became teachers to help others, but I couldn't imagine why teachers would want to work at my school. The kids were mean. Ms. Wood would have done better with a class of Doberman pinschers.

. . . .

The next morning in class, I was determined to turn over a new leaf. In fact, I was so engrossed in being a model student, copying down the new spelling words and practicing them in cursive, that I didn't notice Ms. Wood's menacing expression. She waddled up and down the rows of desks and collected our homework. When she picked up mine, she noticed that there were no drawings.

"Am I to assume," she snarled, "that we are finally done with that comics business, Mr. Schulz?"

I didn't know who Mr. Schulz was. "I can draw one tonight for you if you'd like."

"No thank you," she said, walking forward. "I see that you are also wearing a clean shirt. Did they finally learn to dress you in that zoo you come from?"

"I don't come from a zoo, Ms. Wood," I said.

She turned back to face me. "Pardon me?" she said.

"I don't come from a zoo," I repeated.

She shrugged her shoulders but said nothing.

"And I've worn clothes every day since I started school—they did not *finally* learn to dress me. I've dressed myself since the first day of school."

"Yes. It shows," she said. The other students chuckled, except Elaine. She smirked because she could see something in my face, something new.

"All I ask," said Ms. Wood as she began writing on the board, "is that my students come to class clean and prepared to learn, but I guess that's too hard for some people. I know that I did not get out of bed today for this!"

"Shut up, Ms. Wood," I said.

Her hand froze in midair. She spun around.

"What did you say?" she asked.

"I said shut up. I'm not your patsy." I thought of something my grandmother had told me. "If you can't see that I want to dress myself and be independent," I told her, "then maybe you do need to go back to bed. Better yet, go back to school yourself."

I held my breath. I was practically vibrating in the silence of the classroom. I half expected Ms. Wood to lunge at me.

"Well," she said at last, "that's the first time I've ever heard you put together a complete sentence—and just to hurt your teacher's feelings."

We looked at each other for a long time, her with the chalk still hanging in midair, me trying not to feel guilty.

In that moment I finally understood her. She knew that her clothes were ugly. She knew that her spoiled students all thought they were better than she was. She couldn't come right out and say this—she would have been fired. So instead she looked for a target for her aggression. She picked on me because she was sure I would not fight back.

When class was over, I stayed late to speak with her.

But Ms. Wood ignored me.

In the car Elaine asked if I had gotten into much trouble over the assignments we stuffed under the seat.

"I think they forgot about them," I said. But I was staring at a new assignment with a big red D. She pulled out a failing assignment of her own. "Now I'm in the same boat. Your grandmother called the Heiress, and she said she was going to search me when I come home today."

I tore off a little piece of my homework and popped it into my mouth. I had seen other kids eat paste, so why not paper? Elaine did the same thing, and we shredded our papers, knowing that someone would catch on eventually. But we were both, for the moment, happy.

The Petty Thieves

It was either the infectious post–World War II optimism or a severe oversight on her part—she could never be sure which—but in the 1950s, in a moment of weakness, my grandmother fell in line with other wives and was conned into having children. By that point my grandparents had been married about fifteen years, and she had successfully avoided society's chief expectation for married women. In fact, the only advice my grandmother got on her wedding day could have been a scene taken out of *Fiddler on the Roof.*

Dressed in all black, my grandmother's shtetl-born grandmother waddled over and, in a rare show of tenderness, took my grandmother's hand into her own and said, "Make a good home. Make babies. Lots of babies. Mazel tov."

People gave each other sideways glances. Nobody had heard the old woman talk since she got off the boat at Ellis Island.

Patting her on the hand, my grandmother lied, "I'll get right on that."

To hear my grandmother explain it, she had no intention of ever having children—though initially she had no interest in becoming a wife, either. If I asked why it took so long for my grandparents to become parents, my grandmother would shrug. "I didn't want to rush into anything. I wasn't sure it would work out with your grandfather." Divorce was no stranger to me, but I had no concept of what *work out* meant. What was there to work out? Either you were married or you weren't.

Despite any reservations, my grandmother *did* become a wife and then a mother. First came my uncle and then my mother, five years later. Was my grandmother happy during these years? Hard to say. I know that later in life she often reviewed the critical years of my uncle's and my mother's childhood and adolescence for signs of the disappointment that was to come. She believed that everything started off well—better than she'd expected—but by the time my uncle was fifteen and my mother ten, something had gone seriously awry.

Now, normally my grandparents and I left the Upper East Side each summer, escaping the stagnant heat of the city for either my grandmother's hometown of East Hampton or a small coastal city in France where my grandfather spent summers in his youth. But the summer before my tenth birthday was different. We spent the summer at our apartment on Fifth Avenue, because my grandfather was recovering from his first heart attack and the subsequent triple-bypass surgery. Because of his condition, my grandfather spent most of the summer in hibernation—which wasn't too different from how he normally spent his days. This was a man who turned his nose up at basketball because the games were too noisy to sleep through. But after the heart attack, he had lost weight, and for the first time he started to look his eighty years. His breathing was labored, and he would lean on furniture to take frequent rests during walks around our apartment.

Afraid that my grandfather was really sick and worried about upsetting him, I began to spend more time at Elaine's apartment upstairs.

As usual, the Heiress and the Tennis Player left Elaine in the charge of her nanny while they spent their summer on tour in Europe. Like me, Elaine had difficulty keeping a nanny, but unlike my grandparents, who finally decided to raise me themselves, the Heiress kept hiring new people. This latest nanny was a large Colombian woman named Tonya who had been around since that spring,

but the Heiress was skeptical she would stay. Because the Heiress
was convinced that the last nanny had quit because of Elaine's sleep
deprivation, Tonya received strict instructions regarding the actions
and whereabouts of her ward.

"Remember, Elaine is not to be allowed out of her room before
nine-thirty in the morning." The Heiress had wagged her finger in
Tonya's face, her diamond charm bracelet clanking rhythmically.
"She needs at least ten hours of sleep to be in good spirits."

The first time I heard these rules was earlier that year, five minutes before the Heiress left for a spring holiday in South America.
Elaine had been blackballed by domestic staffing agencies all over
Manhattan, so Tonya had been sent from Boston. Elaine's parents,
relieved that someone was foolish enough to answer their inquiry,
had hired her on the spot.

During Tonya's interview Elaine looked over at me, her blond
curls falling softly around her shoulders. I could tell she was already
thinking of how to bounce this new woman out of the house. Her
mother had tied a pink ribbon in her hair, and Elaine was given a
lacy white dress to wear. She looked positively angelic, the way one
might imagine Archangel Lucifer looking before God hurled him
into that lake of fire. The Heiress did not want Tonya to think her
daughter was like other spoiled Upper East Side princesses who got
whatever they wanted by throwing tantrums and turning on tears.
I'm not sure how the dress was supposed to create that illusion, especially since there were little black shoe prints all over it where,
just before Tonya arrived, Elaine had stomped on it in defiance. Her
cheeks were tearstained.

"Therefore," the Heiress explained, her heavy bracelet keeping
rhythm with her wagging finger, "Elaine [*clank*] must be [*clank*] in
bed [*clank*] by nine [clank] at night."

"But you said that I could go to bed after *ALF.*"

"Elaine, please speak clearly. Mommy has trouble understanding
you when you mumble. You know you have to go to bed at nine;
the doctor says you get too excited if you don't have twelve hours
of sleep."

"But that's half the day, Mommy."

Ignoring the comment, the Heiress walked over to the mirror in the hall and began fluffing her hair. "Please don't give Tonya any trouble. I don't want any phone calls. This is a very important trip; Daddy and I are going to get to know each other all over again."

"Is Daddy going to bring his *friend*?" asked Elaine, raising an eyebrow.

The Heiress dug her expensive heel into the marbled floor of the foyer and refused to make eye contact. "No, it will just be Daddy and I," she said quietly.

One of the side effects of living on the Upper East Side is the strange belief that you can scream at your husband or wife at the top of your lungs and nobody will hear you, least of all your eavesdropping young daughter in the next room. Even though everyone knew about the Tennis Player's indiscretions, the Heiress kept a smile plastered across her own tearstained face. "We're just so happy," she said publicly, and then wondered privately why the Tennis Player filled his days with meaningless girls who kept him away from a loving wife who practically picked him out of a catalog and a loving child who saw right through him.

The Heiress shrugged into a white fur coat. "If you're good, maybe Tonya will take you out to the country to ride your pony. You can bring Matthew. Maybe you can even spend some nights downstairs with Matthew's grandparents."

"But his grandma said we were more trouble than Burt Reynolds in a western."

I nodded. "Yeah, she did."

"Well, then," said the Heiress, "you two can play up here." She gave Elaine a stiff peck on the cheek and left.

Elaine's parents were gone for one month that spring. Contrary to Elaine's track record with nannies, Tonya didn't quit after the first week. Instead a quiet understanding developed between nanny and ward: As long as Elaine didn't make trouble for Tonya, bedtime wouldn't be enforced. Tonya was smarter than we gave her credit for. She knew she had a cushy job. Elaine could be as hellish as she wanted—Tonya just put her orthopedic-soled feet on an ottoman, turned up the volume on *All My Children,* and took a bigger spoonful of her Ben & Jerry's.

.   .   .   .

While my apartment turned into a rehabilitation ward for my grandfather, each morning I padded up to Elaine's apartment, where we watched old episodes of *I Love Lucy* and *Leave It to Beaver* with Tonya, and then, as *All My Children* began, Elaine and I went off to her room to turn on her private television. Using the characters on-screen as inspiration, we'd play with her collection of Barbies, creating love triangles, power struggles, and illegitimate children.

"I need to find a way to get rid of Tonya," Elaine said.

"Why? At least she lets you do what you want. The last nanny I had never let me watch TV. She would've tied me to my bed if I hadn't told on her."

"Yeah, but just the same I don't like her. If she wasn't around, my mother would have to take care of me herself. Like the mothers on TV. They don't have nannies."

.   .   .   .

Whenever we'd go down to my apartment, my grandmother would intercept us. "What fresh hell are you two monkeys going to stir up today?"

Elaine and I would make monkey faces, scratch ourselves, and dance in a circle around my grandmother.

"Whatever you do, don't do it in my house. Go find a street corner and antagonize somebody else."

Elaine and I would shrug and walk back toward the door and play in the elevator.

That summer, out of character, my grandmother occupied herself coordinating a small exhibition of old masters at a local museum to raise money for a children's organization. Since she was not a social woman, a request for my grandmother's participation in anything was usually met with the same response: "Can't I just write a check?"

If told that her time was more valuable than a simple donation—
meaning that they wanted a check *and* her time—she would sigh
into the phone. "Okay, how about two checks?" Because my grandmother had offered her time, and lent several pieces of art, I figured
it was due to my grandfather's condition. My grandmother knew he
was in pain and hated that she couldn't help him, so she volunteered
her time with this museum because she thought she could make a
difference there.

"Listen, Matthew, these people don't care anything about the
children. They just want to be seen and make themselves look less
like assholes. I had to listen to some dumb broad talk about her stupid son at Princeton for four hours tonight." She stood at the bar in
the corner of the living room, mixing herself a gin and tonic. "She
kept talking on and on. Finally she asked where my children were."

I perked up, and my eyes widened. I had wanted to ask about my
mother lately because of my grandfather's illness. I hadn't seen her
since I was three and my grandparents took me to see her get married in London, and I thought for sure she'd finally come home
now—I mean, he was in the hospital and all—but she hadn't. To be
honest, if my grandfather's heart attack hadn't been so close to his
birthday, I don't think she would have known at all. She called only
on our birthdays and my grandparents' wedding anniversary, and
my grandparents weren't the type of people to call with ailments.
Even my uncle, who lived just down in Washington, D.C., only a
few hours away, didn't visit.

I knew they didn't talk often, and I waited for casual references
like these to present themselves so I wouldn't seem too eager, as if I
were sitting around waiting for news. If I mentioned my mother, my
grandmother would shake her head and sigh. "I just don't understand where I went wrong with her. One minute she was a cute little girl picking strawberries in a field, and the next she had Upper
East Side syndrome. She was just another snob asking for a dog to
stuff in her purse."

I often wondered if my grandmother ever attributed my mother's
transformation into an Upper East Side princess to her own absence

as a mother—she was out exploring the world while my mother was at home with the nanny—but I never asked.

"So what'd you say to her?" I asked, hoping she'd let some new information about my mother slip. I wanted to know about my mother, but I didn't want my grandparents to think I spent too much time thinking about her.

"Just to shut her up, I said my son was in prison and my daughter was walking the streets." She sat down on the sofa and took a long sip from the glass. "It was an effective conversation ender."

"I would have laughed if you said that to me," I said, although disappointed that all I was going to get was another sarcastic comment.

"That's because you have a sense of humor, which—thank God!—you inherited from me. The problem with these women, Matthew, is that they're so damn competitive. Every last one of them has something to prove all the time. It's exhausting."

She drained the clear contents of the glass and stared at the bottom for just a moment. What was she thinking? I wondered. Did she miss traveling around the world? Did she think about what her life might have been like if she lived somewhere else? She asked me to pour her another drink, which I did gladly. My grandmother knew that I liked to play bartender. I'd get behind the shiny counter and ask her in a throaty voice, "What'll it be?" or "What's happening, Mac?" She'd laugh and play along, the frustrations of her day dulled by three or four cocktails.

My grandmother was not the kind of woman who waited for cocktail hour before she started drinking, and I knew that sometimes she carried a silver flask with her to events for support. My grandfather, on the other hand, rarely drank anything stronger than coffee, so it's a wonder why it was *his* health that was the issue.

"I'll tell you why he's so sick," my grandmother informed me confidentially. "He was the first one in that damn cult he calls a family not to marry his cousin."

"That's gross," I said.

"You're preaching to the choir, little man. And you know they're all insane. Seriously." She leaned in and lowered her voice, as if we

were co-conspirators, and recited her favorite joke about my grandfather's family. "We're talking about people who've had so much
shock therapy that if they held hands, they could provide enough
electricity for New York City."

She winked and then finished her second drink. "That's the
ticket."

．　．　．　．

One morning in midsummer, I sat watching television by myself, too
lazy to take the elevator upstairs to Elaine's apartment. My grandmother was at the museum, and the nurse was with my grandfather
in the study. The doorbell rang, and—always interested in anyone
masochistic enough to visit our apartment uninvited—I opened the
door before anyone else had a chance and found Elaine wearing a
pretty floral-print dress and carrying two large FAO Schwarz bags.

In my house, mentioning FAO Schwarz was worse than knocking down an old lady. As far as my grandmother was concerned,
FAO Schwarz was the seventh circle of hell. "If I have to go to that
goddamn store one more goddamn time, I'm going to cut my
throat," she'd say every time I asked to go, and then she'd put on
her coat and take me. "I just don't understand why we have to go
every single week. It's the same thing over and over again. And the
crowds!"

I had been left at the store multiple times, refusing to come
when my grandmother called, because I didn't believe that she
would ever leave me. Subsequently I learned the hard way what it
was like to walk twenty blocks uptown after my grandmother took
the limousine home.

"Who's here?" Elaine asked in a whisper.

"Grandpa, Atse, and Gloria. I think the nurse is around, too."

Elaine looked over my shoulder, afraid someone might overhear.
"Come on. Let's go."

"Where are we going?" I asked.

"Shopping." She snatched my hand and dragged me toward the
elevator.

"But I don't have any money," I said. "I'm overdrawn on my allowance for the next ten years." I knew that the Heiress gave Elaine wads of cash to carry around, something I was extremely jealous of. That never happened in my home, where my allowance never rose above seventy-five cents *per week.*

"So what?" she said. "We're just window-shopping."

"Then why do you have two shopping bags?" I asked.

"So we can look important walking around with packages," she said, and I was satisfied with that answer. I liked looking important. When I would go shopping with my grandmother, I would ask to carry all her shopping bags so people would think they were mine. Then I would prance up and down Fifth Avenue, posing every few feet for effect.

The elevator in our building was fast, and soon we were greeted by the concierge and the doorman. Elaine and I came and went from the building often, either for drives or for walks around the city. Nobody ever thought to question us. I thought about how lucky I was to be wearing shoes when the doorbell rang, or I'd be stuck going around Manhattan in my socks. Once outside, Elaine caught sight of her chauffeur, and we bounded off toward the car. It was common for the Heiress to leave Elaine in the care of not only Tonya but three maids, a chauffeur, and a chef.

"We're going to FAO Schwarz," she told the driver.

"Remember, I don't have any money," I repeated.

"Are you a parrot or something?" she said. "I told you that you don't need any, didn't I? Relax already." She blew some air through her mouth in frustration.

My feeling of inadequacy soon melted as the effect of being in the largest toy store in the world took over my body. FAO Schwarz was a jungle of toys in every conceivable shape and color. It didn't matter if you wanted a fuchsia horse or an aquamarine giraffe— anything could be obtained within its marble walls. I stood at the entrance mesmerized by the shelves and sections. I always felt this way at FAO Schwarz; there was always something new and shiny to grab my attention.

Wasting no time, Elaine grabbed my hand once more, leading me toward a selection of toy trains. "Play it cool, all right?" she said.

"Play what cool?"

"Just follow my lead."

Her lead? I had no idea what she was talking about, but I would have followed her anywhere. Most of Elaine's education came from daytime television, but I had accepted that she was smarter and worldlier than I was, and if she said to do something, I did it without question.

Elaine opened one of the large shopping bags and handed it to me. She slid her tongue across her lips, and her blue eyes narrowed as she looked through the selection of trains and accessories. Pulling the items off of the shelves and placing them into the bag, Elaine giggled in exultation.

I had seen people pull items off shelves in shops before, but usually these customers didn't bring their own bag; they waited until a salesperson gave them one. I had heard the term *window-shopping* before, and I was sure that it didn't involve putting merchandise in bags. That was what my family called *shopping*.

"Elaine?" I said.

She looked up, her concentration broken.

"What are you doing?"

"Getting some trains," she said.

"I didn't know you had a train set." I almost mentioned my observation about the difference between window-shopping and real shopping, but I thought she'd get mad at me. I didn't want her to leave me here the way my grandmother had.

Elaine found a track and placed it into the bag. "I do now."

I nodded. "I can't believe your parents leave you with money; my grandparents would never do that. The closest thing to money I get is finding a quarter on the floor, and even then Atse tells me it's his."

"They didn't," she said, reading the box of the train set.

"Did Tonya give you money?" I asked, confused.

"I didn't ask for any."

"Then how are you going to pay for all this?"

She looked at me. "I'm not, dummy. We're going to load up these bags and then leave. Piece of cake."

"Without paying?" I asked, in hopes of clarification.

"Yep," she said, not taking her eyes off the box.

"You mean . . . *steal*?" I saw the two of us wearing masks and robbing banks next, like in *Bonnie and Clyde*. Except, wait—didn't they get shot at the end of that movie?

Elaine looked at me, and her eyes softened in what seemed like genuine pity. *Poor kid,* she probably thought, *they don't teach him anything at his house.*

"I don't think about it that way," she said. "The Heiress spends a lot of money here, and I'm just getting some of it back."

The way she explained it seemed so rational: She deserved the train set. Simple. It was as if she'd been collecting stamps or coupons for all the money spent at the store and it was now time to cash in. Buy ten items, get one (or twelve) free.

But this was not rational, and wasn't stealing wrong? Worried what might happen to me if we were caught, I tried to reason with her. "Elaine, this isn't right. Maybe we should wait until the Heiress comes back and have her buy you a train set."

"All they ever get me are those fucking dolls and stuffed animals!"

I almost dropped the bag. "The F-word?" It was inconceivable that anyone our age could utter that word; I had never heard it happen. "Even my grandmother doesn't use the F-word."

"I don't think that's fair." She thought for a second. A wide grin spread across her face. "That's bullshit."

I did drop the bag that time.

"Listen," she said, touching my chest, "don't you see how they're oppressing us?"

"Oppressing?" I said. I hadn't heard the word used in this particular context before. Oppression was what happened in Third World countries or in Communist Russia, not on the Upper East Side.

"They're holding us back from being our true selves. I saw it on *Oprah*."

"Who's doing that?" I asked.

"My parents, your grandparents." She sighed. "Everyone."

I thought about this for a second, imagining my grandmother dressed as the African dictator whose picture I saw in the *New York Times.* "Do you really think so?"

"When do your grandparents ever give you anything that you don't have to ask for?"

"Never."

"Presents?"

"The last present I got was some dumb sweater that my grandmother paid our housekeeper to knit, and then she passed it off as something she did herself."

"And if they do get you toys, how often are they the toys you want?"

"Grandma says that I should get stuff that's fun for her to play with, too. I don't mind so much. Sometimes she gives me things to use for our wet bar."

Elaine threw up her hands, exasperated. "There you go again, making excuses. You can't even see how much they're taking advantage of you. I can't remember the last time someone read to me who wasn't getting paid to be there. We're stuck in New York while our mothers are off living the high life."

I had no idea what the high life was, but in this context I figured that it was something I was not allowed to have, which meant it was something I should covet.

Elaine touched my arm and pulled me in close. "And don't think I haven't heard my parents talk about sending me away like your mother did to you. I'm lucky I haven't got grandparents, or they would have already sent me packing."

Not able to see that I was being manipulated, I let anger get the better of me.

Elaine knew that the way to get me the maddest was by playing the mother card. I couldn't remember the last time I'd seen my mother, and even though I made excuses for her, I still felt that her not seeing me was a slap in the face. Did she ever think about me? I thought about her constantly: about how she'd left me and never wanted to talk to me. "You're right," I said, suddenly enraged. "They don't . . . *fucking* . . . care about me. My mother never comes to see me. All my grandfather does all day is sleep, and my grand- mother just goes to some dumb meetings. *Fuck* them."

Elaine's mouth fell open, and other customers began to look in our direction.

"Hey, keep it down there, loudmouth," she said. Elaine reached into one of the FAO Schwarz bags, pulled out a smaller folded shop- ping bag, and handed it to me. "Don't let them win," she said.

As Elaine began evaluating her selections, I looked around the store until my eyes fell on a life-size Barbie doll across the floor. I walked over to Barbie and carefully placed some smaller versions of the life-size model into the bag. Malibu Dream Barbie, Rock-Climbing Barbie, Shopping-for-New-Clothes-Because-She-Just-Had-a-Boob- Job Barbie, it didn't matter—I wanted them all. Her perfect world with its beautiful clothes and coy smiles appealed to me, but certainly I could never ask for my own collection. This way, I reasoned with my- self, at least I didn't have to ask. I began grabbing indiscriminately to fill up the bag: clothes, accessories, and even a Ken doll just for fun.

Elaine walked over to me, signaling it was time to go. I nodded and clutched my own bag of loot. We walked casually to the doors, careful not to make eye contact with anyone. Elaine stopped occa- sionally, picking up a toy to examine it pensively; she was the con- summate consumer. The front door was near, and I *could* make eye contact with Elaine's chauffeur, Ben. He stood by the car's back door, holding it open for Elaine and me.

"Let's get out of here," I whispered.

Elaine put down the robotic car she was holding, and we went for the door, but we were intercepted by the store's manager. I had seen this man before; it was he who called my apartment on the oc- casions when my grandmother would leave me at the store. It was he, Mr. Stotes, who would have to deliver the news. "She says walk, and to hurry because dinner's ready and she's feeling very hungry tonight. I must admit your grandmother's methods are unconven- tional to say the least. I don't quite understand them."

"I hear that a lot," I'd say, and then hoof it home.

"What are you children up to today?" he asked us now, puffy-faced and smiling. I could tell from his relaxed manner that he did not suspect us of anything more than being ten years old. We were in the store weekly. We were paying customers. I breathed easier but could not stop feeling nervous.

"Just picking up some new toys to keep us occupied," said Elaine. My eye was twitching, so I just nodded in agreement.

"Young Mr. Rothschild," he said, "where's your grandmother?"

"She's at a museum." My voice was hoarse and cracking.

"Oh? Then with whom are you here? Miss Kensington's parents?"

"Oh, no," said Elaine. "My father's on tour in Europe, and my mother is with him."

"That's right," he said. "I just saw him on television. Great match, very exciting; all that rushing and back and forth."

"Tennis is an exciting game," she said. "He wants to teach me soon."

"All well-bred young ladies should know how to play," said Mr. Stotes. "So whom *are* you two here with?"

"Each other," I volunteered, my voice cracking.

"Isn't it dangerous for your families to give you two large sums of money and then set you loose on the city?" He must have seen this as odd, but the question did not come out an accusation. There was no reason to accuse us of anything. He knew our families. We were good customers. "Mr. Rothschild, I would think your grandmother of all people—"

"Happens all the time," said Elaine. "I keep money in the car with my driver." She pointed to Ben, and I breathed a sigh of relief; she really did have money.

Elaine turned and handed me the bag. "I'll just be right back." She walked through the door and scurried toward the car. She jumped into the backseat and pulled the door shut. The chauffeur walked around to the driver's seat, and they were gone.

Beads of sweat popped out all over my face. Mr. Stotes looked from the getaway car to me and back out onto the street. As the seconds ticked by, I noticed his expression change from confusion to under-standing.

"I think we'd better call your grandmother, Mr. Rothschild."

"Oh, please don't. I'll put everything back where I got it, I swear! Puh-lease don't call *her.*" Images of my grandmother sliding on a pair of brass knuckles danced in my head, and I put my hands together, begging for some kind of leniency.

There was none.

Mr. Stotes sat me outside his office while he made the phone call. My shirt was pasted to my back with sweat. I cursed Elaine. If I hadn't been in enough trouble, I might have let a few more cuss-words slide out. How could she do this to me? How could she make me go to FAO Schwarz, *steal* toys, and then leave me holding the bag? Did my friendship mean nothing to her? And why couldn't I figure out a decent lie the way she could? I wondered how often she did stuff like this—carrying bags to stores and loading up on things she couldn't get by crying or pitching a fit.

"Your grandmother will be here soon," said Mr. Stotes. "Fortu-nately, we won't have to get the police involved. Just wait here."

He walked back onto the sales floor, inspecting shelves and greet-ing customers.

Get the police involved? Why would he want to get the police involved? I saw myself in jail over some stolen Barbies, and a new wave of panic swept over me. Then I thought back to my grand-mother and the trouble I was certain to be in, and I reconsidered my fears about the police. I tried to rehearse some lies to get out of this jam, but not with much effort. She would see through whatever I tried to say and cut through all of the—to use Elaine's term—bullshit. She was probably sitting in the car right now, I thought, swigging out of that silver flask, steeling herself.

I was wrong. I heard his labored breathing before I saw him round the corner: It was my grandfather.

My grandfather was aware of what went on in our home, but it was always my grandmother who delivered the discipline; she could take you from defiance to guilt in three seconds flat, in ways that left my grandfather speechless. He could preach all day long using techniques he'd perfected on politicians, but my grandmother would cut through all the red tape.

Walking with slow, purposeful steps with the assistance of a cane, my grandfather hobbled over and sat next to me. I hung my head and prayed for it all to be over. How was I going to explain to my grandfather, a man who already thought that I needed to spend more time with sports equipment, why I'd been caught shoplifting Barbie dolls?

"What happened?" he asked. I expected him to sound angry, but his voice was soft and without recrimination.

"We put some stuff in some bags."

"And you weren't going to pay for them?" he said.

I shook my head.

"Why didn't you ask for some money? I would have given it to you, you know."

I told him that I didn't know we were going to steal the toys until it was too late. I told him that Elaine said we were just going window-shopping and that it never occurred to me we would be doing something dishonest until I was in the store.

My grandfather thought about this for a moment.

"You must always remember that when you leave our house, you are representing not only yourself but also your grandmother and me."

"Yes, sir," I said timidly. I knew that for my grandfather, hurting his reputation was the worst kind of crime.

"Let me tell you a story," he said. "This was in the 1930s, when I was still a young man, before I met your grandmother. I was living in France—this was before the war—when Hitler started rising to power. My brother was living in Germany, doing business with the Germans, even lending money to the army. He said that the army was a gold mine and that we should concentrate more of our assets toward the German reconstruction—"

"Excuse me, but what's a reconstruction?" I asked.

"The Germans had to rebuild their country after they were

defeated in World War I. Anyway, people said the Nazis were a temporary government—no more than a passing phase—but my brother saw things differently. He saw them as a way to make some money. Even when reports surfaced that Hitler was against the Jews, my brother said otherwise. 'They will make us rich,' he said. I told him that we were already rich, why should we want more? He said, 'Richer than our father ever thought to be.' Keep in mind that our father died when I was a small child, and my brother was really like a father to me."

I had forgotten that my grandfather, like myself, had grown up fatherless. I resisted the urge to crawl into his lap and tug on his arm hair.

"Now, I had begun to hear things—awful things about Jews being blackballed in the cities. Their shops were being closed or looted. Still my brother said to come to Germany. He said he was making money left and right."

"What did you do?" I asked, mesmerized.

"I told him no. I said it wasn't right—that all those people talking could not be wrong—and we had a bitter argument through telegrams, which were very expensive in those days. He said that he would never speak to me again, and I moved to America with our mother. We just barely made it, but my brother did not. We never saw him again."

"He died?"

"Yes, after the Nazis took all his money, they threw him in prison, where he died alone. All because of his greed. He could have seen what was going on, but he didn't make a move to get out. The point of the story is . . ." he said faintly. "What was the point of the story?" It was not a question for me, but I loved my grandfather's stories and helped him out.

"You stood up to your brother and left Europe, even though he told you to stay and make money."

"Exactly!" he said. "You have to be extra courageous and learn how to say no when someone is telling you to do something you know is wrong. Especially if it's illegal. You know that stealing is wrong. And if you really did this because someone pressured you, remember it's always easier to say yes."

"So I should just say yes, then?" I asked. Where was this going?

"No, you should have recognized that it wasn't right, and then you should have left the store."

What would Elaine have said? I almost asked. She would have teased me.

My grandfather positioned his cane, and I grabbed his arm, helping him to his feet.

"Your grandmother doesn't know about this," he said gently. "If it's okay with you, I'm not going to tell her." He looked at me. "She'd kill you."

I was flushed with relief. Looking at my grandfather's exhausted face, it finally struck me that I hadn't really seen him since he came home from the hospital. I had been allowed to go to the hospital only once; his condition had been serious for a week. Once he returned home, my grandfather spent his time resting. He took his meals in the study and spent most of his time alone. I could have gone and sat with him, but I hadn't; I was afraid of seeing him like this. I didn't want to say something that upset him and send him back to the hospital.

I understood then that my grandfather had painfully gotten himself up and dressed to come and get me out of trouble. My stomach lurched, and I felt worse than usual when I did something wrong. I felt even worse about the hurtful things I'd said about him and my grandmother earlier, in front of Elaine.

"Come on, Grandpa. You can buy us an ice cream cone."

We walked toward the front doors, my grandfather balancing between the cane and my shoulder. Mr. Stotes intercepted my grandfather as he was about to leave and explained that in exchange for his not calling the police, I should not come back to FAO Schwarz for a long time.

Nodding his agreement, my grandfather said he thought that was fair. I wanted to cry; my trips to FAO Schwarz were one of the few things I looked forward to every week, but I was so relieved that my grandmother wasn't going to find out what I'd done that I stayed quiet.

Outside the doors my grandfather asked me what I had tried to steal.

"A train set and some trains," I lied.

The next day a train set and tracks were delivered to our apartment, and, true to his word, my grandfather never said anything to my grandmother. But my grandmother was perceptive and saw right away that I was no longer spending time with Elaine and that I hadn't asked to go back to the toy store.

"We had a fight," I said.

"These things happen," she said. "I got into one myself today and almost had to slap that dumb broad with her son that goes to Princeton silly."

The good thing about my grandmother was that she had a way of turning the conversation back around to herself, and I was allowed to forget that Elaine hadn't bothered to call me, either. I did not see at the time that Elaine had pulled that stunt not out of defiance but as an attempt to gain a commodity you can't buy or steal: love. When Elaine told her mother what had happened, the Heiress rushed back from Europe and fired Tonya immediately. Elaine thought she had won, that she would finally have a mother just like June Cleaver. She was too optimistic. True, Elaine got to go to Europe for the rest of that summer, but, as my friend found out, having the Heiress for a full-time mother still wasn't the same as what she'd seen on television.

five

In My Grandmother's Closet

I w a s sure that I could have been a beautiful girl. I had lots of practice. By the end of fifth grade, wearing my grandmother's dresses had become a routine for me. It might have started out as a ploy to get attention from my notoriously bored grandmother, but slowly it turned into a genuine interest of mine.

Actually, truth be told, my infatuation didn't start out with the clothes. It was more about doing imitations. I was gifted with an innate ear for mimicry, and by ten years old I could impersonate almost everyone I saw on television. It just so happened that the people I was most interested in impersonating were women. Go figure.

My grandmother loved the imitations, and they became a staple of her Friday nights. She had Atse pop some popcorn, and the two of them settled onto the sofa in the living room, eager to watch the show.

"Do Julia Child first. Atse loves Julia Child," my grandmother said.

"That's right," he said. "TGIF! Tell us what you'd do to that chicken, Julia."

"Then this is for Atse," I said, winking. "First you take the chicken," I screeched, "and fold the skin over the anal cavity. This makes room for that *delicious* rosemary stuffing. I know I enjoy a bird that's stuffed in more ways than one."

And while my grandmother and Atse would be laughing, my grandfather would be stewing in the corner. "This isn't funny," he'd say. "He could be doing something else, something with a ball. Something in the park."

"Oh, Howard," she'd scoff, "it's Friday night. The only people doing anything with balls in the park are pedophiles. Go on, Matthew. Do something else. Do Zsa Zsa."

My grandfather would throw up his hands and retreat back to the study.

.   .   .   .

I'm not sure if it was a natural consequence of examining the attitudes and personalities of so many women, but I had always been drawn to their clothes and then to the biggest closet in our apartment, my grandmother's. My grandmother's closets had the best mirrors in the house—floor to ceiling, 180-degree angles—and I'd entertain myself there alone. One quiet afternoon, while my grandparents were out and Atse and the maid were downstairs, I slipped on a pair of my grandmother's pumps. My grandmother's feet must have been very petite, or my own abnormally large, because the shoes fit perfectly. Like they were made for me.

But just standing there in Chanel pumps seemed somehow incomplete. I looked around and was drawn to the dresses and skirts. My grandmother had an outfit for every occasion, even for horseback riding. (I never saw her touch a horse.) The clothes called out to me. *Put us on,* they were saying. *You know you want to.*

I hadn't thought of trying on a dress since Elaine brought me that Ms. Wood dress back in the third grade. But these dresses were so different. They were stylish, and I could imagine them floating around me like a cloud if I'd just put them on. I thought girls were so lucky to have such fun clothes. Boys' clothes were all so dull. Nothing boys wore looked like a cloud. Pants were tight until they started sagging in the back. Dresses always kept their shape—at least on my grandmother they did.

So I caressed the lonely fabrics that hung in my grandmother's closet. They were silky and soft, and that just made me want even more to try them on. Still, I hesitated. It was one thing to do female impres-

sions or wear dresses to make fun of your teacher—or so I thought—
and another story to do it in private. Certainly that wasn't normal. It
took me weeks to gather the courage to pull one off its padded hanger.
It was actually my grandmother who suggested I go for it.

I was impersonating a friend of hers. "Oh, Sophie," I said. My
voice was high, and I stretched the ends of my words. "You simply
go to Henri and *ask* him to wash your hair a second time. It's like a
spiritual experience," I said, touching my grandmother's shoulder.
They'd had this conversation during one of the weekly poker games
my grandmother hosted for Upper East Side society women she
wanted to con out of some money.

Recognizing the conversation, my grandmother laughed. "It's a
good thing you live with me, or my life would be all over CBS."
Then, as if remembering something, she got up and went to the
closet. She took down a lavender skirted suit and studied it for a
minute before turning and saying, "Here. Put this on."

I eyed the suit with confusion and desire. Was my grandmother
teasing me? I must have been staring. She soon became exasperated,
the way she did whenever anyone kept her waiting. "Put the goddamn thing on already. You're not having surgery or anything."

I grabbed the suit and carefully slipped on the jacket. The fabric
sliding against my skin was bliss. It was like putting on a whole new
identity. I swore to myself right there that one day I would have my
own dresses like this—maybe makeup, too—but first I knew I'd
have to ease my grandparents into the idea.

This was a start for now, though. I held up my hands, imagining
I was under a spotlight, and then I saw my grandfather standing at
the doorway of their bedroom.

"This is a bad case of déjà vu," he said, and I knew he was remembering coming into my room and finding me impersonating
Ms. Wood.

"What's the matter?" asked my grandmother. "I think he looks
pretty good."

"Good?" he growled. "What is he doing in that getup? This *isn't*
good! Why are you encouraging this?"

She looked at me and shrugged. "I think it looks fine. He just doesn't know what fun is," she said, gesturing at my grandfather. "No-Fun Howard, that's what we'll call him."

Then she held out her arms for a hug, and I ran right into them.

.   .   .   .

I was never exactly starved for physical affection, but my grandmother made me work for it. Hugs weren't free. "What have you done to deserve a hug?" she'd often ask me. She'd lock her arms to her sides or fold them across her small chest like a Jewish genie. It was almost impossible to penetrate the Jewish hug genie. "So tell me what you've done to deserve a hug," she'd say. "These are very expensive."

I lacked the ability to construct a reasonable argument—so much for going into law or politics—so I once threw myself down and grabbed her ankles so she couldn't get away.

"Hug me!" I shouted, kicking myself around in a circle on the floor like Homer Simpson. "Hug me! Hug me!"

"Nope," she said softly, pretending to examine a nail.

"Just give the boy a hug," my grandfather said. "Come here, Matthew, and I'll hug you. Forget about her."

I looked up at my grandmother. She eyed me skeptically. I looked back to my grandfather, whose arms were wide open. I loved my grandfather, but he gave out hugs like John D. Rockefeller gave out dimes to needy children. I didn't want to hurt his feelings, so I begrudgingly crawled over and leaned in.

"That's nice," said my grandfather, patting my back.

"Yeah, it's great," I said. I tried not to sound sarcastic, like my grandmother.

Not wanting to be outdone, she huffed and said, "I might be interested in a hug."

And just like that I tossed my grandfather aside—almost knocking him down in the process—and ran and jumped into my grandmother's outstretched arms. She smelled so wonderful—like

Chanel No. 5—and I would have stayed in her arms forever if she had let me.

. . . .

After my grandmother showed me that dressing up was okay, my imitations became a full-time comedy circuit in our apartment. To create acts, I didn't discriminate based on age or color. Mine was an equal-opportunity muse. I scoured television and film alike, looking for distinct voices and a definitive sense of fashion.

When I finally got the nerve to ask for my own dresses over breakfast one morning toward the end of fifth grade—"for performances only"—my grandmother's face seemed to light up. "What a great idea!" she said. However, my grandfather drew the line. "Absolutely not!" He crossed his arms and then pointed at me. "I've had enough of this business. You. I'm putting you in Little League this afternoon."

I looked to my grandmother, hoping for a reprieve.

She shook her head gravely, obviously nervous that her free entertainment would be lost, and proposed a compromise. "Howard, what about voice lessons?"

My grandfather scratched his chin. "What kind of voice lessons?" he asked softly.

"Whatever kind you'd like. You're the boss." She smiled sweetly. I began to laugh, but my grandmother turned and glared. I shut up. And my grandfather, who loved to be flattered, brightened at her idea. "How about he learns some Sinatra or Tony Bennett? He could be a crooner!" He went back to reading the newspaper, and my grandmother rolled her eyes.

I gripped the table, on the verge of blurting, "But I don't want to be a crooner!"

My grandmother must have sensed this, because she quickly changed to a subject less emotionally charged: politics.

A week later Eric showed up at our apartment. He was a small, androgynous man who, I later learned, played piano in a cabaret downtown. My grandmother asked him to come over when my grandfather was out. Later, when my grandfather asked about my voice lessons, I heard my grandmother lie. "I found a great coach!" she said. "He works with the Metropolitan Opera."

"Great!" He beamed. "Matthew the Tenor. I can see it now."

She smiled. "I had you in mind when I found him."

He paused, reliving his own Plácido Domingo fantasy, and strolled off singing something from *La Bohème* in Italian. I didn't realize I was holding my breath, and I let it out, relieved that my grandfather was happy.

My grandmother shook her head. "There really is one born every minute."

During our first lesson, Eric asked what kind of music I was interested in learning.

"My grandfather says that I should try to learn opera. He said opera or Sinatra."

My grandmother called out from across the room, "How about musical comedy? Don't you think that would be fun, Matthew?"

I nodded. "Sure."

Eric smiled. "That's my specialty." He began playing the score from *Funny Girl* on our piano.

"And he's Jewish, too!" said my grandmother. "Eric, you're perfect. Maybe you could teach him something from *Hello, Dolly!*"

Eric paused on the keyboard. "There really aren't many male singing parts in that show."

My grandmother waved his comment away. "Who wants him singing those parts, anyway? I'm not wasting a Saturday night on Michael Crawford."

"What about Grandpa?" I asked. I was afraid that when my grandfather heard me sing show tunes and not Sinatra, he'd be angry.

"Matthew," said my grandmother, "what do you want?" I looked at her. I looked at Eric. They both watched me. I hated when she asked me questions like this. I just wanted to make everyone happy. I wanted my grandmother to laugh, and I wanted my grandfather to smile, too—and sing along. "I want to sing musicals," I said.

My grandmother grinned and clapped. "That's my boy," she said. "You'll be famous if you keep practicing. You could probably bring back the whole musical genre!"

Famous! If that were true, I reasoned, if that could really happen, then my grandfather wouldn't care that I was keeping this secret. So, after I belted out a number that would make Streisand proud, I kept my mouth shut.

. . . .

Every so often my grandparents would have a "date." They broke open the albums and relived their courtship in the living room, and these were the rare occasions when my grandmother became warm and fuzzy. One evening, shortly after I began voice lessons with Eric, I encountered my grandparents with the albums. I threw myself between them on the sofa, ready to bask in their attention. I sat in awe of the images on the page; I always thought my grandmother was beautiful, but she had clearly been stunning as a young woman.

"She looked just like Judy Garland," said my grandfather. He put an arm around my grandmother.

"Who?" I asked.

"The girl from *The Wizard of Oz.*"

My eyes flashed with recognition, and an idea hatched in my head. That night I sat through *The Wizard of Oz* again, memorizing lines from my favorite scenes. When the movie finished, I hit "rewind." I watched the movie two more times that night.

The next day I discovered that it wasn't Judy Garland's only movie. My grandmother walked me over to the shelf bearing her collection of classic films and pulled out tape after tape. As she dropped the boxes in front of me, my face lit up like a menorah in July.

I spent the next few weeks preparing a new act with Eric: covering the songs of Judy. I practiced daily. I sang in the shower. I sang in the limo on the way to school. I hummed while standing in the lunch line. My grandmother ate it up; she clapped and sang along—"I love that song!" I was her little cherub during those weeks. But my friends thought differently.

After the FAO Schwarz incident, Elaine and I stopped speaking. First I didn't want to talk to her because I couldn't believe what she'd done. Then, when the Heiress found out, she flew home from Europe and made her apologize to my grandparents and me. My grandmother listened to the apology in a state of confusion, as my grandfather hadn't told her about what had happened. Then confusion turned to anger, and she wanted me and Elaine separated.

She called up a friend on the board of another prep school and managed to have me transferred. This friend had a grandson named Ricky who went to the school. And since Ricky seemed like a nice enough kid, my grandmother encouraged a friendship. As it happens, my grandmother didn't have to worry about Elaine influencing me. Shortly after the Heiress made Elaine apologize, she put their apartment up for sale, and they moved out to their country house full-time. There were no teary good-byes, and I wasn't aware they'd moved at all until I was well into fifth grade and ready for reconciliation.

"No, I don't want to hear you sing 'Over the Rainbow,'" my friend Ricky said. "I want to go to the arcade and play." Despite my best efforts, Ricky had been the only friend I'd made at the new school, and this friendship was tenuous at best. We didn't really have common interests, and I'm sure now that if our grandmothers hadn't orchestrated a friendship the previous summer, one would not have sprung up on its own.

I tried to explain that my jazzier version of the song would leave him in awe, but he muttered something about how I'd changed, and turned to leave. I huffed and said, "Ricky, I believe that somewhere, over the rainbow, dreams that you dare to dream really do come true."

. . . .

All my practice seemed to pay off when my fifth-grade teacher, Mrs. Wilson, announced the annual talent show. I liked Mrs. Wilson very much. She was pretty and friendly and always called on me when I raised my hand. And because I liked her—and believed she liked me—I was polite and well mannered. I would have listened to her talk about dog drool, and I was particularly excited to hear about the talent show.

"Last year we had a lot of great acts," Mrs. Wilson began in front of the class. "I hope that some of you will try out. This year the show is going to be in the evening, which will give your parents the opportunity to attend."

That was all the reason I needed. I nodded as if she were speaking to me personally. *Matthew, put your talent to some use,* she seemed to be saying. *Go onstage. Show these chumps who the real talent in Room 3 is.*

"Yes, ma'am," I said. "I won't let you down."

The other kids in class turned to stare. They all laughed. I hadn't meant to say it out loud. My face went red, and Mrs. Wilson smiled.

"I know you won't," she said, placing the sign-up sheet on my desk first. I wrote down my name, my act, and handed her the clipboard. Later, when the bell rang and the class burst into the hallway, I made my way up to her desk. "A singer?" she said. "I didn't know that you sang."

Ricky was on his way out. "Oh, brother," he muttered. "There he goes again."

Ricky had been making comments like that every day, and I always felt embarrassed.

Noticing my expression, Mrs. Wilson asked me to stay. "If you're not in a rush, I could use some help cleaning the board."

I agreed without hesitation and took off my uniform's jacket. The driver was waiting outside, but I figured he got paid to wait as well as drive, and it was only for a few minutes.

She handed me an eraser. "Is there anything going on between you and Ricky?"

I started wiping the board. "I guess he's mad because I don't have as much time to play with him."

"Oh," she said. She was silent for a moment. "What takes up so much of your time? New friends? Sports?"

"I'm working on my act. My grandmother says that if I ever want to be as good as Judy Garland, I have to practice. I have a voice coach, too."

Mrs. Wilson looked puzzled. "Judy Garland?"

"Like in *The Wizard of Oz*," I offered.

"No—I know who she is. I was just surprised that you did, too."

We were silent as I continued wiping the board.

"Matthew, what are you going to sing for the talent show?"

I stopped wiping the board. "I was thinking about doing a number called 'Get Happy' from Judy's last movie for MGM, *Summer Stock*. Gene Kelly's in the movie, too, and—" I stopped and thought before adding, "I think that I could do some of the dances."

"Gene Kelly's dances?"

"No. Judy's."

"You want to sing a Judy Garland song and do some of her dances?"

I nodded, and Mrs. Wilson shifted her weight onto her left leg. "You do realize she was a woman, right?"

.   .   .   .

Preparing for the show consisted of sitting with the musical *Summer Stock,* scribbling down the words, and pressing "pause" when my hand couldn't keep up with my ears. In the movie the song "Get Happy" was performed onstage in a barn. The set looked nothing like a barn, but I was mesmerized by the moves regardless. Judy was great in her long black stockings and clear voice, but I thought the real magic was how the male dancers moved. These dancers wore dark fitted suits and jumped as if the music pumped through their veins. I imagined them dancing around me, the school auditorium rocking rhythmically.

And how fierce would I look in a head-to-toe black stocking?

I waited until the night before the talent show to tell my grandparents I would be performing. We were having dinner. The dining room in our apartment was long, and when I made my announcement, though the room was densely carpeted, I heard the echo as my grandmother's knife screeched against her plate.

"Excellent!" said my grandfather. "Why didn't you say anything sooner?"

"I wanted it to be a surprise," I said. "Surprise!"

My grandmother looked like she'd just been smacked, her eyes globes of terror. If the table had been narrower, I'm sure she would have kicked me. She took a large gulp from a wineglass.

"Wait a minute." My grandfather studied her, frowning, looking like he'd discovered a secret plot. "You two . . ."

My grandmother's face was white. And I knew that somehow I had messed up.

"Did you two do this for my birthday?"

"No. I didn't know anything about this," she said. "This is all his doing." She pointed at me, her bottom lip disappearing. "I can't take *any* credit."

"I know you better than that, cookie."

Food nicknames meant my grandfather was feeling particularly sentimental.

My grandmother was still pointing. "Matthew can make decisions by himself. Can't you, Matthew? Matthew, who I nurtured as though you were my own child since you were born—putting clothes on your back, sending you to the best schools?"

"Yes, but I used the music that you gave me to give to Eric. We've been working every afternoon."

"Well, are you sure you've had enough practice, *sweetheart?*" she asked.

Sweetheart. My grandmother did not usually call me that. The effect was chilling.

"Sophie. You're going to scare him," said my grandfather.

She took another sip of wine. "Howard," she said, glaring at me over the rim, "the world is a scary place."

. . . .

Later that night I watched Judy in my room. I could hear the voices of my grandparents coming up the stairs, and I muted the video. "Are you sure you want to go?" my grandmother was saying.

"Of course! Don't be silly."

"But we have dinner with the Strausses," she said.

"He's been practicing every day, and we're going. Now I'm going to bed."

"All right," she said. "I just want to go check on Matthew. I like to tuck him in."

"Since when?" he asked.

"Who are you, the hall monitor? Since whenever I want."

At the door of my room, she flashed her "be afraid" look. "Hello, *darling,*" she said, her voice loud enough to carry back to my grandfather. She closed the door quietly and ran over to the sofa. She threw herself down next to me. "Schlemiel." She grabbed my hand. "Are you trying to kill me? I'm going to have a heart attack and die right here, and you'll be traumatized for life. Is that what you want?"

I answered that it was not.

"Why didn't you tell me about this?"

"I wanted it to be a surprise." Didn't I say that before?

"Great." She threw her hands up. "Now your grandfather is going to hear you sing and toss us both out on the street. Sixty years of marriage. Over. Just like that."

I watched her moaning. I didn't know what to say.

Sensing my confusion, she sighed. "Matthew, you're a cute kid, but some things you shouldn't do outside the house."

"Like what?" I asked.

"Like wearing your grandmother's clothing. Singing show tunes." She stood up and walked to the door. "Go to sleep now. If we're lucky, he'll drink too much at dinner tomorrow night and I can convince him you're someone else. Good night."

．　．　．　．

The talent-show competition didn't stop with the students. Their parents were in competition, too. Backstage, mothers stood over their daughters and fluffed skirts or coiffed hair. "Now, who's going to go out there and win?" one woman said to her daughter, a third-grade operatic singer. "I am," she said, her eyes blazing. "I'm going to beat everyone." The mother kept picking at her. "Why?" she asked, and the daughter replied, "Because I'm a winner."

The show brought students from different grades to showcase their various abilities. Some of the acts were interesting—kids who did gymnastics or walked on stilts—and some were best left on the subway, to men and women begging for spare change. Backstage, all the participants stood anxiously awaiting their turn. I recognized some of the kids from different classes, and Ricky stood in a corner, apart from the rest of the competitors. He gripped his skateboard with one hand, helmet in the other. Though I was excited about my act, I couldn't help but feel sad watching Ricky. A couple months ago, we would have stood here together.

He saw me and nodded.

I moved to his side so that neither of us could look at the other without turning. We studied the audience from behind the curtain. "Hello, Richard," I said, affecting a British accent meant to convey my aloofness.

"Hey, Matt," he said, completely ignoring my accent. That was the problem with Ricky. He never cared about anything important.

"What are you doing here?" I pretended to survey the crowd. Some mothers were on the edge of their chairs, just on the verge of springing up into wild applause—when their child came on, of course. A few women stood in the aisles videotaping, and I saw one mother gesturing for her violin-playing son to smile. The fathers seemed less interested, and one was even asleep.

"Some of the guys thought we could do skateboard tricks."

The guys? What guys? Surprised, I turned to look at him and realized he was not really standing by himself. There were other guys standing around, and they clutched skateboards, too. They were all boys from our grade, boys who humored me initially because I was friends with Ricky, but now none of them looked at me. I searched Ricky's face, but it was blank. Apparently he was much better at being aloof than I was.

"Good for you," I said, pretending not to be hurt. Why hadn't he asked me to be part of his act? "Good luck," I muttered, walking away.

Ricky's new friends laughed, but I ignored them. Instead I

smoothed out a wrinkle in my school uniform—a navy blazer with gold buttons and khaki pants—and stewed.

I felt someone touch my shoulder and looked up. It was Eric.

"Hey," he said. "I came to wish you luck."

The other kids were looking at him, examining his perfectly moussed hair and skintight leather pants. "And I brought you this." He handed me a brown paper bag. I looked inside—it held the closest thing he could find to a body stocking: long black underwear. "Go ahead, put it on."

It felt as though everyone was looking at me, and I was looking at the long johns, which meant everyone was looking at the long johns. I told Eric, "Thank you, but I'll keep my school uniform."

He shrugged. "Suit yourself. You're going to kill them no matter what you wear." He patted me on the back and left to take his seat in the audience.

I know he was trying to be nice, but I recalled that conversation with my grandparents over dinner and was filled with dread. I had this awful vision of my grandfather's weak heart giving out and him dying in the school auditorium that night, but I felt I *had* to perform—I'd made such a big deal out of it, to my teacher, to Ricky, to my grandparents. How could I back out now?

When the school's principal, the show's emcee, called my name, I walked out and waited for my cue in the middle of the stage. The audience sat stoically. I took a deep breath and launched into "Get Happy" sans tuxedoed dancers.

"Forget your troubles, c'mon get happy . . ."

It had not occurred to me that I might need musical accompaniment, and so my act had none. In the moments I was not supposed to sing—where in the movie the dancers were doing their part or the music was flaring—I just stood silently.

Spontaneous applause, snapping, maybe even a few people singing along was what I had hoped for. But standing there waiting to sing again, I noticed the faces of teachers and administrators. I could *see* what they were thinking: Was this some kind of a joke? It was not the reaction I had anticipated during my rehearsals. Even Mrs. Wilson seemed to bite her lip and knit her brow. I looked out into the audience, nerves crashing into one another. The PTA mothers rested their hands atop neatly folded fur coats. Fathers, who before were only half interested, now eyed me like a circus act.

Then I saw my grandparents. I could see my grandmother in the third row with her hand covering her eyes. My grandfather, dumbfounded, rested his head on his palm. I shut my eyes and belted out the finale to my number. "Get ready—" Skip two beats for the dancers. "Get ready—" Skip two beats for the music. "Get ready—for the judgment daaaaaaaaaay!"

If there was applause, I didn't hear; I ran from the stage. I wanted to hide for as long as I could, so I pushed through the kids backstage and headed for the bathroom. I sat on a toilet in one of the stalls and began to cry.

The door opened, and I sucked in my breath. "Matt?" I heard my name. I looked up. Ricky was standing on the toilet in the next stall, looking down at me.

I let out a long breath and started wailing again.

"Quiet," he said. "You want the whole school in here?"

"I don't care. They all think I'm stupid."

"Matt, I'm sorry I teased you. You sounded good. The song was pretty girlie, but you were all right. You should sing something else next time, something kids our age have heard before."

When I finally came out of the bathroom, I heard my grandparents backstage. I waited behind a wall, attempting to gauge my future punishment.

"—wasn't that bad, really," said my grandmother. "He just needed some accompaniment."

"Like a piano player from a bathhouse?" My grandfather sounded exasperated.

"How did you know about that?" I recognized that tone in my grandmother's voice—it was reserved for shock or battle preparation.

I peeked around the wall. Instead of yelling, my grandfather began chuckling. "I knew what you were doing the whole time. I let it go because it seemed like Matthew was having fun." His smile faded, and his expression turned serious. "You, on the other hand, should be ashamed of yourself manipulating a little boy into lying to his grandfather. And for what? So you'd have some Saturday-night cabaret?"

"I did no such thing! He loved every minute of it."

"Is that's why he's hiding in the bathroom?" said my grandfather. "I don't want you putting any more ideas in his head after this. Let him decide what he wants to do, and we'll go along with it."

"The music teacher wants him to join the chorus," said my grandmother.

"How about football?"

I walked out from behind the wall and stood behind them.

"No football," I said. They both whipped around. I reached up, grabbing both of their hands, and guided them toward the exit.

"How about basketball?"

My grandmother and I both looked at him blankly.

"Tennis?" he said.

"Too much running," I said.

"Golf?"

"Wait a minute," said my grandmother. "You won't let him dress up to perform, but you'll have him go out on the streets looking like a Christmas tree? I don't think so."

My grandfather sighed. "Baseball?"

My grandmother shuddered.

"What about swimming?" I asked.

My grandfather beamed. My grandmother said, "Matthew, swimming isn't just floating and splashing."

"I know. I meant like in the Olympics. There's no sweating, and you get to play in the water." I left out the part about the cute out-fits. If my grandmother really didn't want me leaving the apartment looking like a Christmas tree, she probably wouldn't want me going out in a Speedo.

Jude the Obscure

In t w e n t y minutes my mother was due to pick me up. I could still hear her saying, "Wear something nice, Matthew, and I'll get you in an hour." Wear something nice—it was the first thing I could remember her asking me to do, and I was already messing up. I stood in my room surrounded by clothing designed for fat children, and the only way this stuff would ever slide back on my corpulent ten-year-old body was if I soaked it all in Crisco first.

My mother never came to New York. For as long as I could remember, she'd been perfectly content to stay in Europe amid deposed monarchs and other beautiful people. That's why I was so surprised when she called earlier. "I'm in town! Hello! Would you like to go shopping?" We hadn't seen each other since I was three, and I couldn't even remember that time.

"I'm with my friend, a real live countess, she'd positively *love* to meet you," my mother had said. I was thrilled: Not only was I going to see my mother, finally, but I'd also be hobnobbing with royalty. Surely someone from the press would see us and I'd be on Page Six the next morning.

"Why, yes, Muthah," I said, affecting my best British accent. "I would be simp-ly de-lighted to accompany you and the countess to Bergdorf Goodman's this spring day."

"Excellent!" she said, and laughed. "What a charming accent you have!" I heard splashing in the background and realized she was calling from the bathtub. She must be very important if she could only make time to talk on the phone while she took a bath. Such a multitasker!

She hung up. I ran to my closet to find something suitable, and now look where that had gotten me: Clothes covered every surface of the floor, like some kind of makeshift flea-market rug. I slid down against the closet door, on the verge of tears, when I heard a low whistle. I looked up; my grandmother was leaning against the door-jamb, dressed in all black, her head cocked in wonder.

"What fresh hell is this?" she asked. Her arms were folded across her chest. No matter what she wore, my grandmother managed to look amazing. Give her a burlap sack and some lipstick, she'd still look like a million dollars. Gazing down at my stomach spilling over my gray sweatpants, I found it hard to believe we were related. Where had all this fat come from, anyway? I wasn't always this fat, I could swear it. Pictures from kindergarten indicated I was practically emaciated then. But look at me now. An ungreased pig with kinky hair and a messy room.

I sat staring at her, motionless.

"Well?" she asked again.

"Mother—" I began, but then I stopped. Since I sometimes called my grandmother "Mother," I wasn't sure what to call my real mother, especially when talking about her with my grandmother.

She raised an eyebrow but said nothing. She was waiting for me to finish. I thought carefully about what I wanted to say next. If I said something wrong, I'd surely get The Lecture: twenty or thirty minutes' worth of liberal sighs and eye rolling as my grandmother ranted about irresponsibility and about how "thanks to the influence of your grandfather's family, none of my children ever had a trace of ethics or common sense. They never had a chance!"

Even my grandfather got The Lecture sometimes, and that's why nobody in our home mentioned my mother. But my grandmother was waiting for an answer, and this time I needed to risk it. "Mom called and said she wanted to take me shopping." I cringed inside, preparing for the worst. I had been the first to hear the phone ring and answered it myself.

"Did she?" asked my grandmother. I remember thinking it was strange how unsurprised she was about my mother's being in town. I knew this was one of those questions that didn't require an answer. She scanned my room before letting out a snort. "Looks like your closet threw up."

"I was trying to find something to wear."

"And how," she asked, gesturing to the clothes, "does that translate into your clothes on the floor?"

"Nothing fits!" I hugged my knees to hide my Butterball stomach. "And if it does, it makes me look like a fatso."

My grandmother nodded and picked a light-colored sport coat off the floor. "Didn't I just have this let out?" She picked up a pair of matching trousers. "These, too," she said, wiping off some lint. She laid the outfit on the bed. "Wear them with that blue polo shirt you've got on. It brings out your eyes." She snorted again. "They're your mother's eyes. The narcissist will love you."

"Thanks. . . . Aren't you going to say anything else?" I asked, wondering when to expect The Lecture.

"About the pants?" She shrugged. "You're not a fatso, Matthew. You may be big now, but you'll grow." She motioned vaguely toward my stomach. "All that, it'll redistribute. In the meantime lay off the M&M's for a while."

"Not about that," I said. "About where I'm going. Remember, I'm going shopping with my *mother*? You're not mad?"

"Mad?" she said, shaking her head. "Matthew, it's okay to spend time with your mother while she's in town."

I was stunned. Where was the sermon on responsibility? What about the evil influence of my grandfather's genes?

"Much as it pains me to say it," she said, rolling her eyes, "something would be wrong with you if you didn't want to see her. Besides, how often does she show up? I've seen eclipses happen more frequently." She walked toward the door. "Have her get you some new pants," she called over her shoulder, and vanished into the hall.

"Thanks for your help," I said, but she was already gone. I tore off my sweatpants and put on the trousers and blazer. Surprisingly, the blazer made me look thinner, and the shirt did indeed make my eyes pop out. In a good way, though, not in a crazy, Looney Tunes way. I spent the next half hour trying to tame my Jewfro, and then Atse called up the stairs. The lobby had phoned; there was a car waiting for me.

"Why didn't she come up?" I asked, running down the stairs. My grandparents stood on either side of the foyer.

"Look at you," said my grandfather, eyeing me up and down and smiling. "Very sharp. Where are you two headed?"

Trying my best to sound sophisticated, I told him our first stop was Bergdorf Goodman. "Then we'll probably have lunch at the Plaza before hitting Tiffany's. And actually, it's not just the two of us—we're a party of three. She's bringing *the countess*."

My grandmother rolled her eyes, but my grandfather lit up. "The countess, you say? Well, that is very special, isn't it?"

"They're going to a department store, Howard," my grandmother cut in, "not curing the blind."

"Still," he huffed, "how often does Matthew get to see such important people?"

"If you'd ever let us ride the subway, I'm sure he'd see them every day." She smirked. "There're probably all sorts of broke royalty hanging around in subway stations looking for a sucker to pay for a hotel."

Ignoring my grandmother, he turned back to me. "Your mother is a jet-setter, just like I was at her age. Always on the move. Here one day, gone the next."

"Yes. The very picture of instability," said my grandmother.

I left them glaring at one another and walked toward the elevator. "Don't wait up," I said. I could hear my grandmother sigh as she shut the door behind me. I suspected that I had just abandoned my poor grandfather to The Lecture.

In the elevator I thought about how I'd greet my mother. I didn't want to sound immature, so "Mummy" was definitely out. I caught a glimpse of myself in the mirror. A goofy smile had plastered itself across my face, and despite my best efforts I could not subdue it.

I wanted to look genteel, not insane, but in the mirror I was teeming with rabid excitement. I half walked, half ran to the waiting limousine.

"Mother!" I said, jumping into the car. It was empty.

The driver lowered the partition. "They're waiting for you at the store."

Oh.

I settled back against the cool leather seats and exhaled, just in time for a new set of worries to pop up in my head. How was I going to find my mother in a big department store like Bergdorf Goodman? I went there all the time with my grandmother and knew just how huge it really was. How would I recognize her? I had only seen her in pictures, and all those pictures were old. One was a baby picture on my grandfather's desk, and the other was a picture of her—she was maybe thirteen—all made up, with a small dog. I didn't know what she'd be wearing or where she'd be waiting—what if she were trying on a gown in a dressing room and I missed her completely?

The driver got to Bergdorf's just as another car was leaving. He slid the limousine into a spot in front of the store. "I'll be here," he said as the store's doorman opened the car door. The chauffeur pulled out the sports section of the newspaper.

I entered the department store through a revolving door and started looking for my mother in the cosmetics section. Normally I'd be asking to test some of the creams on my palm, but all I could think about was how close I was to my mother. She could be anywhere. Turning around, I saw lots of pretty women giggling and testing makeup, but none looked like the pictures of my mother. One woman behind a counter called out to me, "Are you all right? Can I help you?"

"I'm looking for my mother," I said, trying to sound casual. The words were foreign to my mouth, and I hoped I sounded normal. Just a regular kid looking for his mom. Children were temporarily separated from their parents all the time in department stores, right? I was breathing heavily, and the woman studied me carefully. She clearly knew I was scared, which I was. I was ten years old, I was about to meet my mother, and I was so close! I didn't want to ruin it.

Her mouth puckered into a small worried O. She pointed across the room to an elevator. "Upstairs, perhaps? If you go up the elevator one floor, you'll find the shoe department and ladies' clothes. If you still don't see your mother up there, come back down, and I'll call for the manager. He'll take you around. How about that?"

"Thank you very much," I said, but knew I wouldn't be coming back down. What would I say to the manager, anyway? "Excuse me. Could you please help me find my mother? No, sorry, I don't know what she looks like these days." I would be mortified. My mother would probably think I'd never been in a department store before! On top of everything else today, I didn't need that kind of grief.

Focus. I walked up the stairs leading to shoes. I looked for a woman resembling the pictures of my mother I'd seen at home. She seemed like the type of woman who'd have lots of shoes, so I started there. There were women crawling all over, but none who looked familiar. A couple of them looked at me and said, "Oh, how cute." I smiled at them, trying to make myself as cute as possible. As I searched, I remembered something my grandmother had told me a few years earlier, when my mother had forgotten my birthday. "Don't take it personally. Your mother can't remember a damn thing."

I hoped she hadn't forgotten I was coming. Or what if she'd already left, because I was too slow in showing up? I started sweating, and suddenly I was nauseated. Then I saw two tiny blondes standing among a sea of black evening dresses.

"You look good in anything," I heard the first blonde saying in accented English. Clad in sunglasses and a skintight skirt suit, she held up a slinky black dress against the second blonde. "Just try it on."

The second blonde laughed. I recognized that laugh. It sounded exactly like the one I'd heard on the phone earlier.

But this woman couldn't be my mother. She didn't look like any of the pictures I'd seen. And my mother did not have blond hair; her hair was dark like mine. It was the only physical characteristic we shared besides eye color.

I needed to get a better look—just to be sure. I snaked through the dresses and spied on the two blondes from behind a rack of sequined Oscar de la Rentas.

"Go try it on," said First Blonde, foisting the dress upon her friend. It looked barely long enough to cover her *pupik*.

"I couldn't wear something like that," said Second Blonde.

"And why, might I ask?" First Blonde lowered her sunglasses and struck a pose—skeptical, incredulous, with her hand on her hip—that I could only dream of pulling off.

"Because," said Second Blonde, giggling. "Look at the neckline. I'd fall out of it the first time I stood up. As it is, the Catholics already think I'm a harlot."

I didn't know which Catholics she was referring to, but I recognized my mother's voice. I heard the same soft wispiness three or four times a year on birthdays and my grandparents' wedding anniversary. My pulse quickened. I was as close to my mother as I could physically be without her seeing me. I could see First Blonde's heavily made up face and the back of my mother's head.

Okay, so if my mother was Second Blonde, that made First Blonde the countess. I looked her up and down. She was certainly stylish enough, but where was her entourage? What, I wondered, was the point of being royalty if you didn't have an entourage? And where was her tiara?

"Oh," said the countess, pushing her sunglasses back up, "I almost forgot. Where is your little man?"

I still couldn't see her face, but I was sure she was my mother, only with different hair. I didn't get why people changed hair colors. Didn't they realize that people looking for them after years and years wouldn't be able to find them? I caught a glimpse of myself in a nearby mirror and pictured myself as a blond.

"Didn't you say your son was coming?" asked the countess. And that was my confirmation. Second Blonde was definitely my mother.

She was staring down at the black dress that Catholics would disapprove of. I crawled behind the row of dresses until I was looking directly at their legs through a rack of creamy, expensive silk.

"He'll be along any minute, I'm sure," my mother said.

The countess was striking a pose again—I could tell by the position of her legs. Her right heel was pressed flat against her left stiletto's arch. "Tell me again. Why does he live in New York?" Her accent made it hard to discern whether she was interested or politely indifferent.

"He lives with my parents," my mother said.

"That you've said, but why? My children live with their father. Why doesn't he stay with his father?"

I held my breath. Crouching uncomfortably on the metal base, I forced as much of myself into the rack as I could. I couldn't see anything above their knees.

"His father . . ." she said. Pause. "I've kept him out of all this." I heard the metal scratch of the hanger as she returned the dress to the rack. "He doesn't actually know about Matthew."

The countess gasped, and I nearly did, too. My mouth fell open. What did she mean? My grandmother always told me, "Your father, he was a bum. He's living out in California. Somewhere! I don't know." I'd always assumed that my father was a man who knew about me and couldn't pick up the phone to see if I was dead or alive.

Now I wasn't sure which reality was better.

"Don't look at me like that," said my mother. "I did the right thing. I found out I was pregnant on the day I filed for divorce. Can you imagine?" She laughed. "Our marriage was over, and I didn't want him hanging around me for the rest of my life. I realize it sounds awful, but you didn't know my ex-husband."

Their legs were facing one another.

"But why with your parents, then?"

A few seconds went by, then a few more. I was sure she wasn't going to answer and by that point I was leaning forward so heavily beneath the rack I almost toppled through. Why hadn't I found a spot where I could see their faces? "Motherhood," she said finally, "wasn't for me. When I was a little girl and all my friends had dolls, I wanted real estate. I didn't have a maternal bone in my body. I still don't. When I found out I was pregnant, all I could think was, damn, that baby will ruin my waistline. And then there was my soon-to-be ex. He'd hang around forever—so . . ." She shuffled, as if her calves were shrugging. "I decided to have an abortion."

Abortion? I knew I'd heard that word before, but I couldn't place it. I tried a vocabulary exercise my grandfather taught me: Take the word you don't know and look at the words around it. Figure out if it's positive or negative. If that doesn't work, associate the word with the tone of its speaker's voice. The words near *abortion* were *divorce* and *real estate,* and my mother's voice had gotten soft, so I assumed it wasn't a positive word.

"Well, I can understand that," said the countess. "Who needs to be tied to an ex?"

"Exactly!" She paused. "But when I told my parents—my mother almost killed me." She laughed. "I thought she was going to claw my eyes out! My father calmed her down. He's always looked out for me, but even he told me I should have the baby."

So that's what an abortion is. She didn't want to have the baby and wanted to get rid of it—me—before I was born. I had heard something on the *Sally Jessy Raphaël Show* once about an operation— now I could remember where I'd heard the word—that could do just that. I took deep breaths to keep myself from crying.

"They wouldn't let me have the abortion. Even my father said it was a sin, and he doesn't believe in God. He said it would bring shame on the family . . . blah, blah, blah . . . that they'd disinherit me . . . blah, blah, blah. They said they'd raise the baby. So, in the end, my mother got her way and a new mind to fuck up. And I got my freedom."

I needed to get up. I needed to get up and leave right away. Actually, I needed to get up, curse these two women with every bad word I'd ever learned from TV and from Elaine and from school and from my grandmother—and *then* leave right away. But I couldn't; I was frozen beneath the silks. I sat under those hanging dresses, sobbing, waiting for my mother and the countess to walk away. My tears made dark pools on my khaki trousers.

"Let's go try these on," said my mother. "We can tell people we're sisters."

They laughed and their stilettos clicked toward the fitting room. I buried my face in my hands, crying so hard I was hiccupping. With my mother safely in the fitting room, I crawled out from underneath the rack of dresses and limped to the front of the store, where the driver said he'd be parked.

.　.　.　.

Of course, I had heard about my birth before—even heard myself crudely referred to as an "accident" on the playground at school. The version I always took for granted was my grandmother's. I was four years old, and it was Mother's Day. I was upset because all my friends were doing Mother's Day things and I felt lonely with no one to play with. "My mother doesn't want me," I said, dejected.

"That's not true at all. We both wanted you," my grandmother said softly, tucking me in. This was in the blissful time before The Lecture had developed. "Yes, we both wanted you, your mother and I, but I wanted you more." She was pulling the blanket tight around my chest. "And I said, 'Give me that baby!'" She dug her fingers into my skinny flesh, and I writhed on the bed, giggling.

"Why didn't my mother say no?" I asked when she stopped.

My grandmother scoffed. "She did! But I locked her in her room until she saw things my way."

That made perfect sense. I pictured the two of them in a boxing ring with me as the prize. My mother was young and spry, but my grandmother was a saucy old dame who wasn't afraid to kick you where the sun didn't shine. My mother would never have stood a chance. It felt good to know that I had been the subject of so much attention.

"You're back early," said my grandfather, glancing at the clock when I got home. I hadn't even been gone a whole hour. I tried to smile. My nose was still congested from crying in the limo, so it must have looked as unconvincing as it felt. My grandmother was in the corner reading the newspaper, a glass of clear liquid resting beside her. So, I thought, they'd had words after I left. Normally they'd sit next to each other on the sofa, and even my grandmother rarely started drinking before noon.

"Well," he said, rubbing his hands together. "What do you say?"

What was I supposed to say?

"Did she tell you?" he asked.

For a moment I was confused. How did he know what I'd overheard? But then I understood that I was supposed to come back from this outing with some other kind of news.

My grandfather's smile slipped from his face. I turned to my grandmother, who put down the newspaper and peered at me over tortoiseshell glasses. "Matthew, did she ask you to go back with her?" she asked softly. "For a visit?"

"No," I said. "I didn't exactly see her."

A worry line spread across my grandfather's forehead. He pursed his lips.

"I couldn't find her," I said. "I looked all over. I walked around, and then I left. Maybe she had left already when I got there?"

"Impossible," my grandfather said, his voice rising. He looked at my grandmother and then closed his eyes. "Did you call the manager?" he demanded. He was rubbing his forehead.

I didn't want him to be angry, but how could I explain what had really happened? He was probably sitting here the whole time, imagining his daughter and her glamorous life of parties and vacations, his daughter who surely wasn't perfect but whom he loved anyway. He knew the truth about me, but that obviously didn't change the way he saw her.

"No," I said, looking at the floor. "I'm sorry."

"She's probably worried," he said. "I'll call the store and her hotel." He rose from the sofa and moved past me, walking more quickly than I'd seen in a long time.

My grandmother was staring at me. "Oh, Matthew. You've got that look," she said.

"What look?" I asked, surprised.

"That look everyone gets after they realize something they never wanted to," she said. She threw the newspaper down on the ottoman and stood up. "Let's get out of here before he gets back. Your grandfather's like a teenager with a crush whenever the subject of his daughter comes up."

"Where are we going?" I asked.

"Just for a walk—to talk," she said. Then, looking at me, she picked up the tumbler of clear liquid, her rings clinking against the glass. "For strength," she said, and then drained the contents. "This is going to hurt like hell."

Trudging over to the candy dish, I shoved a fistful of M&M's into my mouth. "I'm ready," I said. We walked across Fifth Avenue in silence. As we entered the park, I wondered if what I'd heard at Bergdorf's was true, but I couldn't force the question out of my mouth. I was a mass of nerves inside. Outside, I was a morose preadolescent with a weight problem. So I just kept walking next to my grandmother.

I knew that my grandfather was on the phone with my mother by now. At the store I assumed she wouldn't be worried if I didn't show up—she certainly didn't *seem* concerned. But my grandfather's news made me wonder if I'd misjudged her. Mothers don't just ask you to go to Europe if they don't care whether you live or die. Even I knew that.

My grandmother stopped. It was a few seconds before I even realized, and when I looked back, she was half a dozen steps behind me, working a rock on the ground with her shoe, sliding it back and forth across the grass.

"I saw her," I said when I couldn't stomach the silence any longer.

"I know you did," she said, her eyes still on that rock.

"I heard her tell her friend that she didn't want me," I said.

My grandmother's foot froze. "Stupid, stupid girl," she muttered under her breath.

"She said she wanted to have an abortion, but you told her no and that she'd be poor if she did. Disinherited." The tears started again, but I didn't bother to shield my face as I had at Bergdorf's. "She had me because of the money, and she's happy that I'm here with you. She said she was free."

"Stupid, stupid girl," my grandmother repeated, this time more forcefully. She was thinking out loud. She ran her fingers through her silver hair.

"Money," I said. "That's why I'm here."

"That's not true," said my grandmother. She looked up. "Matthew, I won't lie to you. A lot of what she said was true, but you need to understand the whole story first." She walked over to a bench and sat down. I sat down beside her, waiting, and for a moment my grandmother just stared ahead.

"I swear," she said, "I don't know what happened to your mother. When she was born, she was such a tiny little thing. I didn't even want her to walk; I was afraid she'd fall and hurt herself. I didn't let her out of my sight until she was ten years old. Then she went off to Europe to visit . . . your grandfather's family.

"That goddamn cult," she said through clenched teeth. "I still don't know what happened, but when she came back at the end of the summer, I didn't recognize her. She went from being a sweet little girl picking strawberries in a field—she'd eat two for every strawberry that went in her basket—to some vapid little . . . thing! With makeup and a yapping dog. She wore eyeliner and lipstick and suddenly needed her *own* everything. Nothing was good enough for her anymore." I thought about the framed picture of my mother that was in my grandfather's study. She was probably about my age in the picture, clutching a purse with a furry white dog's head poking out. "Fast-forward a few years," my grandmother continued, her face a mask and her gaze fixed on a man playing Frisbee with a little boy. "She was done with husband number two, and"—she shook her head—"I knew *he* was a mistake before I even met the guy. What a *schmuck*. I still don't see what was wrong with Tyler."

Tyler was my mother's first husband, one of the few choices she had made that my grandmother respected. Years after their divorce,

Tyler still called my grandparents and me every week. He lived in London but visited us regularly in New York. Once he even told me that he felt a special connection to me. At the time I wondered if his real motive had to do with my mother—that by being connected to me he could feel he was still somehow connected to her—but that didn't detract from the attention he paid me. He hadn't remarried since my mother divorced him. Meanwhile, she'd remarried three times. But they still talked, my mother and Tyler. It was very European.

"Anyway, she said she wanted an abortion, okay, so that's right." My grandmother frowned, as if what she would say next took great effort. "But you must also understand that she was very young then, Matthew. Only twenty. God, I was almost forty when she was born. She knew she wouldn't make a good mother." She let out a snort. "And if she couldn't do something well, she didn't want any part of it. I wonder who she got that from." She shook her head and looked up to the sky.

I looked up with her.

"She was scared," she said.

"Scared?" I asked. I could hardly believe that. "Scared of what? Me?"

"No," she said, patting my hand. "Scared of messing up, of doing the wrong thing—like I did."

I thought of what my mother had said at Bergdorf's, about my grandmother having another mind to fuck up. Were they talking about the same thing? I wanted to ask my grandmother what she had done that was so wrong. I wanted to tell her that nothing she could do would ever be so bad. But I didn't know how to, so I said nothing and watched the people walking past us in the park.

"She called last week and asked if you could spend some time with her in Italy," she said. "She's throwing a party for her husband—husband number *four*—and she thinks it's time you all finally met. Maybe try to become a family."

"You mean I won't be coming back?" I asked, terrified. I grabbed for her hand and squeezed it hard. "Please don't send me away." I had stopped crying, but my tears threatened resurgence. Plus, the M&M's rose in my throat.

"No," she said slowly. "It would just be for part of the summer. She'd like you to spend more time over there. Of course, that would be up to you."

"Do you think I should go?" I asked, praying she'd say no.

She hesitated. She was staring at the trees across the path, and for the first time I noticed the birds chirping. "I didn't say that."

"What *do* you say?" I asked. Figures. Normally she flooded me with her opinions. Now she had all the clarity of a fortune cookie.

"It's good to have adventures, to see the world. I don't know if you should go alone, is all."

"Then come with me," I said, and immediately regretted it.

She looked at me, and I finally saw her eyes, and I understood that my grandmother was afraid. I was ten years old, too, the exact age my mother was when she went off to Europe for the summer and stopped being the little girl my grandmother loved. She was afraid the same thing would happen to me.

This trip was a test, and it was a test I had to pass. I would show my grandmother that I was better than my mother, that I was someone she could count on. If that meant going to Italy, then I'd go. But I wouldn't stay.

"I'll be fine," I said, wiping my face, the model for stoicism. Her lips twisted into a half smirk. She grabbed at my chin. "I should hope so. I didn't spend all this time on you to have you ruined by whatever orgy your mother's conducting over there. Come on," she said, rising and grabbing my hand. "Let's go tell your grandfather you'll go and make him the happiest he's been all year."

Visiting Mother

My grandmother and I were standing in my room, and we were having a crisis. We sat on it, jumped on it, and even removed some of the stuffed animals, but my suitcase would not close.

"It's only two weeks," she said, forcing her full weight onto the lid. "Do you really think you need all this shit?"

"Yes," I said. "What if she decides we're going to take a little trip somewhere and they have a different climate? That's why I need all my long pants and summer shorts." I didn't admit that the prospect of leaving her and my grandfather was terrifying. I would have stuffed her into that suitcase if she'd have let me.

And there was also the nagging suspicion that this visit might last longer than expected. I was sure that when my mother discovered what a prize I was, she'd be on the phone with my grandmother in a second demanding to keep me. She'd be apologizing to me every day, and I'd make her grovel. And what would my grandmother say to that? Would she say no?

She took out a beat-up old stuffed bear. "And this? Are you having a party of your own when you get there?" she asked, referring to the birthday party my mother was giving for her husband a few days after my arrival.

My grandfather poked his head into my room. "How's everything going?"

"You need to come in here and do something," she said. "That's how it's going. Your grandson has stuffed his whole goddamned room into one suitcase, so it won't close."

"Then we'll get a bigger suitcase," he said, smiling. He called for Atse to go down to the storage closet and get the big Louis Vuitton trunk. That did the trick. My grandmother and I had just repacked everything into the trunk when my mother arrived to collect me. One of the building's doormen took the trunk down, and my grandmother and I descended the staircase leading to the apartment's foyer.

"You'll have so much fun," my grandfather was telling my mother. "Make sure you show him Rome's old city, too. He loves history."

When my mother saw me, her face lit up as if she'd been given a present. I tried to feel good about that, but what she had told the countess was still ringing in my ears. "That damn baby will ruin my waistline," she'd said. "I decided to have an abortion."

"Are you ready, my love?" she asked now, watching my grandmother's face. The two women did not speak, and it was tense.

My grandmother was gripping my shoulders, and I didn't dare move until she let go. Finally she gave me a light shove, and I walked the rest of the way to my mother's outstretched hand. I was ten years old and had never held my mother's hand, but that was fine. It was all part of my plan to make her see what she'd been missing. *She'll be eating out of my palm in no time,* I thought.

My grandfather hugged me and wished me a safe trip. It wasn't until he walked over to my grandmother and whispered in her ear that I noticed her expression, grave and hesitant.

"Call me when you get in," said my grandmother at last.

"We'll be fine," said my mother, gripping my hand. "Don't you worry about us, Mother."

My grandmother did not reply, which I'm sure took an incredible amount of self-restraint.

.   .   .   .

On the airplane it seemed my mother wouldn't stop talking long enough to draw a breath. At some point between describing her husband's illustrious family—in which there were either three popes and two doges or three doges and two popes—and telling me about all the places she was going to take me, I realized I wasn't going to have to put any effort into making myself indispensable to her. From what she was saying, I'd never be farther from her than arm's length. Smiling, I thought how my plan was already working. Then I fell asleep from exhaustion.

"And you'll just love Collette," she said after I woke up, smoothing out her skirt.

"Who's that?" I asked.

She put her hand over her mouth, giggling. "Your sister," she said.

"My what?" I saw random flecks of light swimming around my mother's face, and I felt as if someone had just kicked me in the stomach. How could nobody have told me that she had another baby?

"Your stepsister, really. She's Salvatore's daughter."

A rush of air abandoned my lungs, and the plane stabilized. My mother was smiling, and I laughed nervously. "I thought you meant you had another baby." I laughed some more, wondering what I would have done if she did have another child.

She stopped smiling. "What's so funny about that?" she asked. "Wouldn't you like to have a brother or sister?"

I thought about it for a hot second before deciding conclusively and irrevocably that no, I would not like to have a brother or sister. I didn't even want to have a stepbrother or -sister. I didn't even want cousins. All those people would take time and attention away from me. Besides, if she hadn't been able to be a mother to me, what made her think she could do it for someone else? I turned away and looked out the window at the ocean.

"Would you believe me if I told you that I've been planning this visit for a long time?"

I thought she meant a few weeks, and I smiled politely, but the next thing she said made me realize I was wrong.

"I wanted to have you at our wedding, but your grandmother . . ." She didn't finish the sentence, but I wanted to know what happened. I was torn between not wanting to hear anything bad about my grandmother and wanting to finally know the truth. "Really, none of that's important because we *are* together now, right?" She rubbed my arm.

Just then the plane shook from turbulence, and I was jolted upright. The pilot asked us to refasten our seat belts, and I had a premonition that we would crash and the only person there to comfort me was a woman I knew no better than an airplane stewardess. I swore to God right then and there, while all the passengers buckled themselves in, that if He let me live, I'd get back to New York somehow. I knew that my mother lived in a big house with lots of rooms, and I hoped that some of them would have phones so I could call my grandmother and have her come get me. *This was a mistake,* I'd say. *Please don't make me stay here. She wants more children.*

"What's wrong?" asked my mother, oblivious to our imminent demise. I wondered if passengers on the *Titanic* were this naïve.

"I'm afraid of flying," I said, which wasn't exactly a lie. I was gripping the armrest with white knuckles. She took my hand in hers, and it was warm and distracting enough to make me forget my silent bargaining with God. I loved the attention and settled back into my seat.

"I guess we should get to know each other. How about that?" She smiled down at me. "I already told you about your sister, and if you don't mind, we're going to call Salvatore your father."

"My what?" My father was turning out to be the biggest mystery of all. Before I'd overheard my mother at Bergdorf's, I thought my father didn't care if I lived or died. Then my mother said she'd never even told him about me. In the rush of agreeing to come on this trip and getting ready at mach speed, I'd never asked my grandmother what the true story was.

"I know he's not your real father," she said, "but if you call him Papa or something, he might . . . well, he might want to be. Wouldn't that be nice? You will finally have a mother and a father and a sister all under one roof!"

It sounded complete, like families I saw in the movies or on Nick at Nite, but I wasn't sure I wanted that if it meant giving up my grandparents.

"Do your grandparents ever talk about me?" she asked, changing the subject. "I mean your grandfather. I know your grandmother never does."

I debated whether or not I should tell my mother about The Lecture, but I decided that would only make her feel bad. "They told me you're living in Italy and that you're busy and that's why you never come to visit. Grandma said you were a sweet little girl."

My mother arranged her face into a pout. "That's all, huh? Well, I'll tell you a story. I can remember the first time I was on an airplane like it was yesterday," she said, and her face took on a faraway look. "Your grandmother and I were going to Paris to meet your grandfather."

"What was he doing there?" I asked, expecting to hear that he was attending a conference or visiting a relative.

"He was living in Paris for a while when I was a little girl."

"Living?"

"Your grandparents had separated, and he went to live in Paris to be close to his family. Your grandmother stayed in New York—that is, when she wasn't traveling."

What was she talking about? Were we still talking about the old people back in New York who'd been married for more than fifty years and never went anywhere without each other? I almost put my hand up to her faraway face to see if she were running a fever.

She sighed. "I still remember the night it happened. The night he walked out on us. They had a huge fight—I don't remember the particulars—and he called her a bad name. I think he might have hit her."

"What are you talking about!" I screamed, and the people in the next row over looked at us.

"I thought your grandparents told you everything," she said evenly, with only the smallest hint of a smile, and then shrugged.

"Everything?" *No,* I thought, *they didn't tell me everything.* They always covered for my mother, didn't they? At the time I didn't see the irony in the fact that my grandmother, despite her feelings toward my mother, had always hidden the real truth about her. And here my mother was, trying to confess as much dirt about my grand-parents as possible.

"They got back together. It's no big deal. They're still together now."

"Hitting somebody is a very big deal! So is separation."

"I guess you're right," she said, that same slight smile playing on her lips. "You're very smart. But you shouldn't repeat what I said. I'm not sure he really did hit her. I might have imagined that part. But the rest is true, I think. It was a very long time ago."

"I thought you said you remember it like yesterday?"

She faced forward and closed her eyes. "I was talking about the airplane part."

. . . . .

After we deplaned, my mother steered my shoulders toward the exit and said we would not be spending the night at the villa.

"Why?"

"It's late," she said. "I don't want to disturb anyone. So we're going to spend the night at my friend the countess's apartment. She's not in town, anyway."

She was right; it was pitch black outside, and after doing the time-change math, I realized it was the middle of the night. My mother found her driver, Luke, who'd stayed up late to come and pick her up and deposit her at another apartment before returning to his quarters at her villa. I thought this was strange, but I was also tired and didn't care to ask questions.

"You'll love the apartment," she said in the car, though I didn't see how it mattered much. We'd only be there a night. "It's close to an important square called the Piazza Spagna. I'll show you around there tomorrow."

The apartment itself was opulent, all done in baroque style with heavy furniture. If I hadn't been so tired, I might have walked around and explored. Instead I put on a pair of pajamas I found in the bedroom and conked out.

．．．．

The following morning I found my mother on the terrace over-looking the Piazza Spagna with its famous Spanish Steps. She was standing at the railing with a coffee cup and saucer, staring out onto the square.

"There you are, my love!" she said. My mother had a low, sonorous voice, and the words she spoke seemed like lyrics. Sometimes she lowered it so much that they came out as secret whispers. I've seen her speaking with many people, and the effect is always the same: The words envelop the listeners, drawing them in, making them feel like the most important people in the world. Hearing her talk made me feel like I was in a movie. "Come sit down and eat something." I sat down and looked around. There were pastries and quiche and rolls but no bacon and eggs. I frowned, wondering how I'd get used to Italian breakfasts. I was buttering a roll when my mother said, "I'm just so happy to see you! I mean *here.*"

I still felt strange because of our conversation on the plane and merely nodded, not adding anything that might suggest I was happy, too. I took a bite of the roll.

"I've wanted you to come for so long. I think about you every day."

I chewed slowly to avoid speaking. How could someone who called only four times a year expect me to believe she thought about me every day? Still, I wanted to believe her. I wanted to believe I was special and that for whatever reason she had been unable to show me that she thought so, too, up until now.

"I wanted you to come to my wedding."

Evidently this was a point of contention, as she'd mentioned it twice in twenty-four hours, always followed by the same frown and the same explanation: "Your grandmother wouldn't let you come."

"That's not true, you know," I said, and she looked at me incredulously. "It was Grandpa who wouldn't let us come. I remembered that this morning when I was brushing my teeth. He was mad because you got married to a Catholic. I don't think Grandma cared much one way or the other."

"Oh," she said. "I didn't know that."

Actually, my grandfather had said more than that. What he said was that he would kick my mother's behind from New York to the Vatican before he'd sit through another Catholic wedding, but I didn't see how repeating that would be helpful.

"I'm sorry if I said anything on the flight that upset you. I was pretty nervous."

"Why?" I asked, and she blushed.

"We don't know each other very well, and I want you to like me."

As uncomfortable as I felt, I still wanted her to like me, too. I just didn't want to do it at my grandparents' expense.

"We can get to know each other now," I said.

She smiled. "Yes. Tell me all about yourself. What do you want to be when you grow up? If you do anything. You don't have to, really."

"Really?" I asked. None of my teachers ever explained that that was possible.

Waving her hand, she explained, "We have lots of money. You don't have to do anything. Work only if you want to. I don't work, and see how happy I am?" Stretching her arms high over her head, she let out a massive yawn.

"We ought to plan a day!" she said then, and grabbed my hand. "I want to take you shopping!"

I thought of my grandfather telling her to show me the sights, and I wondered what he'd say to this. My mother told me to go and put on some nice shorts—that it would be hot—and to meet her by the front door.

·   ·   ·   ·

That afternoon I followed my mother around from store to store. It seemed she wanted to visit every shop in the neighborhood. We started up the Via Condotti, came back up toward the Piazza Spagna through the Via Borgognona, and then we went back down the Via Frattina. When we were in Valentino, she made me feel important by introducing me to all the salespeople and then consulting my opinion about dresses. I noticed that all the salesclerks spoke to my mother in English. She must be very important, I thought. Then she took me to Battistoni to have me outfitted for a new suit.

"But I already have a suit," I said.

"Not like this one, you don't. These are perfect for boys. Especially . . ." She paused, choosing her words carefully. ". . . curvier boys."

Curvier? That must have been a nice way of saying "fat." I looked down at my stomach and then at her. She was so thin and beautiful, with her long blond hair. I wondered if my weight problem had something to do with my father and not my diet of M&M's and Little Debbie snack cakes, but I didn't ask.

By the end of the day, she'd walked me around so much that I was exhausted, but not her. She still walked with purposeful strides while I struggled to keep up. All I could think of was a nap and maybe some soda. Until she suggested we stop at a gelato shop. That got my attention. So she ordered us a couple of cones, and we sat down.

I was sitting across from her, licking a tiramisù-flavored cone, when she started talking about family. "I've been everywhere, and all I want now is a home. A home and a family," she said. She was studying me through dark sunglasses, and I tried to look less anxious than I really felt. I knew she was trying hard, and obviously she was hinting at my doing something greater than temporarily jaunting through a European city. But she couldn't want me to live with her permanently all of a sudden, not after being away for so long, right? That was my plan: to make her sorry she ever gave me up. Still, I felt confused. If she'd always thought of me and wanted a home and a family, why hadn't she acted on those feelings before now? I wanted to ask, but I didn't know how, so I changed the subject.

"It must be getting late," I said. "Shouldn't we be heading back to the apartment so we can go to your house?"

"I suppose so," she said, and there was a trace of disappointment in her voice.

. . . .

The pungent aroma of feet slathered in what I could only imagine was olive oil hit me as soon as I entered the marbled villa my mother called home. An artifact of an old man stepped forward to collect my mother's purse and hat.

"God, what is that smell?" I complained, holding my nose.

My mother lowered her voice and touched my shoulder in confidence. "This is an old house," she explained, "and old houses have a distinct smell."

I looked at her. Did she not realize I was from New York? I'd been to lots of old houses, and none of them stank of aged socks and salad dressing. And I'd been to Europe before, too! I didn't want to be disagreeable, so I decided I'd just spend the rest of my time breathing through my mouth. I hoped that I wouldn't go back to New York reeking.

"We should call Grandma," I said, scouting out the place for telephones. It was hard to get a realistic idea of how old the house was, because the inside was completely renovated. The ceilings and walls weren't frescoed like the countess's apartment or others I'd seen in *Architectural Digest*'s Italian Edition, which I'd bought in preparation for this trip. Instead they seemed to be creamy solid colors with the occasional piece of art, a lot like my apartment in New York. This place looked old from the outside, and it looked big, at least three floors. In the great hall, there were lots of tables, but they all bore wilted flowers, their petals spilling onto the floor. Not only were there no phones in sight, but apparently there were no brooms, either.

"Good morning," I heard a voice say in accented English. I looked to the top of the winding grand staircase and saw a pockmark-faced woman wearing shades of gray. Her wiry mop of hair was tucked tightly behind her head, and her eyes glared down at my mother and me both. Her outfit completely clashed with the décor.

"Selma," said my mother with a thin-lipped smile. Selma methodically descended, gripping the banister tightly and testing each step before deciding it was safe.

"We were expecting you earlier," she said, and then looked me up and down. "Is this your liiiiittle bambino?"

I noticed that she lingered on the word *little,* and I wondered if she was in some sarcastic way referencing my weight.

"Yes," said my mother. "Matthew, this is Selma, the head housekeeper."

I looked back to the flower petals on the floor and wondered what this woman did all day. Whatever it was, it sure wasn't sweeping. I wondered if it was hard to get a maid who did housework in Rome.

"It's nice to meet you," I lied, pitying the old hag with her crater face and poor work ethic. She cocked an eyebrow and searched my face. After an uncomfortable silence, Selma shrugged and walked away.

"Albert will show you to your room," she said over her shoulder.

I looked around and realized that the artifact must be Albert. The top of his mostly bald head was peeling in large strips from a sunburn, and the white hair growing in his ears matched the tufts springing free from the constraints of his starched collar. He motioned for me to follow him. My mother said she'd catch up with me later. Albert walked with the same purposeful steps as Selma, and I started to wonder if this house was safe. We took so much time climbing the stairs that it gave me the opportunity to look around.

"How long have you worked here?" I asked him to be polite.

He didn't answer, and I repeated the question louder, in case he was hard of hearing. When he still didn't answer, I was about to fire him in my mind, too, but then I realized he didn't speak English. I had purchased an Italian-language phrasebook from a bookstore in New York, but there wasn't a section on talking to one's domestic staff, so I thumbed to a passage about the weather. "It's a beautiful day in lovely Roma," I said in Italian.

He still didn't answer.

I saw someone peeking out from a door down the hall. As we approached the door, it slammed shut. I turned around and walked backward to see if the door would reopen. It did just before we turned a corner.

My room was the last door in a maze of hallways that traversed the upper bowels of this Italian villa. There was a bed, a desk, a chair, and a dresser, but there was no television. I looked all over the room for one, even one of those tiny portable jobs. Nothing. What did these people do for fun if they didn't watch television? I looked back at Albert, thinking they obviously don't spend much time talking.

Luke, the chauffeur, came into the room and set my trunk down in the corner, then gestured toward Albert and smiled. "Don't pay attention to the old man," he said in English. "He never says two words to anyone, even his wife. He's married to Selma, the maid."

I found Albert's marital affairs to be less interesting than my lack of television. "Is there a TV here?" I asked.

"There's an entertainment room downstairs, but it's not like your American television."

"What's the difference?" I asked.

He shrugged and took off his hat. "It's in Italian."

.　.　.　.

Bored with the monastic opportunities my bedroom offered, I walked back toward what I hoped was the rest of the house. I was humming nonsense to myself when that strange bedroom door from earlier flew open, startling me. "Must you make so much noise?" asked a pimply-faced Italian teenage girl in perfect, unaccented English.

"You could hear me?" I said. Was I really that loud?

"Yes, and people are trying to sleep."

I looked at my watch; it was after eleven. We would be having lunch soon. Who was still asleep?

"Isn't it late to be doing that?" I asked.

"My grandmother is taking a nap, and she'll get mad if you wake her up." My mother had only mentioned one daughter on the plane, so I figured this was Collette.

"I'll be quiet, then. I'm really sorry."

The girl let out an audible sigh and slammed the door in my face. I guess she figured it was only humming that would wake people up. I started to walk away, but the door flew open again. "Wait," she called to me. "I guess I can show you around." Her voice exuded cockiness, and she brushed past me and began her tour. "I don't expect you to understand, but this is a traditional Italian villa. We had a palazzo once, but it's a museum now. You probably saw it when you were in the city."

"I mostly saw the insides of dress shops," I said, trying to make conversation.

"Figures," she said, "that's all your mother does. Shop and spend money."

It took me a moment to register that she'd just paid my mother an insult, and I was surprised. Hadn't my mother said I would love this girl? It didn't sound like she loved my mother. But there wasn't much time to consider this development, as she'd already begun rattling off facts about the villa. I didn't initially mind her droning on about architectural flourishes, which, as she assumed, I did not understand. After a while, though, she started getting on my nerves. She said everything with a sigh, as if I'd begged her to take me on this boring tour. "This is from the Renaissance," she said, pointing to a marble bust. "Do you even know what that is?"

Maybe it wasn't presumptuous for her to think a ten-year-old wouldn't know what the Renaissance was, but I prided myself on being different. Besides, even if art enthusiasts hadn't raised me, *Renaissance* had been a vocabulary word in my world-history class last year.

"You're probably desensitized. Everything in New York looks alike, all concrete and glass."

"Aren't most Roman buildings made out of concrete?" I asked.

She spun around, her eyes narrowed. "What?"

"Didn't the Romans invent concrete?"

"What are you talking about?" Her tone was hard, angry.

"Aren't most of the buildings here from Roman times made out of concrete?"

She rolled her eyes. "I'm talking about on the inside, stupid."

Did she think that New Yorkers lived inside concrete cells? Looking around, I still didn't see any real difference between the decoration here and where I lived—except our apartment was clean and the furniture was different. The furniture here looked out of place. The walls were too light to match all this velvet and heavy brocade. And there were portraits everywhere of the most unattractive people I'd ever seen—even worse than the crater-faced woman. Plus, everywhere I looked, I saw a mess. Layers of dust covered most surfaces. I flirted with the idea of jumping on one sofa just to unleash a torrent of dust particles. The curtains were all closed and the drapes so thick it felt like nighttime.

"Have you even been to New York?" I asked.

I wondered where she was from. Her voice had no accent.

"Anyway," she said, "let's get back to the tour."

I followed her through the labyrinth of art and furniture. The villa, she said, was from the last century. She led me down the stairs and through a pair of open French doors and down into the garden, where I saw my mother and an older gentleman sipping coffee, ignoring each other as though they'd just had an argument. She had changed clothes since we arrived and was wearing a lavender dress—did my mother ever wear pants? My grandmother wore pants all the time, but I had only seen my mother in skirts and dresses.

Looking up, my mother stood and walked-ran over to me, laughing the way one did when one had just heard the funniest thing ever. For a moment I thought she was laughing at me, and then I concluded she must be pretending to be happy—that or she was drunk.

"Has Collette been showing you around?" she asked, pulling me into a sideways hug, which seemed odd. It's not like we'd been separated for more than an hour. The older man looked on with temporary interest.

"Yes," I said, stifling a sneeze from all the dust inside, "it's very nice."

"Come, I want to introduce you to your father." She led me over to the heavily wrinkled old man with thinning white hair sitting at the table. I couldn't tell if he was severe or if his wrinkles made him look that way.

"Matthew," my mother said, "this is your father, Salvatore."

Well, this was certainly an interesting turn of events. I had always pictured my mother married to someone suave and debonair, like Tyler, who everyone said looked like James Bond. But this guy? My grandmother would love this!

As ridiculous as it all seemed, there was also something oddly alluring about the whole scene, this completed family living under one roof. It wasn't anything my family had been able to reproduce, and I was anxious to see how this clan managed it.

"It's a nice place you have here," I said before croaking out an unsteady "Dad." I rocked back on my heels, trying and failing to remember the last time I'd even said the word *Dad,* or *Father* for that matter. Coming from me, *Dad* sounded as hollow as *Mom.*

He nodded, but his face still registered little interest. I held out my hand, and after what seemed like an eternity he took it and gave it a wiggle. He still hadn't said anything in return when Collette ran over and jumped in his lap and screamed, "Daddy!" which, given his frail disposition, brought to mind images of broken hips. But he let out a happy sigh and beamed at his pimply daughter.

Just then I heard a loud human bark coming from inside. I noticed everyone stiffen immediately. Collette jumped up from her father's lap and stood at attention. The old man rose unsteadily, one eye on the door. I looked up at my mother long enough to see her chewing on her lip, the same nervous habit my grandmother had. The voice barked again, and then I heard a tray crashing to the floor and some definite shrieking, then the faint sound of whimpering.

At last the barking voice emerged from the French doors—or are they called something else in Italy?—and I saw a woman no taller than me, but about as wide as a Fiat, as old as time itself, and twice as menacing. Walking with the aid of a cane, the woman had a voice that was deafening, and all in Italian. I didn't understand Italian, but I quickly learned I was responsible for knowing it, anyway, and that she was deadly with that cane. If she thought you were ignoring her, she'd hit whatever was closest. I figured the cane must have been responsible for the falling tray inside and the subsequent whimpering. It was obvious she was the one shrieking.

So onto the terrace she came, this rabid geriatric, draped in black from head to toe in the fierce heat, wielding that cane. If everyone else was scared, I was petrified.

"*Mama,*" Salvatore cooed, and gestured with his hands to the sky, but she wasn't having any sweet talk. Words flew out of her mouth with the kind of tenacity I hadn't seen since Elaine made me watch that possessed girl's head spin in *The Exorcist*.

She looked at me and motioned with her cane for me to come closer. Everyone else looked at me, and I could see a ripple of fear passing over my mother. Her face went white. I stayed put until the old woman beat the cane against a nearby chair and said something I took to mean, "Get your ass over here now, boy!"

She looked me up and down and grabbed my face and tilted it up to her. It took me about half a second to realize the smell I'd sniffed earlier came from her. Her beady eyes bore into mine, and she grunted. Dropping my face, she turned to my mother and barked something else. My mother, who after five years of living in Italy spoke only rudimentary Italian, nodded, and the old woman grunted again. She swatted me away, and I ran back behind the table.

Turning to Collette, my mother whispered in English, "Why don't you take Matthew out to the garden and show him your petting zoo?"

Whether she liked the idea or was just anxious to get away from her grandmother, Collette grabbed my arm and led me down some stone steps and into the gardens.

"Your grandma sure is . . . something," I said once we were out of earshot of the others. We were walking along a gravelly path, and Collette turned and eyed me suspiciously before asking what I meant. I didn't want to run the risk of insulting her by commenting on the way her grandmother terrified everyone, so I changed the subject. "I don't know anyone with a petting zoo," I said.

She seemed satisfied by this. "Now you do. We live in an area protected by the government. You can't build out here, and there's sheep roaming around. So I wanted some more animals. Nobody else has one at their house. Just me and Marie Antoinette. Hers was larger, of course."

"Michael Jackson has one, too."

"If you don't know who Marie Antoinette is," she said, that icy tone returning, "just say so."

I knew exactly who Marie Antoinette was, and I was just about done with this superior act of Collette's. I was only trying to add something to the pitiful conversation, but now I was finished trying. We walked on in silence.

Collette strode ahead of me, and I took this to mean she wanted to be first to the animals. As I didn't much care either way, and since I was already sweating from the heat, I let her go until the distance between us became uncomfortable, almost comical.

"We're not racing!" I called out.

She looked over her shoulder. "Not my fault you can't keep up, fatty."

I stopped walking. "What did you say?" I asked through clenched teeth.

"Fatty, fatty, bobatty," she sang.

"Stop it!" I yelled. My hands balled into fists at my side. I hadn't asked to come to her stupid house with its weird smell and banshee grandmother. I'd played nice when she insulted my intelligence and when I met her geriatric father. I didn't deserve this.

She belted out an encore. "FATTY, FATTY, BOBATTY!"

My chest rose and fell as I walked over to her, stopping just barely a foot from her bulbous, pimply nose. "You're a bitch," I said. The word ended her little song midchorus. Her mouth puckered into a contorted kidney shape, and she turned her head away, almost as if she'd been slapped.

"Bitch," I repeated, my tone low, stretching out the *i*. "You're a bitch like your grandma, and you always will be. I don't want to see your petting zoo." Her mouth fell open as if she'd say something, but nothing came out. "I've got better things to do than to look at your ugly buckteeth again."

Of course that was a lie. They didn't even have television.

"You think you're better than me," she said, completely missing the point. She grabbed me by my shirt and pulled me even closer to her face. She opened her mouth and laughed theatrically, revealing impacted incisors and terrible breath. "You come here from your rich grandparents that can buy the whole world and you think you're better than us." She shook me just once. "You're not, because we have class."

She pushed me hard, and I fell back onto the gravel path. "There," she said.

Looking down, I saw some scrapes on my hands and dirt on my pants. So I picked up a fistful of dirt and rocks, stood up, and threw it in her face. Then I ran.

I'd never run so fast in my life. I knew it wouldn't take long for the shock of the dirt to clear, for Collette to chase after me. I ran back toward the terrace but found nobody. My mother was nowhere to be seen, and I spun around just in time to see Collette tearing up the distance between us like this was a Travel Channel special on the running of the bulls and I was the poor tourist about to be gored.

I took off again and darted into an open door leading to the library. The room was large and ornate, and a huge crushed-velvet sofa sat in front of a large fireplace. Collette was right on my back, so I ran to the sofa and put some more distance between us. "I'm going to kill you," she said, and I believed her. We did circles around the sofa, her going left, me going right, and vice versa. Then her eyes fell on a porcelain music box decorating the side table.

"This has been in my family for hundreds of years," she said, and I was temporarily disoriented. Were we back on the tour? "My father loves it." She opened the box, and its baroque music sounded.

She held the box away from her and locked her gaze on mine. Suddenly I saw what she was about to do, and I called out "No!" just as she released the box, graceful, like someone performing a dance move. It smashed against the terrazzo.

A twisted smile played on her lips for just a second before it spread into a wide, toothy grin. "Daddy!" she called. "Look what Matthew did."

"What's all this noise?" Salvatore said before finding the box on the floor.

Hyperventilating, I backed into a corner by the fireplace.

"Matthew was running around and knocked into the table. The music box fell."

"That's . . . not true," I stammered. "She dropped it on the floor. I saw her do it."

My mother and Salvatore's mother filed into the room. Salvatore crouched on the floor and picked up a piece of the box, turning it over in his weathered hands. He threw it down and shook his head.

"What's happened?" my mother asked, and Salvatore's mother barked something. Nobody answered either of them, and for a moment I didn't know what would happen next. My mother repeated her question, louder this time. I thought the truth might save me, but I shouldn't have been so naïve. I felt Salvatore's hand against my cheek. And for the second time that day, I fell on my behind. The shock to my tailbone was nothing compared to the shock of being backhanded. I rubbed my cheek, where I felt the pain the most, and as tears spilled down my face, I thought, *I've never been hit before.*

"What are you doing, monster?" my mother shouted. She ran up to him and pounded on his chest, and for a second I thought she'd jump on him and ride him like a madwoman. She did not, though, and he turned away from us both. He stood facing the direction of both his mother and his daughter, and I looked up and saw wrinkly grooves crisscrossing the back of his neck. I stayed on the floor and hugged my knees to my chest. In my tearful haze, I looked over to Collette, whose smile had disappeared.

"Don't ever touch him again," my mother said, taking a step closer to me.

Salvatore's mother took her cane and thwacked it on the floor and then turned to leave. Putting his hand on Collette's shoulder, Salvatore guided his daughter out of the room as well, leaving my mother and me alone.

"We have to leave here," I said. "These people are all crazy."

My mother turned slowly and considered me a moment. "And what would we do?" She bent down to me and stroked my face and gazed into my watery blue eyes. "What would we do?" she repeated. "Tell me."

"Go home," I said. "To New York."

She gave me a crooked smile. "This is my home."

What was her problem? I wondered. Couldn't she see what I saw? I wondered briefly if he'd ever hit her, too. Maybe she was in shock, like those women you see on talk shows who had battered wife syndrome and were in denial up until they killed their husbands.

"You have to give them a chance," she said softly. "It won't always be like this." I wasn't buying that, but there was something about the hollowness in her voice that made me think she didn't believe it, either. "It's not any better in New York."

I looked at her. What was she talking about? Nobody ever beat me at home, and sometimes I actually deserved it there.

She was fidgeting with her rings and bracelets. "The best decision I ever made was coming over here. I want you to be happy here, Matthew. I want us all to be a family."

Well, it was official. We had graduated from hinting. Although, if this was exactly what I wanted to hear, I thought I'd feel different once the words were spoken. I thought I'd feel vindicated or accepted, but I didn't feel those things. I felt nothing.

"This is what I've always wanted," she said, and crouched down to me. We were inches apart. She smelled faintly like coconut. "Do you believe me?"

"No," I said, and I surprised both of us with the ferocity of my tone. I paused a second before continuing. "I don't believe you. You say you want to be a family, but I know the truth. I know you didn't want me. I was a mistake."

My mother flinched. "Your grandmother told you that. I never said that."

"Yes you did. And then you said you got your freedom and Grandma got another mind to fuck up. You said 'fuck up.' I remember it. I was at the store when you said it to the countess. I was hiding."

Her mouth hung open, her eyes wide. "But we missed each other—"

"I was there. I heard everything. So don't lie to me anymore. You never wanted to be a family."

For a moment I thought she was going to cry, but then she stood up in one fluid motion. "I . . . I did. It was . . . your grandmother who wouldn't let you come here before now."

"Stop blaming her!" I screamed, and my mother took a step back. "She didn't make you give me up."

"What was I supposed to do?" she asked. "I wish you really understood."

"You'll never have a real family," I said, and she drew in some fast, shallow breaths before turning away and walking out of the room, leaving me to stare after her.

As I sat on the floor replaying our conversation for the umpteenth time in my head, I heard a voice.

"I'm sorry," Collette said, and I looked at her, confused, before I followed her gaze to the shattered music box. "I'll tell my father what happened."

I stood up and brushed my hands on my pants. "Don't bother," I said, and walked past her, back toward where I thought my room was.

"Why?" she asked, following me. "If I tell him what really happened, he'll like you. Don't you want him to like you?"

"Not especially. I just want to go home."

"Do you want to know a secret?" she asked with a look of desperation. "I'll tell you a secret." She put her face close to mine.

"I don't want to hear it," I said.

But she wasn't listening. "It's about Selma. A long time ago, my father and her were married."

"What?"

"It's true. They had sex, and she got pregnant, and they got married. Then she lost the baby, and they got divorced. Now she's the maid."

What kind of freak show were these people running? I wondered. How had my mother gotten mixed up with this family? "Does my mother know?"

"Everyone knows, even Albert. Sometimes I stand outside their room, and she screams at him and tells him how she never loved him because she still loves Daddy."

This was too weird for me to talk about anymore. "I'm going to my room now," I said, and tried to stand up, but she pushed me back down. And then she kissed me. She pressed her lips onto mine and stuck her tongue in my mouth.

I shoved her off me, which took all the strength I had. I was big but not strong, and she was taller than I was, and aggressive. Standing up, I wiped my mouth with the back of my hand. "What are you doing?" I asked, and she didn't answer.

There were people shouting outside, and I went to the window and saw a crew of men putting up tents. "What's that for?"

"The party," she said, still on the ground. "My father's birthday is tomorrow. You didn't know?"

I shrugged. I had forgotten all about the party. I guessed that's why I was invited in the first place. So I could put on a suit and stand with the rest of the family and we'd all look like one functioning unit.

I looked back to Collette, who hadn't moved since she forced herself on me, and shook my head. I didn't know what to think. The maid was married to my stepfather, my stepsister was French-kissing me. My mother wanted me to be a family with all these people? I walked back to my room, wondering how long it would be before someone came to find me, to see if I was all right.

Nobody came, and I went to bed that night without dinner.

.   .   .   .

When I woke up the next morning, I could feel the welt on my cheek, but it wasn't until I looked at myself in the mirror that I saw the bruise. A dozen television specials with attractive, unfortunate teens lying about their abusive parents flashed before my eyes. I could see tragic Jill, who after being pushed down the stairs by an alcoholic mother lies about her broken leg. "Oh, I'm just so clumsy!" she says a little too loudly, fooling most but not the wise teacher, Mrs. Jones, who, one assumes, has seen this sad charade before. By the end of the show, Jill's crying onto Mrs. Jones's shoulder, confessing her lie and begging for help.

I poked at the bruise a couple times, watching the color change and wincing with pain. "I'm just so clumsy!" I said to my reflection. But who was going to ask me about my face who didn't already know what had happened? Luke knocked on my door twice and then pushed it open. "Morning," he said, all smiles. "I bring you suit for party." He hung the tuxedo on the bureau.

"Where's Albert?" I asked, and he shrugged. I muttered a thank-you and returned to the mirror to reexamine my face. Would people notice the bruise at the party?

"You face," the chauffeur said, and got close to me to take a look. "You been fighting with Albert?" He held his fists in a boxing move and hopped from foot to foot.

"I'm so clumsy. I fell and hit my cheek on the door."

He cocked his head and took another look. "No," he said.

I really needed to work on my inflection. I wouldn't have believed me, either.

When I didn't offer any more information, he shrugged. "I go pick up your mother friend now. You want to come?"

"What friend?"

He took out a folded-up piece of paper from his pocket and read the name Tyler Wilson. My face lit up, and I just about ran to the car. On the way to the airport, I hoped that he'd be able to talk some sense into my mother. I knew she listened to him. When Tyler saw the welt on my face, he didn't make a joke like the chauffeur did. I tried to tell him about my clumsiness, but he held up his palm to object. "Tell me the truth." So I did, and he said, "Take me to your mother," as if I could drive us.

He was quiet in the car, but I could tell he was seething. His legs shook, and so did his head. When we got to the villa, he flung open the car door and strode through the front door, almost knocking Albert over. This isn't how he'd normally enter someone's house, even a friend's, and I was scared for Salvatore. Tyler was tall and powerful, and people said he looked like James Bond. "Where is she?" he called.

Selma appeared, and with all the indignation of someone too busy to clean, asked what the fuss was. "I want to see the *lady* of the house right now." He turned around to find me. "Matthew, I want you to stand right here next to me."

"Do we really need to do this?" I asked. I was mad at my mother, but I knew how this would play out for her later, and I was afraid for all of us. If Tyler didn't rescue us, I'd have to face Salvatore myself.

"Tyler, what are you doing?" my mother asked, flushed from being outside in the heat directing workmen.

He lowered his voice. "I want you to explain this to me." He grabbed my face and turned the bruise to her. She looked at it herself and gasped, as if she hadn't realized what the product of yesterday might have been. When she said nothing, that was all the confirmation he needed. "If you want to stay here with a husband you don't love, that's fine, but you don't have to drag your son into it."

Doesn't love him? But wait, if she didn't love him, then what was all that talk about his not being so bad? I had already figured out there was something seriously wrong with this whole setup, but it hadn't occurred to me that my mother might have been a part of it until Tyler said that.

My mother started to cry. "Everyone is always judging me," she sobbed. "Nobody ever gives me a break."

He went to her and touched her face in such a way that reminded me of the movies. I thought he was going to kiss her, but he didn't. "If you want to stay in this prison away from the people who really love you, that's fine. But I'm taking Matthew back to New York. He doesn't deserve this."

She grabbed her stomach as if she were in intense pain and doubled over crying. I wanted to go to her, but Tyler grabbed me. "No," he said, and yanked me toward the door.

"What about my trunk and all my clothes?" I said, and he growled, "We'll send for them later."

I turned back and saw Collette watching from upstairs and wondered where Salvatore was. Had he heard any of what happened? Makeup ran down my mother's face, but she didn't wipe away her tears. She also did not rush after us. She stayed put in her marbled villa.

"This isn't your fault," Tyler said in the car on the way to his hotel, where we'd stay the night before flying back to New York the next morning. "She needs to grow up."

"Are you mad because I ruined your trip?" I asked him.

He shook his head. "I only came to see you, anyway—and your mother, too. I didn't want to go to that party."

I couldn't help wondering if I'd blown my chance to have a real relationship with my mother, but I knew then—without a doubt—that it would not have been like any of my fantasies.

eight

Call Me Pathological

My sixth-grade friendship with Graham Wilson sprang out of a single basic need: I started a new school for middle school and needed someone (besides myself) to talk to. I wasn't really opposed to talking to myself, though walking on the streets of New York taught me that this wasn't looked upon favorably. But I did want at least one friend. And because I was shy and overweight, and because I didn't know anyone at this school, making new friends would be especially challenging. During lunch on my first day, I looked around the courtyard outside the cafeteria where some of the cooler cliques chose to eat. There were the Sneaker-Heads, Gucci Girls, Preps, and Emo-Kids. I scrutinized each of these groups, looking for ways to recommend myself. In the end the only thing that worked was finding the kid who looked as strange as I did, and that kid was Graham.

I didn't notice him at first, partially because he did not belong to a clique, but also because he didn't sit still long enough to be considered. The boy was like a rubber ball ricocheting off walls and sidewalk. If you could pause the scene, you could spot Graham in midjump, but in real time it was impossible. He wafted aimlessly through cliques, unnoticed. In another life, or perhaps his current one, he could be that stranger who appears in someone's vacation photos. Nobody knows who he is, but for whatever reason he's posing along with the family.

When I finally realized that Graham wasn't a twin or a triplet

(Wait, isn't that the guy who was just over there a second ago? I swear he looks familiar), I also realized he was orbiting each group with a plastic bow-and-arrow set. He'd point the suction-tipped arrow at girls, they'd squeal or roll their eyes, and he'd move on. He didn't shoot the arrow and only provided a moment of awkward, random interruption. After he'd moved on, the kids in the clique would act as if nothing had happened. There was no head shaking or discussion about how "some people are so weird!" They just kept on talking about "Ice Ice Baby" and the rise of white rap.

I was in awe. How could all these kids accept Graham's behavior without further comment? There was no teasing, no taunting, no verbal anything. It defied the laws of middle school, a world where adolescents are given special dispensation to act like rabid demons. The only plausible answer was that the students had already known and accepted Graham and found his unique brand of peculiarity familiar and calming.

Immediately I knew I had to make this boy my friend.

Darting out from my perch on the steps leading back into school, I stepped over a dozen kids to put myself in his arrow's line of fire. "Hit me," I said. "Hit me."

He looked at me through thick, Grandpa-like bifocals. "I don't hit anyone."

"Why bother carrying around a bow and arrow, then?"

He shrugged. "Something to do?"

I stepped forward and put out my hand. "I'm Matt."

"I know," he said, and pumped my hand as hard as his scrawny arms could. "You're in my math class. I'm Graham."

I thought back to second period long enough to realize I hadn't noticed him. "Well," I said, "I think we should be friends."

He shrugged again. "Okay. Do you want to use my bow and arrow?"

.　.　.　.

A few weeks into the school year, Graham and I were sitting in math class just after the bell when Mrs. Scobee announced a surprise homework check. Everyone instantly started to panic, with the exception of Graham. All of our homework normally went into a folder, which she collected once a week to stamp and record in her grade book.

"I'm going to come around and ask for an assignment, and if you have it, then you'll get a hundred in my grade book. This is going down as a quiz grade."

I looked at the blackboard. "Mrs. Scobee, the board says you're collecting the folders on Friday. Today is Wednesday."

She looked at me as though I'd raised my hand to share a fart with the class. "I know what day it is. That's why it's a *pop* homework check. Students, remember I can do this anytime."

"Then what's the point of writing the assignment on the board?" I asked, perfectly aware I was flirting with detention.

"Because I want to see who's on top of their work," she said, enunciating every syllable, especially the hard *k,* which produced droplets of spittle over Greg Nelson's desk. "I'll be around with my stamp to look at everyone's folder. While you're waiting for me, go ahead and start on today's assignment."

"What is it?" asked Michael Rogers, two seats behind me.

"Students, where do I put all the information for the day?" she asked nobody in particular, and we all sang, "On the board."

"Except for when she changes her mind," I said under my breath. I hadn't completed any of this week's homework. I was planning on doing it all Thursday. Looking around the room, I saw that other kids in a similar position were attempting to complete some assignments before Mrs. Scobee got around to them. Then I looked over to Graham, his electric blue folder already out and waiting. Mrs. Scobee was three rows over, absently flipping through pages and stamping them, checking one problem per page.

"Graham," I whispered, "you gotta help me."

"Sure," he said furrowing his forehead. "What's up?"

"The sky," I said. "What do you think is up? I need your folder, or I'm gonna fail."

He considered this a moment. "No," he said, shook his head, and went back to work as if nothing had happened.

"No?" I said too loudly.

"No talking," Mrs. Scobee admonished. "You don't have to talk to figure out math. It's solitary." She then returned her thoughts to Paisley Blackwell's folder. "Where's last night's assignment?"

"I don't have it done," Paisley croaked. Paisley was a member of the Gucci Girls clique, and she swung her stilettoed feet back and forth under her desk. She bounced her Gucci tote bag on her lap nervously.

Oh, it's bad when even the teacher's pet doesn't have the work done.

"Paisley," said Mrs. Scobee, touching her chest in horror. "And you, too, Brutus? I'm just so terribly disappointed."

I turned to Graham and spoke through clenched teeth. "Give. Me. That. Folder."

"It's cheating," he said, and adjusted his Grandpa glasses. Was he completely oblivious to my crisis?

"I don't care that it's cheating. If you're my friend, you won't let me fail."

We'd just become friends, and he should have told me to screw off. But he didn't. Instead a worried expression colored his face. His bottom lip disappeared, and he underhanded me the folder, which I took. There were only two assignments, and Scobee was still two rows over. Plenty of time. I balanced the folder on my lap, and I thought I was keeping a decent watch, but Scobee suddenly bamboozled me from behind.

"What is that?"

I felt the spittle from the *t* hit me on the back of my neck.

I knocked Graham's folder onto the checkered linoleum and looked over, where he was already hyperventilating. "Graham!" I cried. "You've dropped your homework folder! Let me pick it up for you, buddy. I don't want Mrs. Scobee to get the wrong idea."

"Nice try, but I've already got the right idea," she said, snatching both our folders and looking pleased with her evil self. "Both of you stay after class today."

I couldn't look at Graham for the rest of the class. At one point I thought I heard him sniffling, and that would've been too much for me. Being caught cheating is one thing, but causing a friend to cry is another.

When the bell rang, as the rest of the class ran out, Mrs. Scobee cracked her knuckles and put on a Cheshire cat grin. "Smug bitch," my grandmother would have said.

"Well, boys, come up here and plead your case." She had a slight accent that I couldn't figure out. It sounded southern, but more Texan than anything else. I couldn't be sure, and it was bugging me.

Dragging his feet, Graham followed about two steps behind me and came to rest at my right.

She crossed her arms. "Cheating can get you expelled, you know."

"Really?" I asked, more curious than afraid. "For a lousy homework folder?"

"I'm so sorry," Graham said, his voice cracking. Even without looking I could tell that tears were streaming down his cheeks, soaking into his shirt. He was making this so much worse than it really was. All we had to do was a little groveling and take a zero on the assignment. I had been at many different schools by then, and it was pretty clear to me that no teacher who wants to write a kid up tells him that she *could* do it. She just does it.

"Mrs. Scobee," I said in earnest, "you have to believe I'd never do something like this unless I absolutely had to." I bit my lip and scrunched up my face in a look of pure constipation, the closest expression to agony I could muster. My voice took on a nasal whine. "I just can't think at home."

Scobee, clearly a novice intimidator, arched her brows and bobbed her head, encouraging me to continue. Her frown was already melting.

"Not since the accident," added.

Graham looked at me, readjusting his glasses.

I inhaled deeply twice, giving the impression I was teetering on the edge of some unknown precipice, when in actuality I needed to buy time. "I just can't talk about it. Whenever I do, I . . . I—"

I spun around and buried my face in my hands, leaving enough of a gap between my fingers to see a slew of kids at the door watching my performance. I heaved my shoulders and sniffled.

"Close that door!" Mrs. Scobee shouted. The kids, of course, did not. She came around her desk and placed her arms on my shoulders in a gesture of womanly compassion, and I knew I had her. "Is it a brother or a sister?" she asked.

I shook my head. *Think, think. . . .*

"One of your parents? Mom? Dad?"

Jackpot. "My mother," I whispered.

"What is it?" some kid yelled in the hall.

"Something about his mother," offered another.

"I said close that door!" Then, with a stern look, Mrs. Scobee dismissed Graham to third period. He touched my arm and went to collect his things.

Mrs. Scobee bent down in front of me. She gently pulled my hands away from my face. "Matthew. Do you need to talk about it?" she asked me.

"I don't think I can. I haven't talked to anyone besides my grandparents. They're who I live with *now*." I was racking my brain for a plausible story line, combing through the plots of countless television miniseries. She'd let me do this nonsensical griefspeak for a few moments, but eventually there would have to be something definitive. That's when I remembered Patty Duke.

"My mother was bipolar, manic-depressive. Before she . . . before . . . the accident."

Scobee wrapped her fleshy arms around my head and pressed me into her chest. "Don't say any more."

Thank God.

By the end of the day, it was clear the news had spread. Everybody knew I was troubled, and I was getting the royal treatment from teachers and kids alike. When I walked down the hall at school, they parted before me like the Red Sea. Ignoring my teachers that day, I focused on what was really important: concocting a story that was certain to make me the most popular kid at school.

"What happened, Matt?" Paisley asked after classes let out, placing her lavender-scented hands on my blazer. I didn't realize she knew my name.

"I'm not ready to talk about it yet. I'm sorry."

She nodded. "Okay, well, when you're ready, will you talk to me first?"

I checked my watch. "Sure. How about we meet tomorrow morning, first thing, in the courtyard? I'll be ready then."

She beamed at me and gave me a hug and bounded off toward her friends—arguably the most *currently* popular kids in school—to brag how she would be the first to hear about the tragedy.

When I got home from school, I was so elated that I forwent my usual slamming of the apartment door and screaming "I hate school!" for the first time that week. I didn't really hate school, but this was an effective way to steal attention and complain that I had no friends aside from Graham. My grandmother, who'd been passing through the hall, stopped and considered me. I shrugged off my backpack, letting it hit the floor with a thud. I winked at the maid as she scurried to pick it up.

"Hiya, Grandma!" I crooned on my way up the stairs, pausing on the landing for emphasis.

"What's with the good mood?" she asked as I ran up the remaining stairs, but I didn't answer. I was on a mission in search of Patty Duke's memoir, *Call Me Anna*. My books were all arranged by subject (alphabetically by author) with celebrity biographies and autobiographies on a special shelf. *Call Me Anna* sat carefully between Bette Davis's *The Lonely Life* and *Majesty: Elizabeth II and the House of Windsor*. Both of those paperbacks were bought used, and the spines showed it, but not Patty Duke's memoir. I flipped it over and examined the back cover. "Manic depression it is," I said to myself.

I was so preoccupied creating a plausible backstory for my mother's accident, that I didn't participate in the usual dinnertime conversation—a smorgasbord of politics, world news, and whatever anyone had done that day.

"Where are you tonight?" my grandfather asked. "She's not

making conversation, either," he said, pointing a fork at my grandmother.

"What do you want from me?" my grandmother said. "We talk
about the same thing every night. I've heard the same conversation
for fifty-five years already. Give me a night off once in a while."

"I was just thinking about school."

"Oh," he said, perhaps assuming I was pondering some profound
lesson. "What are you learning at this expensive new school? How
to become suave and debonair?"

I told him that was exactly what I was learning to do. Sometimes
you have to throw people a bone.

"He's certainly more subdued than when he came home," my
grandmother said, and then lifted her fork. "That school must encourage manic behavior."

There it was again! Manic behavior! It's funny how you can hear
a word and then suddenly it's everywhere. "Do you think my behavior's really manic?" I asked.

"Darling, I've always thought your behavior was manic. It's one
of the few character traits that identify you as a Rothschild. That
and the stuffed-animal shrine you've erected in your bedroom. I'm
just waiting for you to throw a birthday party for your imaginary
friends, and you'll be just like your Uncle Simon. Remember your
brother Simon, Howard, and his imaginary friends?"

．　．　．　．

The following morning, by the time I met Paisley at the designated
place, a stone bench next to the water fountain in the courtyard, I
had the entire story worked out. I decided that my mother should
kill herself. Dog-earing pages of Patty's book where she talked about
suicide attempts, I'd stashed it in my book bag in case I needed inspiration.

"Does it hurt to talk about it?" Paisley asked me, stroking my
hand in sympathy.

No, I thought, but I did not say it.

"I couldn't talk about it with just anyone," I said, and that was true. In middle school the first person one divulges any real tragedy to is a strategic move. It's an exceptionally rare, character-defining moment, as one isn't generally blessed with too many tragedies to use for social advancement. I mean, how many times can your mother kill herself? If I'd chosen some random Sneaker-Head to spill my guts to, what kind of judgment would it have shown? It would have said that I could tell my story to anyone, that I was undiscriminating, that I was uncool. I *was* uncool, of course, but not for long.

"What happened?" she purred, stroking my hand again. It tickled.

Looking as forlorn as I could, I turned away, as though it were too hard to formulate words. I bit my lip. I shook my head.

"I don't even know when it started. One day she was acting one way, and the next she was crazy. She took scissors and cut off her hair and then cut up her clothes. She kept talking like money was the enemy, and then she ran around our house throwing it everywhere."

"Throwing money? That *is* scary."

The bell for homeroom rang, and we got up from the bench.

"I hope you'll sit with me and my friends at lunch," she said. "We can finish our conversation then. You can bring Graham if you want—just try to get him to ditch the bow and arrow."

I nodded and then ducked into the open door leading to study hall. I spent my time imagining how my mother might kill herself, because that was the next part of the story. Sadly, this required knowledge about my mother that I did not possess. How *would* she kill herself? I had to decide on cause of death and in what room said death occurred. It was like playing a reverse game of Clue. Would she hang herself from a beam or sit in an unventilated garage?

Somehow I couldn't see her doing anything uncomfortable, as it'd mess up her clothes or her hair. That left only one cause: sleeping-pill overdose. It seemed as if sleeping pills wouldn't be messy, and you got to fall asleep.

At lunch, Graham and Paisley flanking me, I told the small group of popular students about the sleeping pills. Another member of the Gucci Girls named May half frowned during my monologue, while the rest of the group leaned in with open mouths. When I'd finished, but before the full effect of my words had been seared into everyone's imaginations, she said:

"My mother tried something like that once."

You bitch, I thought. *This is my scene!* If anyone had been looking at me in that moment—like they were *all* supposed to be doing— my cover would have been blown. Oh, I was mad!

"How awful for you!" I said, loud enough to break her spell and re-turn their attention to me. "And I can say so because I know just how bad it is to live with someone like that. Before she killed herself."

"Mine tried, and then she went to a hospital. She's better now." Tears were falling down May's cheeks, bringing streaks of blue mascara. "I don't know what I'd do without her. I feel so sorry for you."

I sat there looking at this girl, who'd just confessed something so personal, displaying her grief so nakedly, and I realized what I was doing. It hadn't occurred to me that real people would kill themselves. I mean, I knew Patty had tried to, but she was an Academy Award winner. Didn't that put her in a different league from every-day people?

I was wondering how I'd ever thought this was a good idea when Paisley grabbed my hand and the crying girl's hand. "I'm so glad you're both my friends." The crying girl nodded solemnly and said, "I don't know what I'd do without you," but all I could muster was a halfhearted "Thanks." I felt disgusting.

Then Paisley looked up and spotted a girl across the courtyard. "May, look at that girl over there. Is that the new Gucci clutch?"

"The nerve," May said, her tears evaporating. "Doesn't she know that we get first dibs and then she can get one? Bitch!"

After school Graham and I were walking to his house to play video games. We walked a few minutes in silence before he grabbed my shoulder. "I have to tell you. All that stuff about your mom; you're really brave. Everyone thinks so. You've never said much about it, but if you ever need to talk, I'm here. Okay?"

I couldn't let this go on. It was one thing to lie to irrelevant kids at school, but Graham was my friend. "Listen, I have to tell you something."

He pushed his glasses up the bridge of his nose. "What is it?"

"Don't get bent out of shape about this, promise?" He nodded, and reluctantly I continued. "My mom didn't kill herself."

"You mean she was murdered?"

"No, I mean she's alive."

He shook his head. "What about the sleeping pills?"

I avoided Graham's gaze. "I kinda made that part up."

I had hoped he'd see my stunt as a good joke, something fun to be part of, a little conspiracy. We'd infiltrated the cool-kid clique! Go us! We'd put one over on Scobee! High five! But looking at his wounded expression, I saw that I should have kept this to myself. I just had to tell someone. That girl from lunch, the crying girl whose mother really did have manic depression—I couldn't get her out of my head, and it was eating away at me.

"Why did you do it?" he asked.

"I knew that Scobee wouldn't bust us if I made something up. Then people overheard, and I was suddenly popular. Understand?"

"You have to tell them the truth."

I gasped. "The what?" I wasn't telling anyone any truth. Was he insane? Why couldn't I just not talk about it anymore? It meant I'd have to find some other reason for the popular kids to like me, but it could work.

I took a longer look at his face and realized that my middle-school career had washed down the drain. I could never come clean. "You're right," I said. "I just need to think about how to do it."

He seemed satisfied with that response and let the subject drop until we were at my house about a week later. "So when are you going to tell them?" he asked.

"Tell who what?" I asked absently before I realized what he was talking about. "Oh. That. I . . . I haven't figured it out yet."

"You have to do it soon. You can't just live a lie."

I tried to reason with him. Surely he could understand my position. "You're so right, Graham. It's just . . . if I tell them, I'm afraid they won't want to be my friends anymore."

"If they're really your friends, then it won't matter. That's what my mom says."

Your mother's a fool, I thought. "She must not be from around here," I said under my breath.

Then, strangely, he changed the subject. "Hey, you have a lot of stuffed animals!"

"That was random," I said, and he laughed.

"Sorry," he said. "My dad threw all mine away last year. He says I'm too big for them now."

"Interesting," I said. "Do you want to play with them? When I was younger, I used to pretend they fell in love and married each other. Sometimes there'd be love triangles with other animals."

It was a diversion, something for him to think about so he wouldn't badger me about the truth. I never thought it would get back to the kids at school.

But the next day at lunch, Paisley fixed her smile on me and said, "So we hear Bob and Esther are getting married."

I looked at Graham incredulously, but he was smiling broadly. Clearly he couldn't see that playing with stuffed animals was worse than pathological lying.

I hung my head and massaged my temples. I could see where this was going, how a full description of the stuffed-animal weddings I conducted as a kid—something I used to distract Graham so I wouldn't have to feel guilty about lying to the popular kids—would surely get us evicted from this group. But I was wrong.

"That's so cool!" the girls in the group squealed. The guys, who in a few years would be high-school muscle jocks, furrowed their brows in something akin to disgust. But the girls were obviously in, so they would be, too.

Then Paisley said, "We should totally have a stuffed-animal wedding, like a real one! We could take pictures for the yearbook!"

"What?" I asked, somehow afraid of where this was going.

"Yeah!" said May. "My animals sleep with me. I'm sure they'd like a day out."

"Besides," Paisley said, "we want to be supportive of Matt and his interests." Then her face lit up. "Matt, you can be the one who marries them!"

"No!" I said. "I don't need to marry them. Besides, this isn't really an interest of mine. It's just that I've never gotten rid of them."

"Matt," she said, "don't hide yourself from us. Let us in."

What else could I do? "Okay," I said, frowning.

After school I chastised Graham for opening his big mouth. "What did you think you were doing?" I asked. We were walking to his five-floor town house in the East Seventies.

He looked surprised. "Paisley asked what we did last night, and I told her. You don't think it's a good idea?"

I stopped walking and faced him right there in the middle of Madison Avenue. "No, Graham, I don't. I really don't think it's a good idea to ask them to give up their interesting plans to attend a make-believe wedding for a puppet and a stuffed bear with a wig."

. . . .

It's strange how one lie leads to another, and then another, until it seems like you can't have an honest conversation anymore. Not that I ever had one with these popular kids before I concocted that bit about my mother, but even when they were attempting to get to know me, everything had to be altered. Making plans over the next week and passing out invitations to the wedding, it somehow occurred to me that my real life story was strange enough as it was. I wondered briefly why I'd been so quick to kill my mother off, but I was too busy that week covering my tracks to self-reflect too deeply.

I wasn't in favor of inviting my grandparents, but Graham did it, anyway. Before any of my new popular friends got to Graham's house, I briefed them on my grandmother's nature. I also told them my grandfather was a wreck after my mother's death and we still hadn't spoken about it.

"I understand," Paisley said, sealing her lips with pinched fingers.

"Good. Would you spread the word? We don't need my grandfather breaking down at the wedding. He's really too sick to come, but he wants to be supportive."

The wedding was a joke around my house. Strangely enough, my grandfather did not heave a sigh or call it a phase. Instead he donned a dark suit and asked what time to be at the chapel, the chapel being Mrs. Wilson's parlor. My grandmother had a different take on the situation. "This is stupid," she said, assuming her seat on the assigned day, and by that point I had to agree with her. It's one thing to pick up animals and dance around your room with them and quite another to advertise your immaturity to a roomful of people. "There's not even a bar for the guests to get tanked. Who are all these people, anyway?"

I hadn't noticed before, but it did seem as if a lot of people were there. There were more kids than I'd invited and adults I didn't know. Wedding crashers. I knew I should be panicked. Any conversation could potentially lead to one's family, especially to my dead mother, but there was a lot going on. I still hadn't practiced my officiator's speech

Graham's mother was mingling with the adult guests, smiling and patting shoulders. Her hair was pinned neatly into a bun, her jewelry demure. "It's for the children," I heard her say, and I was glad to hear that someone besides my own family found this peculiar. Scanning the room for Graham, my eyes fell on my science teacher. He saw me, too, and made a beeline right for me. My grandmother was sitting stoically in her seat, and I walked forward to meet the teacher, Mr. Willett.

"Wonderful little party you're having," he said, all smiles. "Great way to bring students and teachers together." His eyes scanned the room, and he nodded appreciatively. "Nice place here, right? Is your place like this, too?"

"I guess," I said distractedly. "What are you doing here, Mr. Willett?"

"I came with Scobee," he answered.

"She's here too?" I asked, incredulous. Looking at the adults more closely, I now realized where I'd seen so many of them: school. All my teachers were here, and if that wasn't bad enough, so were half the staff who worked in the office and teachers from other grades. The faces I didn't recognize must have been their spouses or spinster cousins.

"Do you want to meet your next-year teachers?" he asked.

I did *not* want to meet next year's teachers, and I did not want them remembering me as the boy who'd had the stuffed-animal wedding! And then there was the fact that I was the boy whose mother had committed suicide, too. Obviously, all of them knew and this would stick with me as long as I was at this school. I began to wonder very seriously if Graham was right, if the only way out of this mess was honesty.

While Mr. Willett was introducing me to his geeky science friend, I looked over to my grandmother and saw Mrs. Scobee sitting in a folding chair right in front of her. I turned white as an onion. I don't remember what I said to the science teachers to get away, but I found Graham standing by the punch bowl.

"What are these teachers doing here?" I hissed.

"I invited them." He filled another cup and set it on the table. "Was that a bad idea?"

"Yes, it's a bad idea!" I waved my arms around. "Scobee's over there right now talking to my grandmother! Everyone's going to know *everything*. Why would you invite them?"

"But you said you were going to tell everyone everything, anyway."

That's because I was lying, I thought. I almost said this out loud, but something else stopped me. Mrs. Scobee stood up, and I watched my grandmother scan the room until her gaze fell upon me. Her lips were pursed, and her head was shaking. She beckoned me with her finger. Even as I crossed the room, I knew I was in trouble. I asked myself, what would Patty do?—but came up blank. Besides, that never would have worked on my grandmother. She could see through me like a piece of cellophane. I was stuck with the truth this time.

Greta Garbo Lives Next Door

After my teachers learned that my mother did not really kill herself, I begged my grandmother to let me switch schools. I figured the kids would soon learn that I had lied, and I wanted to escape that humiliation. She allowed me to, but switching schools did nothing to help my original problem—making friends. By the start of seventh grade, I still had no real friends to speak of, so I often joined my grandmother in a strictly enforced television-watching regimen. There were shows to watch every day of the week, but our favorites were on Fox: weekly episodes of *Beverly Hills, 90210* and the nymphomania that was *Melrose Place*.

"Why don't you have friends like this?" my grandmother asked, pointing at the television.

"Because I don't go to school with thirty-year-olds. Now, be quiet! I think Dylan is going to punch Brenda's father."

Shannon Doherty's pout may have intrigued me momentarily, but it was Luke Perry's post–James Dean bad-boy identity I started wearing around school.

"What's wrong with your face?" asked my science teacher, Mr. Leak. "And what's that jacket you're wearing?"

"What are you talking about?" I pouted, pulling down my Oakley shades and tugging on my extra-large leather jacket.

The day I chose to debut my new look was the day a freak heat wave hit New York City at the end of September. There was no central air-conditioning at this school, and everyone tried to take seats near the open windows. I kept rewetting my hair in the bathroom, trying to keep it slicked back in Luke Perry style, but the humidity frizzed it out of control. Instead of a badass pretty boy, I resembled a lesser-known member of the Jackson 5, Jewmaine. I was in science class, the last period of the sticky day, and dripping with sweat. I could feel it collected in the folds of my stomach and running down my back, mocking my cool exterior.

Even under normal circumstances—when all his Bunsen burners functioned and his test tubes were kept clean—Mr. Leak's moods were erratic, but the sweltering heat drove him over the edge. He was looking for a reason to blow up. I'd like to say his fiery temper ignited with all his students indiscriminately, but that's not true. Since the first day of school, somehow it was always me that set him off.

Mr. Leak glared at me as he handed back our tests. "It has to be ninety-five degrees in this hotbox, Rothschild, and you're prancing around in that leather jacket like this is *Grease*. What's the matter with you?"

"The matter with *me*?" I asked, studying my most recent failing test grade, a product of late-night television and no studying. My grades had been just fine before, but without friends like Graham to do homework with while we gossiped, I lost interest in my classes. "What's the matter with *you*?" I asked. And I immediately regretted it.

He cocked his head and regarded me. I was hoping he wouldn't answer me, because I had nothing to come back with. It was hot, and I was struggling like hell to retain my Luke Perry cool and Shannon Doherty lips.

"Just get out," he finally said, almost dropping the papers. "Take your things and leave."

I stood up and started to throw my things into my bag. I looked around the room at my classmates. "I'm just glad it's me that gets to get out of this 'hotbox.'"

I hoped I sounded like a rebel. Did I look as cool as I imagined?

"Keep it up, Matt," said Mr. Leak, "and you won't be back."

Placing my sweaty palms flat on my desk, I stared at my science teacher through my Oakleys. This was the closest thing to pure aggression I could muster. "What are you going to do?" The words were supposed to sound slow, threatening, almost seductive, but they came out with a croak.

Mr. Leak mimicked my pose. "I guess you'll find out." He pouted his lips back at me.

I turned red and rushed out of the room as the class laughed and laughed.

.   .   .   .

I returned home from school to find my grandparents in the study reading. I took out the suspension notice from school, intending to hand the letter to my grandmother, but my grandfather sat up and coughed. His arm was outstretched. "I'll take it," he said. My grandmother put down her book and looked on curiously as my grandfather read the letter aloud. She crossed her legs and sat back, motioning at my sunglasses.

Take them off, she mouthed.

At least I think that's what she was saying; it was dark in that room. But my grandfather left no doubt.

"Take off those sunglasses!" he shouted. "I've never seen such obstinance." He peered over the top of his glasses and waved the letter around for effect. "Challenging a teacher in the middle of class—" He went on like this a few more minutes, rerunning the highlights of the notice. "You've been in school one month and already: excessive tardiness, dress code violations . . ."

My grandfather hardly ever yelled. I removed the sunglasses and sank into the sofa, hoping to melt between the cushions, but the air-conditioning here worked just fine. At last he caught his breath and said, "What do you have to say for yourself?"

I thought, *It wasn't my fault that I had to put Mr. Leak in his place. It wasn't my fault that the air-conditioning was broken and that he was in a bad mood to start with.* Was it?

"Nothing, sir," I said.

He blinked, surprised. I never called him sir, and I was never without some kind of smart response—even if only to reassign blame. His mouth twisted into a line I hadn't seen before, and deep grooves raked across his forehead. He looked concerned and disappointed and hurt all at once, but he recovered quickly. "Quite right," he said. "Marching all over school in this getup."

"Howard," said my grandmother, "calm down. Don't get yourself all excited. This is not a getup. It's a jacket. He's trying to create his own style and figure himself out."

"Oh, is *that* what he's doing?" he asked, removing his glasses. "Then he can do it in his room for the next week while he's suspended"—he was waving the paper notice—"from school!"

"Seriously?" My grandmother scowled. "For what?" She stood up and snatched the letter from my grandfather, scanning it for details. "For telling someone off? When I was his age, I—"

"I'm very serious," my grandfather said. He sat back and nodded, satisfied. But then self-righteousness made him sloppy. "And I should ground you, too," he grumbled at my grandmother. "After all, this is your fault more than his. You encourage this 'style,' as you call it, and look what happens! He's never been suspended before."

I froze on the couch. There was palpable silence in the room.

My grandmother sucked in her cheeks and squinted before looking over to me. "Matthew," she said slowly, enunciating each syllable, "you're going to have to leave the room now." I pouted at my grandfather and closed the study door just in time to muffle the screaming. The only words I could hear besides my grandmother's obscenities were my grandfather's pleas. "Calm down," he was saying. "Calm down—"

The next morning, after some method of negotiation I was not privy to, my grandmother announced that I wasn't allowed to watch television during my suspension, but movies were okay.

"Really," she said, touching my shoulder lightly, "it was the best I could do. He already feels guilty for doing this. I don't think we should be too hard on him."

. . . .

Over the next few days, my grandfather pretended not to speak to me. He talked over my head at dinner and didn't hand me the style section of the paper, as he usually did. My grandmother shrugged it off, though I noticed she wasn't exactly Chatty Cathy, either. She waited until my grandfather was napping and then visited me in my room, as if talking to me were a covert operation and my grandfather could revoke her TV privileges, too.

"Honestly, I *wish* I had that kind of break from television," she told me. Then the clock struck nine. "Oh!" she said. "My show is on." She excused herself to go watch *Seinfeld.* I was alone again.

At least I had my movies.

On the first morning I was grounded, I went down to the study, where the tapes were shelved. My grandfather looked up, startled from whatever he'd been doing from behind his desk, as I walked into the room. "I'm just getting some movies," I said meekly. He nodded and watched me, maybe wondering what I'd choose. I felt like he was staring holes into my back, so I grabbed the first reasonable thing I saw—*Whatever Happened to Baby Jane?*—and figured I'd come back later when he wasn't there. When I turned around, his mouth was open as if he were about to say something. I waited, but then he looked back to the papers on his desk, and I retreated to my room.

I was watching the movie for maybe half an hour before I involuntarily started imitating Bette Davis and Joan Crawford. Some habits are really hard to break, and for me, imitating female celebrities was one of those habits. I had gone down for the movie out of sheer boredom, but watching it, I actually felt inspired. I grabbed an extra composition book and recorded some choice lines, already intent on how I'd rework them. I'd adapt the characters from middle-aged spinsters with too much makeup to twelve-year-old Upper East Siders with psoriasis. I wanted to read the lines aloud, but then everyone would know what I was doing. I wanted some privacy, so I snuck into the hallway outside our apartment. I figured if anyone came out of the apartment, I'd pretend to polish the furniture in the foyer by the elevator.

In the hall I read all the parts:

BABY JACK: *(Speaking to his drug-addicted brother, temporarily played by Joan Crawford)* Shut up, cokehead.

JOAN CRAWFORD: Baby Jack, Baby Jack, please. I need to go to Bergdorf's for the semiannual pre-sale.

BABY JACK: *(Puts hands on hips while cackling)* Oh, you do? Well, I need to get out to the Hamptons for my BBQ with Barbra Streisand.

JOAN CRAWFORD: *(Sobs)*

I heard the sound of clapping.

I spun around.

There were only two apartments on our floor: my grandparents' and the apartment owned by our reclusive neighbor, a woman whom nobody claimed to have seen more than three times, ever. She'd lived in that same apartment for over thirty years. The only person who entered and left was her scary butler. My grandmother told me he'd only recently been hired, and from what I could tell, he spent the better part of his day outdoors on a park bench sneering at people. My grandparents had tried to buy her apartment many times in an effort to build a home movie theater with plush velvet seats and an arcade, but she'd stood her ground. Some people said that she had once been a celebrity but that her career had ended tragically, and now she spent her days in isolation. Some people said she was Greta Garbo.

Okay, *I* said she was once a celebrity and that she was Greta Garbo.

It was fun to believe that a legend lived next door.

Turning to face the applause, I saw a small, redheaded woman with more liver spots than a dalmatian.

"Take a bow," she said, waving her arms. "That's what we do when the audience applauds."

We? I was intrigued. "Are . . . you an actress?"

Her mane of red hair shook as she laughed. "No, no. Just an old lady."

I was torn between disappointment over her ordinary status and wonder over whether she colored her hair. In the harsh light of the hallway, I could see that her hands were wrinkled and veiny.

"Where are my manners?" she said. "I'm Jimmy Dean."

"Jimmy Dean? Like the sausage?"

"No, no. My name is Janet, but my father always called me Jimmy."

"Did he want the other kids to make fun of you?" I asked.

"No, I think he just wanted to have a son. Say, I was noticing that you're a pretty good actor. You should perform for me sometime," she said. "Would you like that? Oh, you should come in for some cookies. I just had them delivered from Moishe's Bakery."

I was skeptical. Before my suspension I'd been reading *Great Expectations* in English class. "Do you have any adopted daughters?"

Again laughter. "No, I just thought it would be nice to have company. Richard doesn't like to have many people over." Richard, I was to learn, was the butler.

Honestly, it wouldn't have mattered if she'd had an adopted daughter *and* a decaying wedding cake in her apartment. There were cookies and the possibility of an adoring fan, someone who recognized my talent now that my grandmother was more interested in watching television alone than in talking to me. I accepted the invitation and stepped inside her apartment. The place smelled like a pack of Marlboro Reds, and it was decorated in an Asian motif. Samurai swords hung on the walls, and a large brass gong stood in the corner. It was, to my mind, begging to be used. Sitting on an end table was a plate of black-and-white cookies.

"I'll go get us some milk," she said.

I guessed that Jimmy was in her mid-eighties; she looked older than my grandparents, but not by much. She fluffed pillows and moved ashtrays on her way to the kitchen. "Make yourself at home." Lacking a second floor, her apartment was smaller than ours, but it

seemed larger because she sat on mats, not sofas. Sword-bearing nin-
jas, it seemed, were comfortable only with their butts pinned to the
floor.

Realizing she was out of milk, Jimmy returned with a vodka and
tonic and asked if I might like some plain tonic with lime. "I don't
have any stirrers," she said, "but my hands are clean." She reached
down and squeezed the lime into my glass, then stirred the water
around with her finger. I cringed as she brought her finger to her
lips, sucking the remaining tonic water from her cuticle, then offered me a cookie with the same hand.

"Um, not yet," I said, taking a sip of the tonic. She touched my
arm. "Tonic water has medicinal purposes, you know."

Later I repeated this to my grandmother, who asked, "Is that before or after you add the gin?"

"It wasn't gin, it was vodka."

"So you're on a first-name basis with her drink order now?"

"Will you stop talking?" my grandfather interrupted. I thought
he was going to yell at me over leaving our apartment. "I want to
hear more about her apartment. You say there were samurai swords
and gongs?"

I nodded and told him that we sat on straw rugs Jimmy had woven
herself.

"How talented she must be," my grandmother grumbled, but we
ignored her. Incredulous, she asked, "I want to know how someone
who's afraid of his closet visits a hermit who hasn't been outside in
decades!"

"She's not a stranger," I said. "She's lived here for a long time."

"And she hasn't been seen by a living soul since she first moved in."

I shrugged. "Say what you want, but she gave me some old movies
to watch. Which is more than *you* ever do when I refill *your* drinks."

My grandmother snorted. "I'll remember that, little man, when
you're clawing and panting at my door in the middle of the night
because of a *nightmare*." She did have a point. One semirealistic
episode of *Law & Order* and I could be awake all night.

My grandfather laughed so hard he had to wipe his eyes. They may have been laughing at me, but I didn't care. At least my grand-parents were *speaking* to me again.

. . . .

The next day I finished watching Jimmy's movies, and I crossed the hall to return them. Before my hand made contact with her front door, the door swung open. Jimmy stood there in a polyester bell-bottomed leisure suit, a relic of the 1970s. She turned and posed against the doorjamb. "Do you like?" she asked. "I found them in my closet."

"Very nice," I said, but truthfully, everything from the 1970s scared me. In my head the 1970s meant two things: disco and John Travolta. I firmly believed that an era whose biggest superstar was now doing roles in *Look Who's Talking* was reason enough to warrant my distrust.

Jimmy was holding a bag of birdseed and a loaf of bread. "I was just about to go for a walk. Would you like to come?"

I looked back at my apartment. "Not as if I'm doing anything else." I walked toward the elevator, but Jimmy stopped me.

"No, I don't use that one." She lowered her voice to a whisper. "Let's use the service elevator."

A lump grew in my stomach. Whereas the main elevator was oak-paneled and trimmed with gilt taken straight from a Vanderbilt mansion, the service elevator was dark, dirty, and terrifying. "You're joking, right?" I asked. Couldn't she see it was a glorified metal cage?

"There are too many busybodies in this place. And cameras."

She stepped gingerly down toward the service elevator. Reluc-tantly I followed, shuffling my feet. Riding down, I imagined what my grandmother would say. *Which is worse, little man? Being abducted by strangers or being abducted by a woman who's spent the last thirty years avoiding people?*

The service entrance let us out into the alley behind the build-ing, and we had to walk around the corner to get to Fifth Avenue, then on to Central Park. Jimmy walked quickly, and I was barely able to keep up. I decided either she took covert walks when nobody was watching or she was doing laps around her apartment all day. "Walking is excellent exercise," she said over her shoulder. "And I like to give my friends a little treat."

I was too busy catching my breath to wonder who these friends were. Jimmy and I walked into the park, where we found a bench. I promptly sat down, but she remained standing. She pulled the loaf of bread out from its bag and tore off pieces, scattering them onto the ground. She encircled us with bread crumbs and made a second ring with the birdseed. Had the contents of the circle been flammable, I might have been more concerned. I was weirded out enough already.

Gradually a few birds made their way over, pecking at the seeds. One rabble-rouser went after the bread, but Jimmy swatted it away.

"That's not for *you!*" she screamed at the top of her lungs. "That's for *Fidel*."

A family of squirrels came over, but Jimmy swatted them away as well. "You are *not* Fidel!"

I looked around and saw people watching us. One mother shielded her daughter's eyes and walked quickly in the other direction. Other people pointed and stared. Jimmy was oblivious to the attention her outfit and erratic behavior were causing. She sat down beside me.

"You have to watch these animals or they'll eat you out of house and home."

I pictured a swarm of birds and squirrels looting Jimmy's apartment, some holding her at sword point while their friends banged her gong and others ransacked her supply of seed. My grandmother was right. This woman was a bona fide nut. I tried to inch away, but Jimmy grabbed my sleeve. "There he is," she said, elated.

Fidel, it turned out, was a squirrel Jimmy had taken a special liking to. "There's my little Fidel," she cooed. The squirrel stood up on his haunches and waved his paw, doing his best, I thought, to impersonate his namesake. "Oh, isn't he handsome?" she asked, jabbing me in the side.

No, I thought, *he's a squirrel, and you're a nut.* And Central Park is full of squirrels—and nuts too, actually—so how could she be certain that *this* was Fidel? What did she do, tag him? Jimmy stopped talking, and when the silence became uncomfortable, I tried making conversation.

"So . . ." I started, "where are you from?"

"Texas," she said. "God's country." She reached into her pants pocket and retrieved a cigarette. My grandmother had warned me against smokers—"They're pathological liars," my grandmother always said. But people smoked all the time in movies; I thought of Bette Davis. "You smoke?" Jimmy asked.

"Sure," I lied.

Jimmy handed me a cigarette and a lighter. I sat there looking at them, wondering what kind of adult gives a twelve-year-old a cigarette.

"Problem?" she asked.

Yes. I had no clue how to light the damn thing. "I always use matches," I said.

"Matches?"

"I get them at the bar around the corner from the apartment."

Jimmy shrugged, grabbing the lighter and lighting my cigarette. I took a deep puff, and then I was drowning in the sensation that my chest was on fire. The park had turned blurry around me, and I began coughing. "I only smoke lights," I croaked, trying desperately to look dangerous and cool. "Tell me more about"—cough, cough—"God's country." I spit out the cigarette and smashed it in the grass.

She sighed. "Oh, Texas is great. I spent the first forty years of my life there."

"Is that where you met Richard?"

Jimmy shook with laughter, as if I'd said the funniest thing. "No," she said, composing herself. "I picked Richard up in a subway station. He asked if I had any money, and I asked if he could do windows. I don't give handouts. He's been around ever since, but he doesn't really like people." She shrugged. "Which is fine, because neither do I."

I thought about that. Sometimes I didn't like people, either. They so rarely resembled the characters on TV I loved. "Do you have any kids?"

"Yes, I have a daughter. Beautiful, beautiful girl. Of course, she's not really a girl anymore; she's fifty-two."

"Where is she?"

Her face fell, and I knew that I had asked a bad question. "She lives in California with her husband. I see them a couple of times a year when they come to visit."

"You never go out there?" I asked. "I love California. That's where Hollywood is. I'm going to move out there one day."

"Oh, no! I can't get on a plane in my condition. Can you imagine?" She let out a cackle, and for the first time I wondered if she was drunk. "You are so precocious," she said.

I hadn't heard the word before. It didn't sound like an insult, but I didn't want her to think I was stupid for not knowing, so I moved the conversation back to her. "Were you married?"

"I was," she said. "I was married to the same sonofabitch for twenty-five years. Racist pig. My father wanted me married, so he set me up with a young buck in his firm. It took me two years to figure out he was a pig, but by that point I was knocked up, and my parents wouldn't let me leave him. He told me that if I ever tried to leave, he'd take our daughter and I'd never see her again."

This was better than anything on *Dynasty*! "What'd you do?"

She poked my chest with her index finger, bits of the ash from her cigarette falling on my polo shirt. "I'll tell you what I did: I sat there for twenty-two years until my little girl graduated from college, and then I walked out one morning after breakfast." Jimmy took a long drag on her cigarette. "You should have seen that sonofabitch. He said I'd come crawling back, that I'd never be able to make it."

"But you did?"

"Yeah, a couple months later I married an oil guy from Dallas. When he died, the old coot left me a billion dollars, and I moved here to New York. I always wanted to live in New York, but that sonofabitch said there were too many crazies and liberals for us to come up here."

"Mrs. Dean!"

I had been so engrossed in the story that I didn't see Richard running up behind us.

Jimmy froze, a panicked look plastered across her face. I recognized that look—it was the same one I tried to hide when kids at school passed out invitations to birthday parties to which I was not invited. She turned to face Richard. Up close I realized how tall he was—and how greasy his ponytail looked in the sunlight. "What are you doing down here?" he asked.

"I was feeding Fidel and some of his friends," she said.

"I asked the concierge. Nobody knew you had left the building." His eyes narrowed. "I thought I instructed you not to leave."

Jimmy turned to me. "I'm sorry, Matthew, but I must go. Richard was terribly worried."

Richard pulled Jimmy up off the bench, and the two walked back through the park toward our building. Richard looked straight ahead, and Jimmy wobbled alongside him, her confident strides gone.

· · · ·

When I told Jimmy's story to my grandparents that night, my grandfather asked questions at appropriate times, but my grandmother was strangely silent.

"Squirrels ate out of her hand?" my grandfather asked. "They came right up to her?"

"I'm not going to lie," I said, relishing the attention. "It was grade-A strange. I haven't seen something like that since Grandma's cousin French-kissed that horse."

"It wasn't a horse," my grandmother snapped. "It was a whore. And you did not see that—you were eavesdropping on the telephone again."

I shrugged. "I remember hearing about a horse."

"Maybe you should leave Jimmy alone," said my grandfather. "It sounds like she's not in the best health."

"That's just it," I said. "She was fine until the butler took her away. That's the strangest part!"

My grandparents traded a quick glance.

The next afternoon I knocked on Jimmy's front door, but there was no answer. Later that night I found three classic movie tapes on the welcome mat outside our door. I watched them immediately.

"I don't understand," I told my grandmother. "Why doesn't she answer the door?"

My grandmother rolled her eyes. "I don't know, Matthew, maybe she was carving up somebody else's grandson. Stay away from her. She's probably got a cult made up of people she took home from the subway."

. . . .

The next day I tried again. And once again before my knuckles made contact with Jimmy's front door, it swung open. Richard stood in the doorway, staring down at me. He was dressed casually in a Hawaiian shirt and shorts, carrying a feather duster.

"She's napping," he said, and slammed the door on my face.

I knocked again. When Richard opened the door for the second time, he was clearly annoyed. "Young man, I said: She. Is. Napping." His mouth barely moved at all.

"She left these for me," I said, holding out the movies. His attitude made me nervous. "I wanted to return them. In case she misses them."

"Oh, she did, did she?" He snatched the tapes. "I'll make sure they find their way back to the proper place. Thank you." He shut the door in my face for a second time.

. . . .

Later that week I flopped onto the sofa next to my grandmother. She was watching *Matlock.*

"Richard won't let me see Jimmy," I said.

She turned up the volume on the television.

"Wait a minute," I said.

My grandmother put her finger over her lips, then pointed to the television.

"But I have a problem!"

"You'll still have it in ten minutes, so let me watch."

"But I want to talk now."

She turned off the television and faced me. "You're right, Matthew. Let me give you my undivided attention so that you can tell me how you're worried that something is wrong with our crazy neighbor. Will that make everything all right?"

"Yes!"

"Go tell your grandfather." She switched the television back on.

Across the room my grandfather grunted. I stood up and kicked the couch and shouted, "I'll bet Jimmy would listen to me if *she* was my grandma!" I had never raised my voice to my grandmother before, and for a moment she simply sat there, dumbfounded.

But then she exploded.

"Jimmy! Jimmy! Will I have no peace around here because of that woman? All I ever hear about is how great she is. Ask her how she manages to live all alone in peace and quiet next time you talk to *her*."

"But something is wrong," I said, exasperated.

"We don't know that," my grandfather said.

"*I* know it! What else do you need?"

Apparently they needed more conclusive evidence, because they did nothing.

The next week I returned to school and my television privileges were reinstated. I still didn't give up on Jimmy, and over the next few weeks I discreetly knocked on her door, but nobody ever answered, not even Richard. There were no more movies on my doorstep, and after two months I wasn't even sure anyone was still living inside. Sometime after Thanksgiving, but before Christmas, I came home and found policemen milling around outside her apartment. The door was wide open.

"What's going on?" I asked my grandmother.

She paused a moment. "Jimmy's dead."

The downstairs neighbor had called our building's super because of a strange odor emanating from the ceiling. When he used the master key to unlock Jimmy's apartment, the super was almost knocked down by the smell and called the police.

"They don't know how long she's been dead," she said. "She was already rotting and drawing flies."

"Where's Richard?" I asked, and she shrugged.

I was so mad, I kicked the wall. I rushed past her into our apartment, screaming, *"I told you so! I knew something was wrong!"* She called after me, but I slammed my door shut. I sat alone in my room that night, refusing to eat dinner.

My grandfather knocked on my locked bedroom door. "What could we have done, Matthew?"

"For starters you could have cared enough to listen to me!" I yelled, my voice full of bitterness. "You never did anything to help her. And now, look—she's *dead*. For someone who made a living jumping into other people's business, you sure dropped the ball this time!"

He said nothing else.

.   .   .   .   .

An autopsy was done, and the official cause of death was listed as heart failure, a testament to her old age and a preexisting condition. Still, nobody could find Richard, and skepticism over Jimmy's death arose when her will was read a few weeks later. In a wobbly but still-legible hand, Jimmy had left most of her fortune to her butler—and some squirrels. When Jimmy's daughter contested the will, it came out that Richard had isolated Jimmy from her family and friends. In the end, Richard, a homeless man Jimmy had met on the subway, flew to the Bahamas with $10 million and left behind Jimmy's incensed daughter and many raised eyebrows in our building.

"Don't get any ideas," my grandmother told Atse after Jimmy's daughter settled with Richard. "My children aren't that generous."

Atse raised his fist high into the air and cried out, "Foiled again!" before doubling over with laughter. "I guess Christmas bonuses are going to be small on the Upper East Side this year."

My grandmother agreed, and Atse went back to the kitchen. She and I had been watching television again but not really talking; I hadn't said much to either of my grandparents since Jimmy died.

"So what was it about Jimmy that you liked so much?" my grandmother asked.

It was a good question. Was it the attention? I found myself thinking about it for longer than I should have. It seems like if you're friends with someone, you should be able to spit out a few key reasons for the friendship. "I felt bad for her because she was alone."

"Mercy friendship?" she asked, looking directly into my eyes. I searched her face for the meaning of the question. Her tone was soft but not curious, and I couldn't figure out exactly what she meant.

"I did feel bad for her. And she was nice. But, you know, she was weirder than me. Like, she was so weird that she didn't think I was weird. It wasn't like the kids at school."

"The kids at school think you're weird?" she said. "I didn't know that."

I hadn't ever mentioned this detail. I didn't have many people hanging around with me at our house, but I usually had at least one friend, so it never looked like I was isolated, just that I was a loner. She sat back and stared ahead at the television, perhaps filling in some of the blanks on the ticker tape of time.

"I guess the kids thought I was weird, too," she said, "when I was in school. Hell, they do now, but do you know what I say every time one of those high-society broads looks down her nose at me?" I shook my head, and she glanced around to make sure we were alone before continuing. "I say fuck 'em."

I gasped. My grandmother cursed, but she rarely used the F-word.

"Just don't tell your grandfather or he'll ground me from TV, too."

The Wandering Jew

By the time I was thirteen years old, I had all but lost my passion for impersonating women. It might have been the Elvis-like chops or the thick facial hair I shaved daily—the Jewish hair gene already taking root all over my body—or the change in my voice, but I had passed the point where a boy wearing designer evening gowns was cute even to my grandmother. It's hard to say what tipped me off first. Was it my grandfather's insistence that I act more like a boy? Was it the strange look I would get from teachers when discussing Judy Garland's heyday at MGM? Who's to say?

If my grandparents wondered why I no longer walked around the house dressing up and singing show tunes in the voice of Carol Channing, they kept it quiet. My grandmother wasn't the kind of woman who pried, and my grandfather appeared happy that his original assertion was correct: Cross-dressing had been a phase. I could tell he was relieved.

"Mark my words," my grandfather said, helping my grandmother into her coat as they were leaving to go out for dinner. "It's just a matter of time before he's out running and playing with the other boys."

I'm not sure what he meant by "running and playing," but if it was something that interested the jocks from my gym class, I was sure I wanted no part of it. But I did want to be accepted and to make friends. Maybe playing sports was the answer?

So one day shortly after I started the seventh grade, I decided to give sports a try. Gym class was mandatory, and I had full intentions of participating in some football or basketball, but I didn't get that far. The gym-class bullies, a group of six muscular eighth-graders, intercepted me on the way out of the locker room. "Why don't you go home and wear a dress?" their leader, the perfect oxymoron, Mark St. Joy, taunted. He elbowed his friends, and they laughed. "A dress!" they echoed.

"I'd like to," I said, staring at my feet, "but you got it dirty when you were prancing around Central Park in it."

His friends went silent. They looked at him, waiting for a retort, and he glared at me. He stood silent for what seemed like an eternity. Then he spit, "You're just a faggot."

Now I was speechless. I looked up from my spotless gym shoes, too stunned and too proud to cry.

His lips were twisted into a Joker-like smile. The guys stood in a semicircle, dangling limp wrists before walking away to throw around a football. "Faggot," they echoed.

"You can't even spell *faggot*," was the first thing I could utter, and not until they were safely away. It was important to appear unfazed, but I felt as if the wind had been knocked out of me. I sat down to focus on not caring; to care would be an admission that what they said was true.

I turned to the other boys sitting nearby, who looked at me in something resembling relief. Today had been my day to be taunted, which meant they were free. Hovering close to the wall, we all refused to participate in gym class and sat out of the way of stray balls that might "accidentally" hit us. Some of these boys had buckteeth or skin disorders. To pass the time, we played cards or chess, much to the chagrin of our gym teacher. Some of us were fat, some skinny. All of us were uncoordinated. None of us could catch a football or make farting noises with our armpits, but I was the one targeted as "faggot."

At the time I didn't know that middle-school gym jocks are demons sent by Lucifer to torment the rest of us, and their calling me "faggot" had little to do with sexual preference. If there was any truth to the comment, it was purely coincidence. But at the time I was petrified that everyone knew a truth that I had not accepted. I knew I was interested in things that did not interest other boys—reciting every album Barbra Streisand had ever recorded, for instance—but how did that make me a faggot?

I had to find out if there was any truth to these accusations. I needed advice from someone older and wiser, and the logical choice was my grandmother. She was worldly. My grandfather was more sympathetic, but I couldn't talk to him about this stuff. He was so busy imagining the equipment I would need for my new career in athletics, how could I ask him to truthfully verify my sexual status? No, I needed my grandmother. She was the only person who ever really listened to me—regardless of subject—even if it was during commercial breaks. However, I would have to be smart about it. I couldn't just come right out and ask her, "Am I a faggot?" Somehow I had to work it into conversation.

"I can tell that you're cranky," I said to her that night. She was sitting at her makeup table applying lipstick. "Maybe you shouldn't go out tonight, and we can play Scrabble instead."

She snorted. "Like I have a choice."

"But why do you have to go?" I whined. "We'll have a quiet night in. Let Grandpa go alone."

"I'll be damned if I know. All I said was that I was getting hungry, and somehow your grandfather thought it meant I wanted to go to dinner with every goddamn politician in the city." She shrugged. "Go figure."

I paced behind her chair. Did I need to wring my hands and tear out tufts of hair for her to see that I was a mess? Why wasn't she paying attention? I decided to bluff. "Maybe I won't be here when you get back," I said, folding my arms across my chest. "If you're not going to be here, why should you expect me to be? I don't have to sit around and wait for you, you know."

She put her lipstick down and raised an eyebrow in the mirror. "Matthew, I don't see why you're getting so bent out of shape. It's an election year. You know that your grandfather has pimped me out to every goddamn charity dinner in town this week."

She went back to applying her lipstick.

"Why don't you sit yourself in your room and have a nice bath instead?" she asked. "It'll be quieter. You like the bubbles."

Although this was true—I adored bubble baths—she was completely missing the point. I wanted to spend some time with her. I needed to ask some guiding questions and fool her into giving me advice on handling the bullies at school. I wasn't trying to be difficult. Why was she turning this into a joke?

"Maybe I'm too much trouble for you. I'll just leave home, then," I said, sitting on the bed. I had been talking about running away a lot lately.

She sighed. "You do this all the time."

"Maybe this time it'll be for good."

.   .   .   .

My grandmother was fond of telling people that I began running away from home almost as soon as I could reach the doorknob. She especially liked to shock her poker buddies, a collection of four other Upper East Side dowagers she invited over to rob blind.

"I give him a bag of bread crumbs and he leaves himself a trail in case he gets lost between the apartment and the basement. So far it's worked fairly well."

"But aren't you worried?" asked one of the poker buddies, Mrs. Pierce.

My grandmother shook her head. "The first time was a bit stressful. Matthew was three years old, and I was on my hands and knees looking everywhere."

"Where was he?" asked Mrs. Pierce.

"Hiding in the elevator." She rubbed her knees like she could still feel the burn. "Two thousand years we can live in houses, and I have to get the Wandering Jew." She sighed. "Oh, well. My husband always wanted a Bedouin. Anyhow, he still runs away."

"You're very brave," said Mrs. Wolff, shaking her head. "Hit me!"

Apparently these women didn't see that worrying wasn't Grandma's style. Her way of showing concern was through practical jokes, and each time I made a break for it, my grandmother placed my dinner in a dog's dish—with the name "Matthew" written in stylized black capital letters—and placed it outside the front door of our apartment for anyone to see.

My grandfather disapproved. "You just have to advertise, don't you? Everyone needs to know our business, I suppose?"

"Oh, get off the cross, Howard," she said, staring down at a glass of Tanqueray.

Being relegated to the classification of "business" didn't thrill me, but I stood silently by, waiting for someone to beg me to stay. It never happened. Huffing and puffing, I'd sob, bang around in my room, make a big show of how "I am never coming back!" but after a few hours away, hungry and bored, I'd wander back upstairs. The bowl with my name was in its usual place outside the front door, and I would sit in the hall and eat dinner.

"My children always threatened to run away," said Mrs. Pierce. "It used to worry me, but then I told them that was fine by me, they just had to leave my home the way they came in: naked. They wouldn't be taking anything I bought for them, that's for sure." Mrs. Pierce puckered her old-lady lips and went back to her hand.

"I'm not going anywhere naked," I called across the room. "It's cold outside."

My grandmother, finally looking up from her cards, said, "Don't give him any ideas."

"Just the same," said Mrs. Wolff, "you know once you leave for good, you can't ever go home again."

"That's the point," I said.

. . . .

When I turned thirteen, however, running away became more of an annoyance than a quirk. I mentioned it with increasing regularity whenever I thought my grandparents were ignoring me. But up in my grandmother's bedroom, watching her apply lipstick in preparation to leave for the night, I didn't want to talk about running away. I wanted to have a real conversation. I was getting desperate.

Just then my grandfather came in. "Hello. Are you almost ready?" He tousled my hair and sat down on the bed.

"Yes. Do something with your grandson. He's distracting me."

I stood up and glared at her reflection in the mirror. "Oh, I'm a distraction now. I'm definitely leaving home. Tonight."

"Fine," she said, exasperated. "Fine. Go."

"This wouldn't be happening if he had more friends his age. He needs the right kind of friends, of course." He turned to me, "Matthew, if only you'd think about soccer or something like that. It would help you lose weight, too."

My grandmother bowed her head and closed her eyes, waiting for my reaction. She knew I was sensitive about my weight. She might have expected tears or a full-fledged tantrum, but I exploded with fury.

"Don't you get it, old man? I'm not playing sports! I hate sports! And I hate kids my age! They suck! Why doesn't anybody understand me?"

I had never screamed at my grandfather before. He looked as if I'd slapped him. He breathed deeply and looked to the floor, but I wasn't done ranting. I turned to my grandmother, also in shock, and said, "You're right. I don't need to run away. I need to kill myself to get some attention around here!" I grabbed my grandmother's cuticle scissors from her makeup table. "That's what I'm doing tonight while you're out at your little party. How's that?"

I'm not sure exactly what reaction I thought I'd get, but I know it wasn't rage. My grandmother was still speechless, but my grandfather's face contorted in anger. He stood up, his eyes as big and round as silver dollars, and I knew he was about to have an explosion himself. And my grandfather was a big man. While he was normally sweet, I was still scared of him when he got angry.

"You're not going to blackmail me, you manipulative son of a bitch!" he shouted, and my mouth fell open. Then he started walking toward me, and I had a vision of getting backhanded. So I ran into their bathroom and locked the door. He pounded and pulled at the knob. Then he pounded louder, and even though he wasn't in the best of health, I thought for sure he'd rip it right off its hinges. I got into the shower and curled up in the fetal position and started to cry. The kind of crying that induces hiccupping, not the elegant kind you see in Ingrid Bergman movies.

"Howard!" I could hear my grandmother say. "Howard, please! Calm down."

But he kept pounding and pounding on the door. Until he suddenly stopped. And there was quiet. I thought for sure he had dropped dead. I thought, *He's dead, and I killed him. I killed my grandfather by yelling at him.* So I cried harder.

Nothing happened for a while—I'm not sure how long; I lost track of time—and then I finally heard a feeble knocking on the door. It was my grandmother.

"Open the door," she said.

"No," I called, still crying.

She paused. "Your grandfather's downstairs. It's just me here, and I'm worried about you." She paused a moment. "Listen, I need to get your grandfather out of here. It's not good for him, Matthew. He can't get upset like this; it's bad for his heart. Tomorrow we need to talk. All of us."

I'm not sure if I was more afraid or angry then. I couldn't believe they were still going out. My grandmother was more worried about my grandfather than she was about me. I was the one with the sharp object in a locked room! They really didn't care if I lived or died. What kinds of people leave a suicidal boy at home to go off and party? And then there was that bit about talking tomorrow. I wasn't doing that, either. Not after they'd had at least twelve hours to think about what had just happened.

I let more time pass before I finally opened the door and peeked out. I was alone in their bedroom. I went to the door and looked into the hall. Same thing. Then I went down to the staircase and peered down. Nobody. They'd really left! It wasn't a ruse to lure me out of the locked room. The maid was off for the night, and we were between drivers so Atse had to drive my grandparents. I really was alone.

I sat down on the bottom stair and cried some more. What was I going to do? I was in so much trouble. And for what? I thought people were supposed to be sensitive around kids who said they were suicidal. Tears fell down my cheeks, and my anxiety grew until I started to wonder what it would actually be like to kill myself. I wouldn't be in trouble if I did. And, oh, my grandparents would be so sorry. They'd feel guilty forever. My grandfather would be traumatized. He'd be too busy sitting around and sobbing to ever want to attend another party again. My grandmother would probably go insane. She'd roam around the apartment, refusing to speak to anyone. And if I killed myself, I'd never have to go back to school!

I smiled for the first time. What did we have around here that I could use for suicide that wouldn't hurt? My grandparents didn't use sleeping pills like the ones I'd said my mother had overdosed on. I walked around the kitchen. There were knives, but I wasn't a cutter. This was supposed to be about *them* suffering, not me. I thought about poison.

I had just seen an episode of *Alfred Hitchcock Presents* on Nick at Nite where a mistress poisons her lover's wife. It seemed to be fast and relatively painless. Did we have poison? I tried to remember where I'd seen the skull-and-crossbones logo and found myself looking underneath the sink, where I found a small box of rat poison in the shape of a cheese slice. On the counter, though, was the most miraculous thing I ever saw in my house: cash. No doubt they had left it for Atse—a one-hundred-dollar bill with a paper-clipped note. *"For incidentals,"* it said. I took the bill and the rat poison and grabbed my coat and left the apartment.

Once I stepped off the elevator, I buttoned up my coat and thought about where I'd go to eat the poison. It was already dark.

"And where are you off to, young sir?" asked the concierge, Joe. He was the oldest of all the concierges, and the nicest.

"I'm going over to my friend's house. My grandparents are out, and I'm going to spend some time over there."

"Be careful," he said, opening the front doors for me.

As I crossed over Fifth Avenue and walked into the park, I looked for my favorite bench. I usually sat here during the afternoon, but Central Park takes on a different mood at night. People walked faster than usual, and nobody made eye contact with me. I sat down on the bench and broke open the fake slice of cheese. The poison itself came in greenish pellets, no larger than a baby's fingernail. They were hard and odorless, and I sniffed one before popping it into my mouth. It tasted like chalk. I thought rats were supposed to be smart. I didn't understand why they would eat some odorless, chalky pellet when they could go after trash, but no matter. I ate one after the other and closed my eyes, waiting to die, thinking all along how sorry my grandparents would be that they'd gone out to that stupid dinner.

. . . .

Aside from some nausea, I was still alive and well after the first hour and then the second. Occasionally people walked by, but nobody said anything to me. I looked at my watch—it was about eleven o'clock, and I was cold, and my misery was wearing off, and I realized that maybe this wasn't such a good idea after all. I turned the box over and saw the "Warning: If swallowed" message. You were supposed to induce vomiting, and as much as I hated throwing up, I stuck my finger in my mouth and tried to gag until I vomited. I did this a few times and sat dejectedly for a little while longer. This was all because of those stupid kids at school, I thought. If they hadn't called me a faggot, none of this would have happened. I stuffed my hands into my coat pockets and found the money I'd taken. What could I do with this? I closed my eyes and thought, *I can go to Forty-second Street and find a prostitute. A prostitute can tell me if I'm gay or not.* I didn't want to have sex with one, but if I could find a nice enough lady who was having a slow night . . . Maybe she could help?

I caught a cab in front of the Met and asked him to take me to Times Square. The driver was indifferent to my age and took off down Fifth Avenue like he was racing in the Daytona 500. He rounded Seventy-ninth Street, and we headed through the park. Traffic was a breeze until we hit Seventh Avenue, and then we crawled down to Times Square. The cabdriver squawked when I handed him the hundred-dollar bill until I told him I'd give him a ten-dollar tip.

It took me about fourteen seconds walking down Forty-second Street to realize I was in over my head. The whole area was synonymous with sleaze, and I'd heard enough jokes in the locker room at school to know that it was full of sex shops and sex workers. I was walking past the triple-X stores, and I watched heavily made up and scantily clad women yelling at one another, stopping briefly to invite male passersby for a little recreation. Growing anxious, I was just about to head home when a middle-aged white woman with frizzy hair and a leopard-print miniskirt called, "Hey, little boy."

I thought she looked as good as any of them, and she had already said hello, so I went up to her. There were bags under her eyes, and her breasts looked like they'd spring from her low-cut halter at any moment. "What are you looking for?" she asked.

"I need an opinion," I said.

"An opinion?" She looked me up and down, confused. "About what?"

A few other women were already gathering around us. I didn't really want to ask my question within earshot of a crowd. I wanted to run, but I reminded myself that I had come all the way here from the Upper East Side and I needed to know the truth. Especially in case the rat poison was really slow and the vomiting didn't work.

I took a deep breath. "I need your opinion if I'm gay," I said.

The woman with frizzy hair blinked. Another prostitute burst out laughing. "I've never heard that line before!" she said. "Donny! This little boy wants to know if he's a fairy!"

My face went hot as a short, thick, black man with cornrow braids came through the crowd of women. He was wearing a black suit with a white dress shirt. He grinned. "You definitely came to the right place, my friend. Any of these lovely women would be happy to show you a good time. You won't be a fairy for long!"

They all laughed.

"No, no," I said. "I just came for an opinion," I said. "Not sex."

Donny scratched his head. The first prostitute tapped me on the shoulder. "Opinions cost money, little boy. You got money?"

I dug out all my change from the cab ride and handed it to her. I waited, expecting some questions, like when I went to the doctor, but she only looked me up and down again. Then she nodded. "Fruit," she said, and the other women laughed and hooted, "Fruit! Fruit!"

I knew immediately that I'd been cheated, but I was too mortified to argue. Donny took the money from the woman's hand and put it in his pocket. "Now get outta here," he said, "before you get yourself hurt. Not everyone's as nice as we are." He gave me a shove, nothing hard enough to hurt, just hard enough to push me back in the direction of Times Square and let me know he meant it.

. . . .

By the time I got home, it was after midnight.

"You're out late," said Joe, checking his watch.

"My grandparents back yet?" I asked, and he said no. I took the elevator up and went to sleep. The following morning when I woke up, my grandparents were both in my room by my bed. My grandmother held the box of rat poison I'd stuffed into my coat, and my grandfather held his head.

"What are you doing in my room?" I asked.

"Matthew, your grandfather and I have made an important decision," my grandmother said.

My grandfather looked up and smiled brightly. "We've decided to get you a dog."

Damn Static

W h e n I was eight years old, my grandparents took me to see some cheesy movie about a girl who, because her father wishes on a star, is transformed from an ungrateful heiress into a humble maid. I'm sure it was probably entertaining, but the only thing I can remember about it now is the inescapable feeling that someone was trying to tell me something. But at eight years old, I lacked that kind of self-reflection. Instead I focused on the main point of the movie: If I wished upon a star, I could get anything I asked for.

"I wish I may, I wish I might," I began, standing at the living-room window.

"Oh, brother," said my grandmother, rolling her eyes.

"Have this wish I wish tonight. . . ."

"Ever since you took him to see that goddamned movie," my grandmother complained, "all he does is sit around and make wishes on his Lite Brite. Look at him now. Wishing on a streetlamp."

"It's harmless," said my grandfather.

"Wait'll he wishes for new grandparents—then we'll see how harmless it is."

My grandfather laughed. "Just a phase," he said. "And what's so bad about some innocent wishes?"

Of course these were no ordinary wishes; I had a plan. I wanted a new puppy. A puppy that would be all mine. A puppy that would follow me around everywhere and love me unconditionally.

But after months of solid wishing on everything I could find that was bright enough to be a star, I realized I'd been conned. Since my stargazing hadn't produced the puppy I desired, I turned to making demands.

"I want a dog," I said, flopping down next to my grandmother on the sofa.

"That's nice," said my grandmother, and turned up the television volume.

"I want a dog," I repeated.

"Is there an echo in here? Am I deaf? I heard you the first time. What do you want me to do about it?"

"Why can't I have one?"

"Who says you can't?"

"You did."

"Oh," she said. "Just checking."

Fine, I thought. If demanding things did not work, then annoying her would. "Grandma," I whined.

"Listen, you may have as many animals as you'd like, as long as they're stuffed."

I turned to my grandfather, who tried to take my side. "Why can't he have a dog? They're so furry and adorable. It'll be nice for him. He can have a friend, and it'll teach some responsibility."

"Responsibility!" shouted Atse from the kitchen door, clad in latex gloves. "I'll tell you who's gonna clean up after that dog and feed that dog. Responsibility, my eye . . ."

"Two against two," said my grandmother. "Sorry."

This conversation sounded largely the same for the next six years: I would ask for a dog, she would say no, my grandfather would plead for me, but we would both be rejected. Until the night I ran away and ate the rat poison in Central Park and consulted the prostitutes in Times Square. My grandparents were clearly at a loss to understand what was bothering me so deeply, and my grandfather saw a dog as a way to bring me back into the fold. "It'll give him steady companionship and might give him some exercise besides," he told my grandmother.

But two months after they said they were getting me a dog, none had appeared, and I figured the conversation was still going nowhere. The dog was clearly my grandfather's idea, and, like in the past, since my grandmother didn't want a dog in the apartment, we weren't getting one. And that was that. Then one day my grandfather told my grandmother that he and I would be home later, we were going shopping. "Ah." She nodded knowingly, assuming we were shopping for her upcoming birthday. She practically rushed us out of the apartment.

We were half an hour outside Manhattan before I asked where we were going. When I was younger, he used to take me on rides through the country, but he hadn't done that in a long time.

"There's something I want to show you in New Jersey," he said. In an uncharacteristic move, my grandfather hadn't waited for my grandmother's approval about getting me a dog. Instead he had secretly reserved a dalmatian puppy from a breeder out in New Jersey. It's still not clear to me why he thought I'd like a dalmatian, but that was the year Hollywood was remaking the classic Disney film *101 Dalmatians.* Kids everywhere were going nuts over dalmatians. Maybe he thought I'd want what everyone else did.

It was the only puppy left in the litter—all the others had been sold—and when I saw his little rolls of fat and Jell-O mold face, I fell in love. Seeing me, his soul mate, the puppy rolled onto his back, practically begging me to rub his brown-spotted belly. At the time my grandfather and I thought it endearing; my bundle of love wanted attention. In hindsight I see that I probably should have kept playing the field. Other puppies I had seen came to people for attention, often placing their heads against awaiting hands, but this puppy made me come to him. Then he peed on me while I petted his belly.

I lifted my new dog out of the pen and set him on the ground, thinking that he would follow me, but when he made contact with the ground, he took off running, much the same as my grandparents described my own first steps. This, again, was another signal that I completely missed. My grandfather laid down some cash, and we took the dog, a crate, and some puppy food.

"What did you do?" asked my grandmother when the dog jumped on her.

"Happy birthday!" said my grandfather.

She shook her head. "There'd better be enough room in that cage for the both of you, because you won't be sleeping in my room tonight," she said.

My grandmother did not want an animal messing up her apartment, and she definitely was not picking up any dog droppings. I told her that I would take care of him, but she wasn't convinced. To her this puppy was another generation of all the pets she had allowed her own children to adopt years ago. More beasts of burden.

"Sure, they're cute for a few weeks, but after that you have to potty train them, then send them to obedience school. It's just like having children—I let your grandfather talk me into that, too. Atse never stopped picking up after them, either. Did you, Atse?"

Atse just stared at the dog. "I'm not speaking to any of you," he said, and walked back to the kitchen.

But in the end my grandmother threw up her hands and said, "What's done is done." The dog stayed.

My grandfather and I had won.

·   ·   ·   ·

So I was more than a little annoyed when the dog took an immediate liking to my grandmother. I tried various names for my new friend, each more ridiculous than the last. My grandmother rejected Aristotle and Pubert, and finally it was she who gave our new dog his name, Static.

"Like static cling?" I asked. Then I laughed. "Because he's always at your side."

"No, like the static you get on the television when the cable goes out."

I should have known; my grandmother had been watching television, and when the picture turned to fuzz, she began beating the remote control against the sofa. "Damn static!" she shrieked. Unfortunately, since my dog refused to leave my grandmother alone, this

became the only call he would acknowledge: a banging sound rid-
dled with screaming obscenities followed by his name. Static.

Having missed the opportunity to give him a name, I set out to
train Static. I wanted him to learn every trick I had seen dogs do on
television. Static, however, was having none of this and just yawned
when I demonstrated how to play catch. One time during our lesson, he stood up, and I thought he was going to play, but he only
walked to a shady part of the park to nap. He must be tired, I
thought. All this learning was wearing him out.

My grandmother, the strict disciplinarian, warned that if we did
not send Static to obedience school, we'd have an anarchist on our
hands. "And you can't teach an old dog new tricks," she'd warn.
"Just look at your grandfather."

But I enjoyed Static's rebellious nature; he was a free spirit. Of
course, animals are already free spirits—that's the point. What I did
not realize was that the only thing separating my dog from some
coyote was learning how to sit. People told me that dalmatians
tended toward the dumb side, but Static put this theory to rest early
on; he was smart enough to know what you were saying, and depending on who you were, he was smart enough not to care. When
my grandmother told him to sit, he sat. When I told him to sit, he
laughed at me. Seriously. His little doggy lips curved into a smile,
and his cheeks swelled with air. It was disturbing.

And there were many things about having a pet I didn't expect.
As a puppy, Static would playfully nip at me. I grew tired of this
quirk very fast. When I'd had enough, I started biting him back.

"That's what you get for biting Daddy when he just wanted to
try your food," I told him.

While I was at school, he and my grandmother grew even closer,
which, I suppose, was quite nice, except it was not supposed to
happen. Static was *my* dog, not hers. My grandmother did not encourage the dog's affection; he just flocked naturally to her, which
infuriated me. I tried to bribe him with food or doggy cookies, but
he just snatched them out of my hands and ran back to my grandmother. When I came home ready to play, Static would sniff me up

and down like some stranger and walk away. Sometimes Static would be sleeping when I came home, so I would wake him up to play, but he didn't like this and would nip at me. For years I had wished for a dog, a best friend who would love to spend time with me, and what I got was a new poker buddy for my grandmother. The jocks at school paid more attention to me. "Be careful what you wish for," my grandmother teased, petting Static.

"We are not talking, old woman, until you do something to make him like me."

"Oh, Matthew, it's only because you're not here all day, and he's gotten used to me. Just the other day, he jumped into the bathtub while I was having my bubble bath and brought me his rubber ducky." She turned to Static. "We had a lovely time in the bath, didn't we, baby? I washed your little ears and paws, huh?"

"What is the matter around here?" I said, exasperated. "What the hell happened?"

"He's my little, *wittle* baby," she said. This from a woman who probably made phone calls to Cruella de Vil the first day she was alone with the dog.

This will just never do, I thought, and I began making pitches for Static's attention. I was a fourteen-year-old boy looking for approval from a six-month-old puppy. I would bring him into my room— against his will—to sleep with me, and wake up in the middle of the night feeling him gnawing on my feet. Some mornings I would wake up and there would be books or magazines scattered on the floor, glorified chew toys for his pleasure. He never did this to my grandmother's belongings.

The final straw was when I came home from school on the last day of classes before winter break and saw that I no longer had a bed.

"Static ate it," said my grandmother, shaking her head.

I had a vision of him roasting my box springs.

"His ball got trapped under the bed, and he tried to dig it out." She patted Static's head in sympathy. "It's okay, boy, 'cause Mommy got it out for you, didn't she?"

I rubbed my own head, trying to soothe the headache that was fast approaching. Who was this woman, and what had she done with my unaffectionate shrew of a grandmother? This was a woman who made me plead my case whenever I wanted a hug, and here she was practically rolling around on the ground with the dog I'd waited six years for!

I complained to my grandfather, who answered my whining with, "I'm sure it's just a phase."

Static had almost turned a year old, and my grandmother busied herself making plans for a small party in the park with some of his friends from the elite doggy day care on the Upper East Side she used when she felt he needed socialization.

"Everything has to be perfect," she said over dinner the night before the party. "Howard, do you have confirmation from all guests?"

My grandfather put on a thoughtful face, trying to be serious, and then he laughed. "Everyone has RSVPawed."

"Matthew, I'll need you on hand to help with refreshments," she said.

"What refreshments? You put some kibble in a bowl and you're done. Atse does it every night." What I didn't know was that my grandmother had hired a caterer who specialized in these kinds of affairs and had specialty dog cookies and cupcakes that needed to be served. "You're nuts," I told her.

"Just remember, he's your dog." She petted Static's head and cooed sympathetically.

"He's not my dog! You hijacked him!"

"Do you hear this, Static? Daddy doesn't want you to have a good birthday. He's fighting with Mommy right here at the table."

Static looked at me and gave a low growl as though he understood and agreed.

"Fine," I said. "I'll do it."

"Now we know it'll be a *good* day," my grandmother said, scratching behind Static's ear.

And it would have been, too, had we all not forgotten that Static and my mother shared the same birthday. On my way out of the apartment to join the party in the park, I heard the phone ring and answered it.

At first I was excited. I was alone in the apartment, and my mother was on the phone. I wouldn't have to share her with my grandparents or worry about my grandmother listening to our conversation. Maybe we'd finally talk about what had happened in Italy? But then I started to panic. She only called on birthdays or anniversaries. Well, it was nobody's anniversary and I found it hard to believe she'd called to wish the dog happy birthday.

"Some people seem to have forgotten something," she said.

I thought for a second before admitting that I didn't know what it was.

"My birthday!" she said. "Where are your grandparents? Why didn't they remember?"

I couldn't help smiling. "They're out in the park right now with Static."

"Static?"

"Static the dog, yes. Did you know you share the same birthday? Grandma is having a party for him—in the park. She's been working on it for weeks. It's catered. Grandpa verified the guest list. He said they all 'RSVPawed.' That's where they are now. Anyway, I'm here. Happy birthday."

I started to tell her I knew just how she felt. Since the dog arrived, my grandmother had no time for anyone. Static had usurped every one of us. I would have told her all this and more had she not already hung up on me.

Intrafamily Feud

My grandmother had a strict policy about visits to or from my grandfather's family: They were strongly discouraged, but allowed on a case-by-case basis—birthdays, weddings, or the occasional heart attack. However, they were forbidden to take place during a meal. "I should waste a perfectly good meal on a group of people who consider incest a hobby?" she'd say.

"Cousins can marry each other," my grandfather would huff. "Look at Eleanor and Franklin Roosevelt. It was a family tradition for them, too."

"Yeah," said my grandmother, shaking her head, "I know so many families where the cousins are also siblings."

I found these debates entertaining—if not slightly gross—but I didn't participate. They started long before I was born, and it was clear to me that nobody was changing my grandmother's mind.

If a member of my grandfather's family called, whoever it was always hoped my grandfather might answer the phone. My grandmother treated telemarketers better than Rothschild relatives.

"Oh, you're stopping through the city? That's nice." She would roll her eyes. "You'd like to come see us? Whatever for?"

I never got a straight answer as to why my grandmother hated my grandfather's family, but from what I understood, this feud had been going on since before my grandparents were married. When my eighth-grade social-studies teacher assigned a family-history project, I decided to figure out how this feud with my grandfather's family—or "the cult," as she christened them—really began. The project meant I had an excuse to interview my grandparents, which I did in the study, the unofficial spot where all our family meetings and discussions took place.

My teacher had given us worksheets with sample questions to ask our families, and we were supposed to take all the answers and spin them into a fairly benign expository piece. I thought I could spice the whole thing up by supplying a narrative rich with family gossip. That way my teacher wouldn't be bored and I'd finally have some answers.

With my grandparents in place on the sofa, I balanced a notebook on my lap and looked down at the first worksheet. The questions read, "What are our family's origins? How far can we trace our family back?"

Who cares about that? I thought, and instead pretended to read off a question. "It says, 'Why does your family hate your wife?' Isn't that funny?"

My grandfather looked alarmed. "What? It says that? Let me see that paper," but I kept it out of his reach, and my grandmother answered for him. "They hate me because I'm not a hemophiliac," she explained. "Your grandfather was *supposed* to marry someone else—someone who would keep the bloodline *pure*—and they never forgave me."

"*Pure?* What's that supposed to mean?" I had a vision of blood as clear as springwater running through my grandfather's veins and water as polluted as the Hudson in my grandmother's.

My grandfather let out a heavy sigh. I could tell that this was an argument he'd had many times before with my grandmother. "In families like ours, people prefer not to marry under"—he looked at my grandmother—"*what they consider* their rank." He turned away, waiting for my grandmother's reaction.

"Their what?" she said. "Their rank? What is this, the military? No. Write this down, Matthew. We were all Jews, and that was their 'rank.' Your grandfather's family had more money, but they were never treated any better than the hordes of Jews living in the ghettos. They had more money, and they pretended they were better. Pack of snobs."

I had been scribbling on my notebook furiously until she said that part about pretending to be better. I looked up at my grandmother and wondered if her anger came from an inferiority complex. I knew that her father had made his fortune in pots and pans in America, but by that point my grandfather's family had been around so long they were buying titles in Europe.

Trying to assuage my grandmother's temper, my grandfather laid his hand on her arm. "I was engaged to someone my mother had picked out, but I called off the engagement as soon as I met your grandmother. Some of my relatives," he conceded, "never got over that. It's taken them a while to warm to your grandmother."

"Fifty years and counting," she said, patting his hand.

"So it's like the Duchess of Windsor and the rest of the royal family?" I asked, applying my knowledge of Kitty Kelley biographies.

"Exactly," she said, her face furrowed. "Nobody would have been good enough for them, except one of his twenty-five sisters. All those children." She shuddered. "At least my parents had the good manners to stop after two."

"Why do you always say that?" my grandfather asked, becoming exasperated. "There weren't twenty-five. It was five," he'd say decisively each time she did this, but then doubt would creep in.

"Are you sure?" my grandmother would ask dryly.

"Or was it seven?" he'd ask, staring at the space above my head. "I know it's a prime number—hold on. Eleven?" Then he'd start counting on his fingers, starting with the dead siblings. "Helene, Charlotte, Max . . ."

Like my uncle and my mother, my grandfather had been an unexpected late arrival for his parents. Unlike my mother and my uncle, my great-grandparents had had children early in their marriage, so there was a wide gulf in age between him and the rest of his siblings (his eldest brother was twenty years older than he was), most of whom were dead before I was born. Their children never had a real relationship with my grandparents, either, and as far as my grandmother was concerned, that was just fine.

Whatever the real reasons behind my grandmother's feelings, I grew up never having met most of my grandfather's siblings or any of their umpteen children.

Except Irene.

.   .   .   .   .

My grandfather's niece Irene was the one exception to my grandmother's cold shoulder. Irene was a thin, dwarfish woman with a mouth like a truck driver. She was ashamed of nothing. Any and all topics in her life were up for discussion, and since Irene lived on the Upper West Side, we saw her more than anyone else from my grandfather's family.

Shortly after I turned thirteen, Irene and her husband, Mickey, were over for a routine lunch. My grandfather was showing her some coins he'd recently purchased from an estate sale. He was an avid collector, and these were small gold ones from ancient Rome.

"I love them," said Irene, holding the coins in their plastic cases. Normally my grandfather wouldn't allow anyone to hold his coins. If I tried to touch any of them, he'd scream, "Have you washed your hands?" or "Put on some gloves!" I felt immediately jealous as I watched Irene studying the coins. I stewed, waiting for her to leave.

"They're so small," Irene said. "Just like my tits." She held the coins up to her blouse and pressed them against her breasts. "Mickey, aren't these like my tits? Sophie, what do you think?"

My mouth fell open. My grandmother was already howling with laughter.

"Oh, Irene!" My grandmother slapped her palms against her lap, barely able to breathe. "You're always! So! Funny!"

Irene nodded. "I was thinking about getting them lifted; Mickey might start looking somewhere else if I don't."

Mickey turned bright red. My grandfather coughed and quickly gestured at me. But my grandmother and Irene obviously didn't care how inappropriate the joke was. I watched them across the room, mesmerized. Here was a middle-aged woman, probably married over thirty years, telling my grandparents that she wanted to have a *boob job,* and my grandmother was encouraging her. *What a freak,* I thought. *I love her.*

Suddenly Irene smacked the arm of the sofa. "Guess what Bernard's done?" Bernard was Irene's younger brother, who, because of his interest in family reunions and gatherings, was never welcome in my grandmother's home.

The question was clearly rhetorical, because she continued breathlessly, "He put together a directory of everyone in the family—like a telephone book. He's sending them out to all the relatives."

My grandmother rolled her eyes. "Why the hell is he doing that?" she asked.

"You know how he is. He wants an excuse to call everyone and show off his Ph.D. God, remember that last big family reunion back in the seventies?" She looked at my grandmother expectantly before answering her own question. "What am I talking about? You'd never have gone to one of those. Anyway, Bernard saunters up to Uncle Max and says—get this—'You have to call me "Dr. Bernard" now.'"

My grandfather's eyes widened. "What happened?"

Irene buried her face in her hands, laughing. "Max slapped Bernard upside the head. Then he cursed him for standing in his way to the buffet table."

After he finished laughing, my grandfather said, "Well, now that we're listed in Bernard's book, maybe we'll hear from all my relatives."

I perked up. Maybe I'd be able to intercept some of these long-lost relatives. They could finally tell me what had *really* happened between "the cult" and my grandmother.

"Perfect," said my grandmother. "Now I'm going to have to change my number, or your uncle will have every fifth cousin over for dinner with all their livestock."

Irene laughed, and my grandfather mumbled, "We don't have livestock."

The livestock part was a stretch, but I saw her point. My grandmother just didn't want to be bothered. She had raised two children of her own, already attended more family functions than she cared to, and was now comfortably waiting for the next heart attack or funeral to reunite her husband's family.

Whether it was prophecy or coincidence, my grandmother was right about Bernard's directory. A few days later, my grandfather intercepted a call from a woman claiming to be his long-lost niece. Her name was Edie, she said, the daughter of his dead sister Helene and the product of the extramarital affair that led to Helene's divorce. After this divorce Helene ran off with the guy she'd taken up with and was disowned by everyone in my grandfather's family. Except for my grandfather, who, because his sense of loyalty outweighed his sense of propriety, had stayed in touch with his banished sister until her death.

"She says she doesn't want any money," my grandfather told my grandmother over dinner. "She just wants to meet us. I think it would be nice."

"Me, too!" said my grandmother, her eyes as big as saucers. She clapped her hands together. Atse had been serving, and he stopped and placed his hand on my grandmother's forehead. "You sick?"

I looked at my grandmother, afraid that she'd finally lost it, but my grandfather understood exactly what was going on—this niece was a golden opportunity for his wife to rub scandal in her in-laws' faces.

"Sophie," he said crossly, "if you do anything . . ."

"Watch your blood pressure," she told my grandfather. Her lips were stretched into a wicked smile. "I want to have her over for lunch—for a visit."

. . . . .

When the day for lunch with Edie arrived, my grandmother chose her most maternal outfit—a white linen suit and some sensible shoes—and even told the maid to take the leaf out of the dining-room table. "It'll be more intimate that way," she said, and she was still instructing Atse on the menu when the doorbell rang.

I tried to run to the hall to get a look, but my grandmother grabbed my shirt, snatching me back. "Oh, no," she told me. "You go play in your room. I'll call you for lunch when it's ready."

"Why?" I asked, offended.

"Because you're a snoop. This woman doesn't need her life broadcast all over CBS."

"This is from Miss 'I'm sorry, Brooke, I don't know who told everyone that you had your eyes lifted'?"

She gave me her most menacing look. "Why, you little—"

While my grandmother and I were bickering, my grandfather opened the door and welcomed Edie inside. She was a small, round woman with long silver braids and a facial expression that could only be likened to that of a deer in a Land Rover's headlights.

The minute Edie stepped inside the apartment, she grabbed my grandfather in a tight hug and burst into tears. "My uncle!" she cried into his shoulder. "I'm so . . ." she sobbed even harder.

My grandmother and I fell silent. I wasn't used to such an embarrassing outpouring of emotion. I quietly asked, "What is she *doing?*"

My grandmother swatted me. "Shut up! Don't you know we're about to see a real show?"

Normally my grandmother waved at visiting family from the comfort of a three-foot block of personal space, but today she practically galloped over to shake Edie's hand. "Hello! I'm Howard's wife, Sophie," she called, her arm outstretched.

Edie then forced my grandmother into a ferocious hug. It reminded me of how I saw snakes kill their prey on TV.

"My aunt!" Edie cried in my grandmother's arms.

"Now. Hush. . . . Let's not get carried away," my grandmother tried to say, but the words came out in gasps.

My grandfather guided Edie into the living room, and my grandmother smoothed out her suit. She turned to me. "I'll have to send this out to be cleaned. Think twice before you say anything that might start her crying." She firmly straightened her jacket— she looked like Captain Kirk on *Star Trek,* about to set foot on a new planet—and walked into the living room.

Before lunch Edie and my grandparents rehashed memories of

the few visits my grandparents had made to Edie's parents' farm in upstate New York when she was a child.

"It was like having a movie star come to your house," she told me. "Your grandparents would come, and my mother would serve on our best china. There would be a ton of food; my mother wanted to impress them. And your grandparents always gave the best gifts."

I looked over to my grandmother. "What happened? The best present I ever got was a pair of socks."

"You're about to get a one-way ticket to your room," she said, winking to the other adults.

They all laughed, and I sank deeper into an armchair.

"You had a brother, didn't you? How is he?" asked my grandfather.

Edie kept smiling, but her gaze fell to the floor. "He's dead." The words came out quickly. Even I could tell that she'd delivered this news too many times and didn't want to rehash any details.

But I was too curious to care. "How did he die?" I asked. I didn't know anyone who had died. A mysterious dead cousin would be great news to share at school the next day.

My grandfather bit his fist.

"Matthew!" my grandmother said, gripping the sides of her chair. "Don't be rude."

I wanted to reply with something snappy like, "When did Mother Teresa show up?" but my grandmother sucked in her cheeks and squinted her eyes—and I knew that look. I took the hint. "Edie doesn't have to talk about that—unless she *wants* to tell her Uncle Howard and Aunt Sophie." My grandmother touched Edie's hand and smiled.

I glanced at my grandfather. He was glaring at my grandmother disapprovingly.

"He died about three years ago," Edie said. "It was suicide."

I straightened up immediately. A suicide! I would have been happy for a case of malaria or leprosy, but suicide—this was huge.

My grandmother groaned sympathetically, but she also sat back and subtly rubbed her hands together. Suicide pointed to mental illness, which proved every theory she'd ever had concerning her in-laws. "That's horrible," she said. My grandmother was a professional manipulator. "Would you like to talk about it? I'm sure it would make you feel much better." She turned to face me and blinked rapidly. She nodded toward the other room and blinked again.

Damn it! I got up and walked slowly out of the room but stood just on the other side of the doorway.

From where I was standing, I couldn't hear everything, but I still caught most of Edie's story. Her younger brother, Greg, had been depressed for most of his life. Though he'd been institutionalized many times, he never recovered full stability. His mother, Helene, was his anchor, but after she died, Greg's condition worsened, until he took his own life.

Later, after Edie left, my grandmother sauntered past my grandfather flashing a victorious smile. "I realized that your people were crazy, you know," and then she recycled her favorite joke about my grandfather's family. "I mean, your cult's had so much shock therapy that if they held hands, they could provide enough electricity to power New York City."

My grandfather was silent, and meanwhile I was planning how to use this information at school. I thought of the stories I could spin about my poor, long-lost cousin who killed himself. I knew from previous experience that nobody would be able to top a suicide! Later that night my grandmother called Irene to blab everything, and I listened in on the extension. My grandfather was sitting next to me.

"So get this," my grandmother was saying. "Some woman named Edie calls your uncle out of the blue. Says she's Helene's daughter."

"Doesn't surprise me one bit," said Irene. "Helene was a tramp. As much sex as she had, I'm surprised there aren't a few more Edies floating around with their hands out." Irene paused. "No, no, I'm thinking of Aunt Elise. Edie was Helene's daughter by the plumber. God, was *that* a scandal! Running out on her family in the middle of the night so she could go bang a plumber in the mountains. The woman died of shame!"

"Or too much sex," mused my grandmother.

"There was a son, too. I can't remember his name."

"Greg," said my grandmother.

"The suicide!" laughed Irene.

I was surprised by this reaction. Do people normally laugh when a relative kills himself? If that were true, I might have to rethink how I told this story.

"Yes," said my grandmother. "She told us all about it."

My grandfather was tugging on my sleeve. "What are they talking about?" he whispered.

I covered the mouthpiece. "Your dead nephew," I told him.

My grandfather stood up quickly and went into the other room to glower at his wife. After fifty-plus years of marriage, my grandfather understood that she could start family wars with a single rumor, and it was his job to preempt this damage.

"Greg killed himself a couple years back," Irene was saying. "Went totally mental one day and hanged himself. You know, I heard it was because he was *gay*."

I gasped. Edie hadn't mentioned *that* during lunch. "Gay?" I asked out loud, then immediately regretted it. I cringed.

The line went silent. Then my grandmother screeched, "Matthew! Are you listening in on the other line? I never have any privacy with Liz Smith around here!"

"Anyway," continued Irene, "that's what I heard."

"That's so horrible," said my grandmother. They seemed to have forgotten I was listening. Or just didn't care.

"He couldn't handle it. He even tried one of those conversion programs."

"Those what?" my grandmother asked.

"Conversion programs. Where they try to un-gay you."

Un-gay? How did that work? I wondered. Was there an operation involved?

When my grandmother told Irene that Edie was coming back for another dinner the following week, Irene invited herself over as well.

"Irene wants to know if she can come to dinner, too," my grandmother said.

She was talking to my grandfather, who was suddenly on the line as well. "No," he said. "Irene, you do not know how to behave around company."

"What company? She's family!" said Irene.

"It's not called family when you haven't seen them in forty years," I said.

My grandmother burst out laughing. "No, it's called smart," she said.

My grandfather warned the two women, "Irene can come as long as she behaves. Don't chase this woman away, Sophie, or you'll answer to me."

When the topic of their conversation changed to soap operas and my grandfather hung up, I lost interest. I went up to my room and flopped onto my bed. Was being gay really the type of thing that made someone kill himself?

It's not that I considered myself gay—but there were those kids at school who called me a faggot. And there was my staring problem when boys with big calves walked by. . . . I rolled onto my back and stared at the ceiling. I wondered, *Is it possible that I'm gay, too, and just don't know it?* I needed to know more.

The following day I pulled out my grandmother's phone directory and dialed Edie's number. She sounded delighted to hear from me, and I searched for a way to ask her about Greg. I didn't want to tell her about my grandmother's gossiping, but I was desperately curious about homosexuals, and I needed to investigate. I already knew I had a cousin who was a magician, one who was a ballet dancer, and another who wanted to marry his dog, but no homosexuals. Who else was I going to ask?

Edie's reaction was not the answer I was looking for.

"That bitch," said Edie. "She doesn't have enough to do, so she has to talk about my dead brother? Is that it? Is her life that boring?"

"Haven't you met Irene?" I asked.

I heard footsteps behind me. "Is that Irene?" asked my grandmother.

"Is that your grandmother?" said Edie. Her voice was seething with anger.

I felt my cheeks burning up.

"Matthew?" said my grandmother.

"Matthew?" said Edie.

"Give me the phone."

"Give her the phone!"

My grandmother took the phone, and slowly I backed out of the room. As I ran upstairs, I heard my grandmother's voice. "No, Edie, I would never tell someone. . . ."

My grandmother, of course, blamed everything on me the minute she hung up the phone. My grandfather had been standing behind her for most of the conversation, and he was fuming. "This is all the boy's fault," my grandmother said, pointing at me.

"Oh, no," he said. "*You* were the one who called Irene. I told you to leave it alone, and now I have to fix this mess."

"Well, whoever's fault it is, Edie said she doesn't want anything to do with us."

My grandfather pondered this a moment before nodding toward the study, a sign he wanted to speak with my grandmother privately. After he'd walked away, my grandmother grabbed my collar and pulled me along behind him. "Don't you think I'm going down alone," she hissed.

Sitting at his desk, my grandfather looked up suddenly. "Okay," he said. "This is what we're going to do." He decreed that my grandmother would call both women over to the house, and they would all discuss it like rational adults.

My grandmother frowned, but she nodded and made the arrangements.

"I'm not forgetting about this," she told me after she hung up the phone with Edie. "When we accidentally lose the key to your room and you're locked in it, you'll know why."

"You're going to give me a complex," I said.

"You'd better believe it," she replied, shaking her head.

. . . . .

My grandmother arranged to have each niece come to our house for dinner on a Thursday. This was the most neutral night for her television schedule. That Thursday, Edie arrived first, looking every bit like an unhappy Hummel figurine. Two steps behind her was an unexpected sight: a large black man. "This is my husband, Rich," she said tersely.

I considered this latest development. He was a giant compared to the rest of us. I wondered why she didn't bring him the fist time she came over, the way Irene usually dragged Mickey along.

"Oh, this just gets better and better," said my grandmother under her breath. She was far from racist, but my grandmother knew that when "the cult" heard about Rich, they would die from embarrassment. Knowing she could be the one to make that happen filled her with the kind of joy usually reserved for ethnic foods and open bars.

My grandfather introduced himself and shook Rich's hand. "You are very welcome," he said warmly, and guided everyone into the living room. Edie's face gave nothing away. She didn't say hello to me, and I was standing right there.

My grandmother tried to be social. "How's your work?" she asked.
Edie remained guarded. "Fine."
"Was there a lot of traffic on the road?"
"No."

Rich complimented my grandparents on the apartment, and they started chatting about the weather, but the real questions were obviously *out* of the question. The sound of chewing filled the air as we snacked on pâté and shrimp cocktail. When at last the doorbell rang, I jumped. Atse opened the door, and Irene rushed past him, without Mickey for once.

"Good to see you, too, Miss Irene," Atse said, rolling his eyes.

"Helloooo?" she said to nobody in particular. She threw off her coat and fell into a chair. "That fucking cab," she moaned. "It's getting so bad that I have to look into the cabs before I get in to see what kind of driver it has. Every one of those goddamn towelheads tries to take me to the cleaners."

"Where's Mickey?" I asked.

"I gave him the night off," she said, smiling. "So—"

"Irene," interrupted my grandmother, "this is your cousin Edie and her husband, Rich."

Irene's eyes lit up. She jumped up from the chair. "Really? Edie! I didn't know you were coming! This is great." My grandfather almost dropped his plate. It was obvious my grandmother had not told Irene that Edie would be over. And if she had left that part out, then I concluded that my grandmother also hadn't told Irene that Edie knew about Irene's spilling the beans about Greg. I knew exactly what my grandfather was thinking: This was going to get ugly soon. He opened his mouth to offer some kind of warning, but Irene cut him off and turned her attention to Rich. "And you are? Edie's *husband?*" A *black man,* she almost said, drooling.

"Where did you meet?" my grandmother asked, giving Irene a stern look.

Edie stared at the parquet floor, and Rich answered for her. "At a mosque. Edie came to an information session at the mosque where I work."

"Wait," said Irene, "you're . . . You work for a *mosque?*"

"We're both followers of Islam," said Edie.

"Oh, are you?" said Irene. "I guess it takes all kinds."

.   .   .   .   .

In the dining room, when Edie found out that Atse had prepared a small feast with several different types of meat, she announced she was a vegetarian. I thought I remembered her eating meat at our house during her first visit, but I didn't dare comment.

"We have asparagus soup and salad," said my grandmother. "You can have a larger bowl."

"She can have mine," I volunteered. "I hate asparagus."

"Problem solved," said Irene, sitting down. Then, turning to Edie, "Now I want to hear all about you. Tell me *everything.*"

Edie, who had been spreading her napkin over her lap, turned to Irene and looked her up and down. "Oh, you want to hear everything, do you?"

My grandfather interrupted, clearing his throat. "I think, ladies, some things were said that need addressing. Things that were inappropriate, and an apology is deserved." Here were his famous diplomacy skills at work. I watched, fascinated.

There was silence around the table.

Finally Irene asked, "What happened?"

Edie exploded in rage. "You said my brother was *gay*! That's what happened!"

Irene sat back, clutching her chest in mock surprise. "What's so bad about that? He *was* gay."

"He wasn't gay," said Edie. Her face was red. "He was sick."

"Of course he was gay!" Irene said. "I met Greg at my grandmother's funeral, and that man was fruitier than a Judy Garland medley sung in the Village—no offense, Matthew." She glanced over at me apologetically.

I looked to my grandparents, wondering if I'd just been called gay. Neither of them paid attention, and I still don't know if they caught the reference or were trying to spare my feelings by not acknowledging the remark.

"He was not . . . gay," said Edie slowly.

Irene threw her hands up in the air. "A forty-year-old single man who lives with his mother, never has a girlfriend, and he isn't gay?"

"He was *Jewish*."

Irene sighed. "Oh, you're full of it."

Edie stood up and faced Irene. "No, you . . . you are full of it. And I'm done with this." She smacked Irene across the face so hard that it echoed down the hall. My eyes widened, and my mouth fell open. My grandfather shot up to intervene, but my grandmother just sat back and smirked. *Finally,* she must have been thinking, *the show I've been waiting for.*

"Edie," said my grandfather, "you can't slap people you disagree with. Civilized people discuss their differences—"

Irene lunged out of her chair and started pummeling Edie. Irene was wiry, but she was much too small to do any real harm. The two women fell onto the floor and began kicking each other. It was Rich who separated them.

"Edie! Pull yourself together," he said. "You're going to let some bitch get the best of you in your uncle's house?"

"What uncle?" she said loudly. She was panting, scrambling to fix her hair. "Get me out of here. It was a mistake to come in the first place!"

"Oh!" Irene shrieked. "But you didn't think it was a mistake when you called my mother and asked for money?"

"Irene!" At last my grandfather lost his cool. He looked furious. "I am not going to have you bad-mouthing anyone else in our family. Now, please. Just shut up."

My grandfather was usually a happy, even-tempered man, but when he was angry, people took a step back. Personally, I felt like hiding behind my chair.

"Howard," said my grandmother, "calm down. Please don't get excited." She turned to stare at Edie and Irene—Irene was still lying on the floor. "Do you both want to see him in the hospital? Do you want to come to his funeral?"

The women, still breathing heavily, glared at each other.

"Now," my grandmother said at last, "I think it's time to continue our dinner."

But Edie had started to cry. "How are you going to tell me anything about my brother? Were you there when he was in the hospital? Were you there after he had taken too many pills and the doctors couldn't save him?"

Rich hugged her, trying to hush her sobs.

"Being gay is nothing to get upset over," said Irene, rubbing her own cheek.

"Edie, let's leave," said Rich. "We don't need these people, and we don't have to have anything to do with them. Just let it go."

Edie sidestepped Irene and padded off behind her husband.

Irene struggled to her feet, and my grandfather grabbed her by the back of her neck and guided her to the door after Edie and Rich had let themselves out.

"What are you doing?" she cried. "I'm your niece!"

"Not tonight you're not," he said, and slammed the door behind her.

My grandmother stayed at the table, twisting her linen napkin around her fingers. A few seconds later, I heard the study door slam, a signal that my grandfather wanted to be alone. I walked upstairs to my room and quietly shut the door, worried. I knew there were problems in my family, but I felt like this latest skirmish was entirely my fault. I thought, *When they calm down enough to talk to me, I'm sure they're going to ask why I called Edie in the first place.* And what would I say? How could I possibly tell them the truth after seeing the night's spectacle? How could I tell them I feared I was gay, too?

It's Nothing Personal

Boarding school is only a hop, skip, and a donation away." It was a threat my grandmother had made for years, but I never took her seriously. Then one afternoon, just after I started my freshman year in high school, I came home from a walk in Central Park to find my suitcases packed and sitting at the foot of the staircase. When I asked my grandmother why, she let out a heavy sigh and mouthed the words *Boarding school.*

I looked down at the suitcases. Was this a practical joke?

"Do you understand?" she said.

"What's to understand?" I said. "You don't love me, and you're sending me away." I sat down on the bottom stair and tried to cry. If I cried, she might at least feel bad about sending me away.

"I didn't say that." She ran her hands through my hair, pulling at my curls.

"This is about the Super Glue, isn't it?" I asked, looking up at her.

She sat down next to me and shrugged.

. . . .

This was not my fault.

A popular kid in my English class, Johnny Byatt, who honestly had the face of a mouse, found a tube of Super Glue next to his father's stash of porn. So what does he do? He brings the glue to school and whips it out while our teacher, Mrs. Wolff, is walking around during silent reading. "What does Super Glue have to do with porn?" he asked. "I just don't get it."

"It's a metaphor," Mrs. Wolff was saying to a kid a couple rows over. "Why don't you get it?"

A few of us sitting near Johnny looked at the Super Glue skeptically, as if it unlocked the secrets of adult sexual desire, but I was the only one who had something to say. "It means your dad's a perv, is what it means," I whispered, glancing back to see Mrs. Wolff in her stocking feet helping another kid a couple rows back. "Put it away before she busts you for talking about your perv dad and his pornos."

The other guys around us laughed. I had been doing pretty well at this new school, making new friends by making jokes.

I went back to reading but soon heard sniggering and looked up to see that Mike Jones, captain of the lacrosse team, had nabbed Mrs. Wolff's shoes and was using his pencil to spread glue inside them.

I nodded appreciatively. She was forever taking off her shoes and massaging her bunions. She'd walk around barefoot, stinking up the classroom. Every math class was a show starring the ten corn kernels she called toenails. As the bell rang, he threw the tube of glue over to Johnny and then flung the shoes on my desk.

"I'll take these," Mrs. Wolff said, snatching them out of my hands. I was about to say something, but when she tried to drop the shoes to the floor, they wouldn't budge. She shook her hands, and the shoes wobbled but wouldn't fall. They were stuck to her hand. Johnny and Mike ran into the hall, laughing wildly as they escaped. I couldn't move; I could only watch my teacher's face graduate from mild curiosity to panic to anger.

"Matthew!" she screamed. That was my cue to run. By the time the principal found me in third period, I had a whole story worked out in my head. It involved a science experiment and a new kind of bunion cream. I was still polishing the finer points, but he wasn't interested. I had been expelled.

. . . . .

"Maybe we could offer the school something to let me back in?" I suggested after I'd been sent home to my grandparents.

"What something?" my grandmother asked. "You and a box of grapefruit? You can't glue people to their shoes and expect a thank-you. Now I have to go and buy your teacher a pair of shoes so her kids or her cats or whatever the hell she has won't go hungry."

I tried in vain to explain that it wasn't me, but they wouldn't listen. My grandfather was mortified. The only thing he could say was "expelled" followed by "the shame," and I couldn't tell if he meant me or the actual expulsion. I assumed if I waited long enough, he'd run out of steam, as usual. He would come around and realize this wasn't such a big deal. It was high school—didn't people pull pranks all the time in high school? The only thing that kept nagging me was that *this* prank hadn't even been my idea!

But I expected that kind of reaction from my grandfather. It was my grandmother's take on the expulsion that surprised me. "This is so disappointing," she said, shaking her head. "You go from one school to another: I don't know what to do anymore."

Now, looking at my suitcases by the front door, I realized that had been a lie. She knew exactly what to do.

"It's nothing personal," she said, attempting a joke, but I didn't think being thrown out of my house was very funny. Was she seriously looking me in the eye and telling me to leave? If there was something wrong with me, surely she was to blame! I had watched *her* throw tremendous fits in department stores all my life. *She* encoded whatever genetic defect I was programmed with that kept getting me expelled from Manhattan's finest schools. Yet *I* was the one being sent away.

"Listen, it's not me. This comes from upstairs," she said, and pointed to the sky.

"*God* told you to send me away? What kind of medication are you on?"

"No," she said, "your grandfather. He's upstairs sleeping."

So my grandfather had been pulling these strings. That didn't really surprise me, but it still stung. What had happened to him and me? I wondered. We used to be so close, and now we fought all the time over nothing. Okay, so being expelled from school isn't nothing, but did it really warrant sending me away?

"I guess he won't be coming down to say good-bye."

"He's not feeling well. In a few days, he'll call you, and you'll make peace. You know he can't stay mad at you. Maybe you can work out a deal. If you show him you're improving, he can try to get you back in a school here. As it is, no school in the city wants you. You'd think there was some kind of list."

The next day, as we were driving out to the school, I learned that I hadn't already been accepted. My grandmother was taking it on faith that I would be, and so she had packed my bags prematurely. I was hopeful the school might still reject me, allowing me to return home, but my grandmother laughed at that. "Matthew, these schools are run by businessmen. It'll cost me, but there's no way they'll say no. They're too greedy."

．　．　．　．

Located in the heart of Connecticut, this boarding school had been my grandmother's choice because of its reputation for taking in "talented youths," which was code for bad seeds and morons, and assisting them in making "fine choices."

My grandfather stayed home and left the task of enrollment to my grandmother.

As we waited outside the headmaster's office, I looked around the walnut-paneled anteroom. An American flag stood in the corner next to a picture of President Bush. "I heard that teachers beat kids in places like this," I said.

"Me, too," my grandmother said, flipping through a magazine. "Your uncle went here."

After the headmaster reviewed my transcripts, his secretary called us into his office. From his expression I could tell he wasn't pleased.

He greeted my grandmother warmly, then turned to me and scowled.

"It's not that we . . . doubt your grandson's academic ability. I can see by his test scores that he's a gifted student." He put down a thin folder and picked up another, this one at least an inch thick. "But his disciplinary record, Mrs. Rothschild, is also very impressive."

My grandmother nodded. "My Matthew is an active boy, it's true, but—"

"You see," the headmaster interrupted, "we just had the lawns replaced, and I don't think we could risk a brushfire."

My grandmother caught his attempt at humor and laughed too loudly at the joke. "He is quite spirited," my grandmother said, casting a glance at me.

"Ponies are spirited. Children who glue their teachers' hands to their shoes are what we call *troubled*."

She sucked in air through her teeth. "Troubled. That has such a negative connotation, don't you think?"

"And I'm not troubled!" I broke in. "I didn't even do it!"

My grandmother reached over and pinched me. She winked at the headmaster. "This is all because of television. Nowadays all the kids are watching television, and it's giving them these crazy ideas."

My mouth fell open, and I looked at her in amazement. Was she seriously blaming my problems on her main form of entertainment?

"That's why in my house we rarely watch television. If we do, it's the occasional PBS special. However, when Matthew started attending his last school, he made some dangerous friends. That's what led to all these shenanigans. I know that this is the best place for him now. It worked wonders with my son when I brought him here in 1968. He's very successful now."

I could not believe my ears. She was lying—totally bullshitting this man—and he sat back and nodded, as if they had some secret understanding about "troubled" children like me. I was enraged, but I knew better than to speak out against my grandmother, so I stood up and walked to the window, where I surveyed the new lawns on the quad. They *were* quite green, and it was still warm enough for kids to be sitting under trees, reading. Some of the leaves were already changing color in anticipation of fall.

"I don't know," said the headmaster. "It will be a hard sell to the committee."

I saw my grandmother's patient smile evaporate. She whipped out her checkbook, and at that moment I knew I was here to stay. "Hello, new school," I said under my breath.

"Okay. What's this going to cost me?" she asked. "A tennis court? A library? Just don't be unreasonable, please. I've already underwritten one losing lacrosse team this year."

The headmaster folded his hands underneath his chin, framing his face like a cherub who's seen holier days. He licked his lips. "When I was last in New York attending a conference, I had the opportunity to take in some of the museums."

"Yes?" said my grandmother, her eyes narrowing.

"I had the chance to admire a lovely miniature van Gogh that I seem to recall belonged in you and your husband's own collection. . . ."

She sat back in her chair and exhaled loudly. "You want me to trade a painting for my grandson?"

This is exactly what he wanted, a glorified insurance policy. But he couldn't say it out loud, so instead he laughed. "No, I want you to loan it to our museum here at the school. I know that our admissions committee would look favorably upon your application if they understood your deep commitment to the school."

She studied me, and I could tell she was weighing her options. I shook my head. She returned her gaze to the headmaster. "Fine. It stays as long as he does."

"Mrs. Rothschild," he said, "four U.S. presidents have passed through this campus. This school has been the alma mater of senators, governors, and princes. We pride ourselves on retention."

My grandmother closed her checkbook and stood to shake the headmaster's hand. The headmaster said he'd take care of the committee—I could start classes the next day. My grandmother and I walked outside to her limousine.

"Three hundred years your grandfather's family had to toil in the ghettos to afford that painting. All so that you could bribe your way into this *goyishe* high school." She threw her hands up and laughed. "I don't even want to think what college will cost."

I watched our driver unloading my suitcases. This was starting to feel a little too real for me. "Why can't I just go to school closer to New York? That way I could still live at home."

She snorted. "Matthew, schools in the city don't have museums."

"I'm sure they could all use a van Gogh," I replied. She started to say something, but I put up my hand. "I know, I know. It's nothing personal."

She hooked her arm through mine. "I hope in time you'll understand. You realize that this is all your grandfather's fault. . . ."

I laughed and rolled my eyes.

She smiled. "Try this time. Please," she said, and adjusted my collar. "It's hard to keep bragging about my grandson when he gets kicked out of every school he attends. Not everyone considers that an accomplishment. And if you straighten out, I can probably talk your grandfather into letting you live at home again."

I helped her into the car and then waved good-bye as the driver pulled away.

. . . .

My dormitory was a converted Georgian affair that reeked of disinfectant, a smell neither better nor worse than that of pubescent boys all living together under one roof. My room was on the third floor, and I dragged my suitcase up the stairs even though the brochure for this joint boasted "every modern convenience." They must have meant every modern convenience invented before 1900.

"Elevators?" I said to myself. "No, sir. Climbing stairs builds character!"

By the time I reached the third floor, I was winded and sweating.

"Those stairs'll give you a real workout," said a man with an oversize smile and a crew cut. Certainly he could see that I was five foot seven and two hundred pounds and that I had no real interest in working out, so I guessed he was joking. I didn't laugh.

He cleared his throat and extended his hand. "I'm Mr. Crawford. You must be Matthew? The headmaster's secretary called to say that you'd be here."

"Yes," I panted. "And that's my suitcase."

He grinned and picked it up effortlessly. "I'll show you to your room. It's right down the hall! You're lucky we had this vacancy."

"*Very* lucky," I said, and he looked back to determine my sincerity. I smiled sweetly.

He pointed to a door at the end of the hall. "My wife and I stay in that room."

I had heard that teachers slept among the students at boarding school, but I hoped it was a rumor. It certainly gave "I know where you live" a heightened sense of meaning. My room turned out to be the messiest I had ever seen. Clothing spilled out of drawers and the closet, papers littered the desk and every inch of the floor, and it smelled like a locker room. Who—or what—lived in here?

As I stood at the door, afraid of being sucked into this chaos, I heard a voice behind me.

"And you are . . . ?"

I whipped around, ready to recite a lecture on the merits of cleanliness to this Philistine—when my mouth fell open, dumbfounded. This guy, my new roommate, standing at an easy six feet, had to be the best-looking guy I'd ever seen. Blond hair spilled onto his forehead over eyes so blue they were almost glacial. His T-shirt bulged with muscles, and his suntanned arms were dusted in light blond fuzz. He was like a walking advertisement for Abercrombie & Fitch.

"This is Matthew," Mr. Crawford said, giving me a friendly shove into the room.

"Matt!" I corrected. I couldn't have this god thinking I went by my full name. Nobody went by his full name. The only people who called me Matthew were my grandparents, and that was only because Matt sounded weird when they said it. "Oh. I'm Steve." He held out his hand. I shook his hand. *I got to touch him.*

He brushed by me and flopped onto his bed.

Mr. Crawford winked at me. "Sorry, I meant Matt. I'm just tired. You two can get to know each other before dinner. Steve, will you show *Matt* how things work around here?"

"Definitely."

"You'll be fine." Mr. Crawford smiled and clapped me on the shoulder. He disappeared down the hall to his room.

Steve took out a tennis ball from underneath his pillow and tossed it into the air. I shut the door and walked over to the empty bed. It was covered with his clothes, but I pushed them aside carefully and sat down. "Uh, where are you from?"

"California," he said, continuing to toss the ball effortlessly into the air. I admired his coordination. If it'd been me, the thing would have fallen and smacked me in the eye.

I couldn't think of anything else to say, but, fortunately, Steve just kept talking, smoothly and comfortably, all about California and about the school and the other students there. I watched his mouth open and close, but I didn't pay much attention to what he said. Too busy wondering if living with Steve would be a blessing or a curse, I was torn between silently thanking God for Johnny Byatt and his Super Glue and wringing my hands in fear that my secret desires would finally be discovered.

". . . sorry I was a shit when you came in."

"Huh?" I said, snapped out of my worries. "I didn't notice."

"I was just hoping that nobody would replace the Fag."

"What?" I said, flinching like I'd been slapped. I was instantly transported back to my sixth-grade gym class, with those jock boys shouting "Faggot! Faggot!" in my face. So much for considering this a blessing.

He laughed. "My old roommate. That's what we called him. The Fag."

"Why? Was he . . . gay?"

"I don't know. Probably." He shrugged. "Anyway," he continued, getting up from his bed, "it's almost time for dinner. I gotta shower. Wait for me and we'll go down together, okay? I'll introduce you around."

He grabbed his towel and shower caddy and left. When the door shut, I balled my fists and hit the pile of his dirty clothes on my bed. I got up, looked up at the ceiling, down to the floor, paced the room back and forth, and took stock of the situation. What was I going to do? I was a fourteen-year-old closet case living in the same room as Michelangelo's inspiration for *David*. Actually, I didn't know if I was really a closet case; that would imply I was truly gay. Truth be told, by that point I was praying for something called bisexuality. I had seen enough cable television to know that bisexual men had relationships with both men and women interchangeably. I mean, I was interested in girls. I was—

Wasn't I?

I enjoyed looking at fashion magazines and *Cosmo*. Did that count?

Unfortunately, when it came to the nitty-gritty of bisexuality, I'd been unable to locate the hard-and-fast rules. I mean, was there a man-to-woman ratio I had to sustain in order to keep this bisexual status? Could I still be bisexual if 99 (point 9) percent of my fantasy partners were men? Or did that mean I was gay and the occasional Cindy Crawford fantasy just made me greedy?

Cinemax didn't go into those details. And the one time I dared myself to check out the human-sexuality section at the New York Public Library, the librarian gave me such a funny look that I fled.

Muffled voices out in the hall disrupted my pacing. I heard someone giggling—a girl, maybe? There was a guy's voice, too. Then the door flew open, and Steve charged in. He was wearing only a towel and a wide grin. Droplets of water still clung to his muscular chest and arms.

"Hey, buddy!" He grinned and broke into jock talk. "Ready for some foo-foo-foood?"

"Yeah. Girls are allowed on this floor?"

"Oh, that was Mrs. Crawford. She was telling me to get a robe before I blinded someone." Steve dropped his towel, and I turned away faster than I should have. I'd been around enough half-naked guys to know that when a guy strips, the normal thing to do is protest, "Put some clothes on, dude." You're not supposed to react as if a naked boy will turn you to stone.

Steve didn't seem to notice. "But I know she likes it," he called out. "She was always looking at me in class."

"Is she a teacher here?" I asked. My back was still to him. I started to sweat.

"She was my history teacher last year. She's totally got a thing for me." I heard him moving close behind me. And then he clapped his hand on my shoulder. I jumped. "She was always asking me to stay after class or come early, if you know what I mean."

He laughed again and walked back toward his dresser.

I thought about Mr. Crawford. He wasn't a bad-looking guy, but Steve was much hotter, hands down. Suddenly I was scared. If Mrs. Crawford couldn't control herself around Steve, then how could I?

I looked over at Steve's side of the room and wondered what had happened to his last roommate. Had he made a pass at Steve one late night? Had he leered at him over wire-framed glasses?

The next morning I got my schedule. My first class was English, and, using the campus map the guidance counselor had provided, I made my way over to the English department.

My new teacher stood by the classroom door, smiling broadly to anyone who walked past. The three hairs left on his bald head were wrapped around his skull like a thinning turban. His ample jowls sported a thick white beard, and his gut was so large he could rest his arms on top of it. Also, he was wearing a kilt. Now, I wasn't one to judge anybody's cross-dressing, but didn't this man know he wasn't supposed to do this sort of thing outside the comfort of his own room?

"Good morning, young man," he said to me. "You must be my new student. You're in for a real treat today! It's Kilt Appreciation Day."

I stood at the back of the room and waited for the other students to arrive. I took an empty desk in the back of a row.

"What is he wearing today?" I heard a whisper. I turned to see a pretty girl next to me. She was talking to another pretty girl sitting in front of her.

"He stole your mother's skirt." They both laughed and looked at me. I smiled.

"Hey, I know you," said the first girl. "You're Steve's new room-mate, right?"

I realized we'd met last night at dinner. She and her friends were cheerleaders who ate with Steve and his buddies.

"Carrie, right?"

She smiled and introduced me to her friend, Jackie.

"How do you like it so far?" asked Jackie.

"It's all right. I've never been to boarding school before."

"You'll get used to it," said Carrie. "We'll teach you everything you need to know."

"Stick with us," said Jackie.

With his back to us, Kilt Man started writing sentences on the board and diagramming them. He wrote, "When wearing a kilt, it's best to have ample support." Then he walked up and down the aisles and called on people to identify parts of speech. "Isn't this great?" he said, grinning to the entire room. "Nouns, verbs, adjectives. The words dance on the board!"

"I hope they have proper support," I said, much too loudly. The class laughed.

Kilt Man didn't seem fazed. "I should hope so," he said, smiling.

When class was over, Carrie and I discovered we both had world history together, so she helped me find the room. "You'll love Mrs. Crawford. Everyone does."

Mrs. Crawford? I looked back down at my schedule. "I think she lives on my floor," I said. "And her husband." I thought about Steve in his towel and blushed.

When Mrs. Crawford saw me, she smiled warmly and extended her hand. "I was wondering if you'd be in my class! Everyone on the floor is a sophomore, except for you."

"Really?" I asked nervously.

I hadn't met the other guys on the floor yet, just seen them in passing. This explained why everyone looked so much older than me. I was already a young freshman—just shy of fourteen—and now I was living with a bunch of fifteen-year-olds?

"It's a good group of guys." She smiled. "Especially Steve."

I forced my lips into a polite smile and sat down next to Carrie. When class started, Mrs. Crawford wrote "WAR" on the board.

"When is war justified?" she asked.

"Why does it have to be justified?" called out a guy in the third row.

"Typical response by someone who hasn't done his reading and wants to stir the pot," she said, smirking. "Dave, why don't you take out last night's reading and skim over it while the big kids talk?"

The class laughed.

"Okay, everyone. Same question: When is war justified? Think about what you've read and take a position."

"How about for peace?" said another student.

"Okay." She nodded, as if considering this. "So you're going to make war, saddle everybody with posttraumatic stress disorder, ruin the economy, and make mayhem to bring peace?" She rolled her eyes. "Somebody else? Anybody awake this morning? I'd like to hear something besides fantasies."

The other students began peppering her with responses.

"Freedom."

"Religion!"

"Property?"

She sat on top of the teacher's desk and swung her feet back and forth.

"What about ego?" she asked. "What about, 'I'm tougher than you. My guns are bigger than yours?' Come on, think outside the box."

"Isn't war necessary?" asked Dave, the guy who didn't do his homework.

"I don't know," she said. "What do you think?"

"Well, I think it is," he said.

"Why?"

Dave had no response.

"Don't make an assertion until you can back it up. Keep reading."

I felt myself smiling as I leaned back in my seat. When class ended, I realized there had been no lecture. No notes on the overhead. Just a conversation about viewpoints and values with some facts interspersed throughout. This was different from any class I'd ever been to, where the teacher just throws up some dates and reads from a textbook.

"She loves that kind of stuff," Steve said that night when I was telling him about my first day. "There's no wrong answer, as long as it's thought out beforehand." I could tell he was mimicking Mrs. Crawford.

"I loved it! Everyone was talking and thinking. I love that 'no wrong answer' business."

He raised an eyebrow. "Calm down there. Anyway, I've got an answer for her that I know she loves."

I threw a sock at him. "That, my friend, is something I don't need to think about before dinner. By the way, that girl you introduced me to, Carrie? She's in Crawford's class and English with me."

Steve nodded. "Definitely a hottie. I'd do her, if she wasn't still getting over her ex-boyfriend. He dumped her when summer ended. I think he swims for Phillips."

"Swimming," I echoed. I had tried swimming for about a minute back in fifth grade, but I was cut from the team—missing too many practices. Splashing around wasn't worth not knowing who was on *Oprah*.

"Yeah," Steve said, "but you'd never think he was a swimmer. He's jacked and cut. And," he said, winking, "Carrie likes her men big." He lingered over the word *big*.

I felt my face go red. Steve smiled and watched me.

．　　．　　．　　．

I ran into Carrie the following morning walking to English. "What do you think about swimmers?" I asked. Her face got all dreamy before she recomposed herself. "They're okay, I guess."

"I'm thinking about going out for the team myself," I said, trying to sound casual. "I used to swim, and I could stand to get back into shape." I coughed. She turned to examine me, probably searching for vestiges of musculature under my fat.

She smiled. Then she told me where to find the swim coach.

I found the coach after classes, but he sounded less than enthusiastic. "It's late in the season. You won't be able to compete this year. We practice every day."

"Even if I don't get to compete this season, I'd still like to practice for next year. It's important to me." If I slimmed down and put on some muscle, Carrie might want me to be her new boyfriend. Then I'd have something to take my mind off my roommate. It was the perfect solution.

The coach removed his baseball cap—it was emblazoned with the school's name—and studied me up and down, scratching his head and grunting. "We'll give it a try."

"You won't be sorry!" I said, already fantasizing about my new body. I had only been at school a couple of days, and I was waiting until I had some good news before calling home for the first time. Joining the swim team seemed like something my grandfather would appreciate, so I picked up the phone. "Appreciate" turned out to be an understatement. He was wild with enthusiasm. "I'm so proud of you," he said. I couldn't even remember the last time he'd said that, and I was even more pleased with my decision—it felt like I'd done something right for a change.

But my grandmother was skeptical. "I must be getting old," she said, "but I can swear we played this game once before."

"Let him try," said my grandfather on the extension. "Don't be so negative. He'll make the right kind of friends."

"He can do what he wants," she retorted. "I'm not the one who wasn't supportive of *all* his interests."

"Bah," scoffed my grandfather.

"Such an eloquent response," she said. "Did they teach you that in the foreign service?"

I begged off the phone. "I've got homework," I said, and for a

moment there was stunned silence on the line. Even my grandmother was impressed.

.   .   .   .

We had a paper coming up for Mrs. Crawford's class, so I had books
spread out on my desk when Steve was suddenly behind me.
"What're you doing over here?" he asked, then started massaging
my shoulders. I was sitting in my boxer shorts; I didn't need the
kind of reaction a massage from him would likely produce. "I have
to take the Roman Empire and argue how it influenced the Found-
ing Fathers."

"Over my head," he said, continuing the massage, rubbing harder.

"Didn't you ever do anything like this?" I started shaking my
legs nervously.

"I'm sure. But I got my grades for other things."

I shot up and reached for the pair of shorts hanging on the desk
chair. "I'm going to shower now," I said as I fled from our room.

.   .   .   .

I spent a lot of time with Carrie over the next few weeks. After practice we met in the library to study and talk, but nothing was materializing between us romantically. I kept telling myself I wanted a
girlfriend; I just didn't know how to go about getting one.

Two months after I started swim practice, Steve and I were in our
room. I was studying. Steve was flipping through *Sports Illustrated,*
and he said, "Hey, Matt?"

I looked up from my math problems. "Yeah."

"Swimming's paying off for you. You look a lot better than when
you first showed up."

I couldn't breathe. "Thanks," I finally said. I felt intensely self-
conscious. Normally we'd talk about Steve and his perfect body as
he paraded around our room, or the entire floor, shirtless. I turned
around in my seat. "You really think so?"

In all honesty, I *had* noticed changes in my body, and they
seemed to be happening rapidly. My clothes were practically falling

off. When I was at home during Christmas break, the first thing my grandmother said after hello was, "What, do you have some kind of eating disorder?" I had taken it as a tremendous compliment.

"I think he looks fantastic," said my grandfather. "See what some good old-fashioned exercise can do for a body?" I'd also brought home my first report card, and they were both clearly impressed, but my grandfather was especially pleased. "I knew it," he said, "I just knew it. That school was the right place. I knew it."

At that, my grandmother scoffed, "Yeah, what you knew could fill a shoe box."

When she took me clothes shopping, we learned I'd lost six pants sizes, and I beamed. My grandmother was not as enraptured.

"This just isn't normal," she said. She frowned, studying my waist.

"I know!" I shouted, dancing laps around her. "It's a miracle!"

· · · ·

The new clothes gave me confidence. I noticed stares from girls at school. Carrie already sat with me at lunch, but she had started putting her head on my shoulder. She was laughing louder at my jokes, too. It was just after Valentine's Day, so it had taken five months, but I finally asked her out on a date.

"So what did she say?" asked Steve.

"She said yes," I told him, my face reddening.

"So it's finally happened!" He slugged me in the arm, and I fell down on my bed laughing. He wiped away a mock tear. "Matty has a girl. Now you can stop beating off to all my stories."

I just kept laughing. It was too close to the truth for me to actually respond.

"I think your bed is softer than mine." He plopped down on my bed and shoved me off. "Give me a massage," he said, rolling onto his stomach.

"A what?"

"A massage. I had a hard practice."

Was he being serious? "So did I," I said.

"Then I'll give you one after."

I couldn't move.

"What are you waiting for?" he asked.

I was waiting for my body to communicate with my head.

"Hurry up," he said.

My hands shaking, I pressed into the muscles in his back.

"Harder," he groaned. "Get on top of me, rub it that way."

"Hey," I said. I searched wildly for something to say. "Did you see what Carrie was wearing today? It was this hot—"

"Do you think Ted's gay?" Steve asked.

Ted was a swimmer on my team, and he worked out with me at the gym. We had become good friends. My hands froze. "I don't think so. Why?"

"He works out a lot."

"So do you," I said. Steve sat up and pushed me down on the bed. Then he began rubbing my back. "I think he could be," he said.

I was afraid of what my next words might reveal, so I closed my eyes and pretended to be dozing off. Steve stopped talking but continued to knead his fingers into my back. When he stopped, I didn't open my eyes as he lay down next to me. My bed was a twin, and there wasn't much spare room. After his snores came, I scooted to the edge of the bed, looking at his side of the room. I wanted to get up, but I was also excited by having him in my bed. Minutes ticked by, and then an hour, and I still hadn't done anything. I must have fallen asleep at some point, because the next thing I knew, I'd woken up with his arm around me, his chest against my back.

And there was something else: Steve had an erection, and it was pressing against me.

Get out of the bed, I told myself, but I didn't move. I only pressed more firmly into Steve.

He groaned and held me tighter.

Get out of the bed.

Maneuvering out of his arms, I sat up. Steve rolled onto his back, putting his hands above his head, and spread his legs. I had left the light on—probably the reason I'd woken up—and I could see the outline of his erection through his shorts.

My pulse was racing. I left the room and went to the bathroom, where I stood at the sink, splashing water on my face for a good twenty minutes. I stared at myself in the mirror. *Don't be stupid,* I told myself.

I hoped that Steve would move back to his bed when he heard the door open and close, but he didn't. He'd often claimed the ability to sleep through anything, and now was no exception. He was still lying in my bed, hands over his head, but now his shorts were on the floor. He was naked except for his button-up boxers. I walked over to my bed and touched his biceps. I shook him gently. He wouldn't budge.

"Steve?" I whispered.

Nothing.

"Steve," I tried again, louder.

He was still.

The nagging voice in the back of my head told me to switch off the light, get into Steve's bed, and go to sleep. But I couldn't stop myself. I was like the creepy friend they show in movies who becomes the date rapist because people are too blind to recognize he's a pervert. My grip on his arms got harder and, on its own, turned to groping. I snatched my hand back, half expecting him to wake up. *What are you doing?* I imagined him saying. *Get your hands off me, fag!*

But he didn't. I put one hand on his chest, the other on his erection. I held my breath. He arched his back and pressed his pelvis against my hand.

The room was totally still—and then the fear of discovery was too much for me. I stepped back, flipped the lights off, and lay in his bed. But I couldn't sleep. I was unable to take my eyes off him.

This would not be the last time that Steve found a way into my bed, and each time over the next two weeks my hands went further and further. I wasn't ready to confront these desires, but I couldn't stop myself, either. The pattern was set: I spent my days in class with a cheerleader girlfriend, and I spent my nights taking advantage of my roommate, who apparently had a sleeping disorder. I was obsessed with the idea that this was one more stop on the road to homosexuality.

There was something else, too. Steve was spending less and less time in our room. And when he *was* in our room, it seemed like we didn't talk anymore. Carrie told me he was seeing a new girl, but he never bothered to tell me about it.

One Saturday in early March, while Steve was out at an early-morning baseball practice, I found his journal on his desk. I had seen him with the book often enough to know of its existence, but I didn't know how much he wrote—or what he wrote about. I knew that he wouldn't be back for hours, so I picked up the notebook. In a dorm, privacy is a luxury.

I started scanning through the pages and stopped when I found my name. He wrote that we hadn't been getting along, that we were fighting, and he attributed this to my being gay.

And that's when it hit me: He hadn't been sleeping.

All those nights that I thought he was asleep—or at least when I told myself he had been—he'd been awake the entire time. I started sweating. What if he told other people? What if they believed him? There were a few openly gay guys at our school, but they were mercilessly teased, and I had no interest in joining their plight. I put the notebook back where I found it—right there out in the open, feeling like I would be sick. How was I going to keep living with him?

The phone rang.

"Rothschild," the headmaster's voice huffed into the phone. "I need to see you in my office—now."

I swallowed hard and put the phone down. I knew that this meant I was in trouble for something, but what? I ran down a list of possible grievances. There were none. My grades were fine. I was respectful to the teachers. No cutting class. I hadn't set anything on fire. The only answer was Steve. He must have said something. I dragged myself into the headmaster's office and took a seat. He sat behind his oversize desk and fidgeted. He clearly had something unpleasant to say. I had seen this kind of behavior from school officials before, and it always came right before I got the boot. *He's trying to figure out how to say it,* I thought. I briefly considered what I would tell my grandfather.

The headmaster finally opened his mouth, but no words came out. Only air.

I licked my lips and began shaking my legs nervously, hoping that he wouldn't write a letter to my grandparents listing deviant sexual activity as the reason for my expulsion. "I'm very sorry," he said at last, and then he paused as if giving me a moment. "It's your grandfather. He passed away early this morning."

I couldn't have heard him correctly.

I was about to ask him to repeat himself when he apologized again. "I'm never very good at delivering news like this. You'll have to forgive me. I know you were very close, and this can't be easy."

What was this man talking about?

I pressed my hands down on his desk. "I think you've got the wrong kid. My grandfather can't be dead. I just talked to him last night."

"He died this morning," he repeated.

I froze, leaning on his desk. "Yeah," I whispered. "You said that already." I slumped back into my chair, and my eyes drifted out the window. My stomach grumbled, and I started gulping in deep breaths. The headmaster grimaced, as if I might try to argue with him. Or scream.

I thought back to our conversation the previous night, trying to remember if my grandfather sounded different on the phone. We didn't discuss anything important, but at least I ended by saying, "I love you."

"Who am I going to go to with questions now?" I said.

The headmaster looked puzzled. "Your grandmother," he said.

I didn't realize I'd spoken out loud.

"My grandmother?" I snapped. "You don't go to my grandmother with questions. She'll make up the answers and then laugh when you make a fool out of yourself. Last year she told me that the Battle of Waterloo was when the French catapulted toilets onto the Russians."

The headmaster looked strained. I couldn't tell if he was trying to say something comforting or trying to suppress his laughter.

"Go on and laugh," I said, shaking my head. "It's what she did when I came home complaining about my dumb teacher." I paused. "What am I going to do now?"

"We've arranged a car to take you to New York. I'll tell your teachers, and your work will be here when you get back. You probably won't be gone longer than a few weeks. I'll hold your room. There's no problem there."

My room. Steve and his journal! I'd forgotten all about that. I heard myself involuntarily chuckle from embarrassment and relief. Embarrassment because I thought I was getting expelled over Steve, when the reality was so much worse. And relief because now nobody could ever tell my grandfather I was gay.

I stood up. "I guess I'll go back and wait for the car."

The headmaster opened his mouth to say something but then snapped it shut. *Big help you are,* I thought, imagining how my grandmother would probably have said that out loud if she were here. I walked back to the dorm, wondering what I'd tell everyone. What if Steve were back? Surely he left his journal open so I'd read it. What if he'd told people to humiliate me? What if . . . I stopped. *What if I don't come back?* My head felt flooded, and I sat down on the stoop of the dorm's entrance to collect my thoughts. My grandfather was gone now, and he'd been the one who wanted me to come here, not my grandmother. If I were smart, I'd never have to come back. I could convince my grandmother to let me stay in New York, and I'd never have to see Steve again.

I was so distracted by my own thoughts that I didn't see Mrs. Crawford at all until she touched me on the shoulder. "Earth to Matt," she said, smiling. "What's got you thinking so hard?"

"I'm leaving school," I said. "My grandfather died this morning."

She sat down next to me. "I'm sorry. Was he sick?"

"Yeah. He's been sick for a long time, but this year was especially bad. He's been in and out of the hospital a lot."

"Oh," she said, and nodded. "That's why you haven't been yourself lately, right?"

What was she talking about?

"Since you started dating Carrie, I've noticed you haven't been the same in class. Your grades have slipped a little, too." I hadn't really thought about it before, but I saw she was right. It's just that it had nothing to do with Carrie. It was Steve, but I couldn't say that. "When you come back," she continued, "I want you to come and see me so we can get your grades back up. I don't want your average to fall."

"Why are you being so nice to me?" I asked, wondering what she'd say if she knew the truth.

"Because I see something in you. When you first came here, I was worried because I'd heard about your last school, but you were nothing like what I thought you'd be. You're considerate. And smart, too! You have so much potential, if you'd only start using it."

No teacher had ever said anything like this to me before. She put her arm around me just as the town car the school had hired to take me home arrived. The uniformed driver rolled down the window and called my name. Mrs. Crawford and I stood up, and she pulled me in for a hug before making me promise that I'd see her just as soon as I got back.

"I will," I said, and then walked toward the car as she stood at the dorm's entrance watching.

"Any bags?" the driver asked.

I hesitated. What was I going to do about my stuff? Was there anything I really needed up there that was worth facing possible humiliation? The answer came fast. I had clothes at home and nobody in New York would miss my luggage right now. After I convinced my grandmother to let me stay, we could either send for it or replace it.

"Bags?" the driver repeated.

I looked back at Mrs. Crawford, thinking about how nice she'd been to me. Then I turned to the driver and said, "No. I think I'm done here."

Howard's End

On the ride back to New York, I tried to figure out where my grandfather and I went wrong. It didn't seem that long since he'd been the center of my universe. Every morning until I was about seven or eight, I woke up before the sun to intercept him before my grandmother or Atse could. It might have been because he napped constantly, but I had never known him to sleep through the night. So by the time I'd find him in his study at around 6:00 A.M., he would've been up for hours. The *New York Times* and the *Wall Street Journal* would be lying around him in pieces, already read and reread. As soon as he saw me, a wide smile stretched across his thin lips. I liked to think he was waiting for me.

"Come sit down," he'd say, patting the spot next to him. "I saved this piece of the paper for you."

Then, picking up the closest section of the newspaper, he'd sum up what was going on in the world and how he would change things. He did not agree with President Reagan or President Bush, saying, "We tried that already, you know. Let me tell you about Star Wars and the SALT Talks."

After we read the newspaper, as we waited for my grandmother to come down for breakfast, I watched my grandfather give himself his first shot of insulin. There were two shots a day, the first one at breakfast and the second at dinner, and Atse delivered the insulin and a fresh syringe on the same small silver serving tray as the orange juice. In the morning, if it was just my grandfather and I, the injections happened in the dining room. If my grandmother was around, or we had company, he retreated to the privacy of his study. I was the only one who got to watch.

I didn't understand diabetes, so I always sat perched in my chair, watching him curiously. To my mind, diabetes was an exotic affliction he'd picked up in some foreign country while brokering for peace, not a hereditary illness aroused by rich sauces and too many pastries.

"Can I do that for you?" I asked every morning, watching him prepare the needle.

As usual, he laughed. "No, I have to do this myself, Matthew."

The tip of my tongue poised just outside my lips, I would watch his face as he sank the needle into the soft flesh around his middle. If it were me, I'd be howling like a wounded animal, but not him. He never even winced.

"Doesn't it hurt? Don't you want to cry?"

He laughed again. If there was something disconcerting about his young grandson's fetish for pain, he never said anything.

As my grandfather put the cap back on the needle, my grandmother invariably walked in, as if on cue. "Oh." She touched her chest in mock disappointment. "Did I miss the festivities? I really tried to get here on time today."

Pleased with herself—she told the same joke every morning—my grandmother chuckled and sat down at the breakfast table. "I swear, this is like the Addams Family. Any day now I half expect Matthew to ask if he can perform surgery on you with a butter knife."

"You just don't understand," I said, and exchanged a knowing look with my grandfather. My grandmother rolled her eyes and turned her attention to the carafe of boiling coffee set at her place.

"Oh, I get it, all right. I just think it's sick the way you're drooling over needles and pain. Then again, I guess everyone needs a hobby."

But while I could remember the newspapers and the needles and my grandfather's silences in the early morning, I realized I couldn't recall when they ended. As I grew older, I stayed up later watching television with my grandmother, and those early mornings probably came to an unceremonious end. By the time I was in middle school, my grandparents were already sitting at breakfast when I got up, engrossed in their own conversation or reading the newspaper (the third time for my grandfather, for my grandmother the first). My interests also shifted. I cared about dolls and fashion and my grandmother's shoes—not politics and business—and my grandfather interacted with me less and less. I couldn't pin down exactly when or how, but soon it seemed as if all he ever said to me was, "Do you want to go out and toss the ball around?" Or he would be ignoring me because I'd gotten into trouble at school.

.   .   .   .

When the town car docked in front of our apartment building, I saw four limousines parked along the curb, like some kind of luxury deathwatch. It hadn't occurred to me that there'd be anyone else at home besides my grandmother. When I got out of the car and stepped into the building, the lobby was unusually crowded, too. People were sprawled politely all over the decorative furniture that I had never seen anyone use before.

Joe came from behind the front desk and placed his hands on my shoulders. "It's a tough break, I know, but you hafta keep a clear head right now." He pursed his lips. "Your grandma needs you to be strong and help her through, okay?"

I nodded.

He continued, "You know as well as anyone that there's nobody else who's gonna help her, and I don't care if the queen herself comes and pays condolences."

I gave him a weak smile and wondered briefly which queen he was talking about.

He looked around the lobby—crowded with our neighbors—and lowered his voice. "I'll do my best to keep these vultures away from her. They've been asking about the police and the men coming and going all morning."

"The police? Who's up there?" I asked. I hated surprises, especially when they were family. I wanted to know if my uncle or my mother was already here.

"Don't know. Dark-suited types. Lawyers, maybe? The cops came earlier this morning and left. Gloria didn't know what to do, so she called them first."

I recoiled. Was there already business to conduct?

"Just remember when you get up there, you hafta look after her now. It's what he"—Joe pointed to the sky—"would have wanted."

I nodded my head as if this had all been planned and rehearsed. Of course my grandfather would have wanted that. Of course.

But in truth, aside from one recent telephone conversation, I couldn't remember when my grandfather had last confided anything in me beyond disappointment, and that wasn't a well-guarded secret. I could only imagine the shocked expression on his face if he knew that people were assuming I would be my grandmother's guardian. It seemed like a sad joke.

When I entered our apartment, the first thing I noticed was how normal it smelled. It was the same smell as always—that mixture of lemon-scented furniture polish and fresh linen. The heavy draperies were still closed, though, and the only light came from dimly lit lamps in the living room. This is how our apartment looked when we all went to bed and how it stayed until eight o'clock in the morning, an hour my grandmother considered reasonable for sunlight. But this was already afternoon.

A group of men in dark suits—just as Joe had mentioned— stood huddled near my grandmother, who, still in her robe and pajamas, sat motionless. She just stared toward my grandfather's study. The men were all waving their hands, discussing something in hushed tones, but I was fixed on my grandmother for almost a full minute. I couldn't remember the last time I'd seen her in pajamas.

I cleared my throat.

The men squinted at me from across the room but did not stop talking, even as I walked over and shook their hands. They were a chorus of condolences: "Very sorry." "Terrible tragedy." "Great man."

Static was lying next to my grandmother's feet.

My grandmother did not shift her gaze until I moved directly in front of her. She looked up and blinked. For a moment I thought she was trying to remember who I was. Her hair looked different—layered and cut short, it was nice—but the bangs hung over her eyes.

"I knew it when I woke up," she said. "I knew something was wrong."

I leaned down to kiss her on the forehead.

"I guess it's just us now," she said. "You should maybe go say good-bye. He's in the study."

She must have read the surprise in my expression. "The undertaker we'd chosen was out at Fire Island for the weekend. He's on his way back, but I told them not to hurry. Though, I suppose, if they wait too long, we'll be able to have the viewing here."

I was suddenly reminded of a conversation between my grandparents a few months before. It was after my grandfather had just been released from the hospital, and I was in town for the weekend, helping him get comfortable back in the apartment.

"Next time this happens," he said, waving at his chest, "don't bother with the ambulance. Just call the man who is going to fry me." I didn't know what to think, so I looked to my grandmother for an appropriate reaction.

"Fantastic," she said, rolling her eyes. "Should I get the number from you then, or can you give it to me now? I'd like to put it on speed dial."

The two of them burst out laughing, and my grandmother smacked his shoulder. "You're sick, old man."

"I am a sick old man," he said, and they only laughed harder.

And they wondered where I got my morbidity from.

My grandfather's body sat propped up on the sofa in his study. Somebody had wrapped him in a series of intricately patterned blankets that made me think—instantly—of a sleeping Navajo and one of the wise men in a Christmas nativity scene. The warm, pinkish color had drained from his face, replaced with a shade of blue, or maybe gray, giving him an almost metallic look. I touched his forehead, expecting him to wince.

Nothing. It was cold. He'd become a block of ice.

Why all the blankets? I wondered. It's possible that he'd wrapped himself in them. Maybe death came on like a sudden chill, and he'd used the blankets to warm himself before his heart just stopped. I marveled at their careful arrangement, all the way up to his neck. They were so perfect, so neatly placed—had he just fallen into death as if he were falling asleep? Could death really be such a calm . . . thing?

Scenarios popped up in my head. How had it happened? I wondered. Had he been awake and felt the whole thing? Had he been asleep and felt nothing? Was he dreaming? I looked around and couldn't find his newspaper, which meant he probably had been dead a very long time. If he'd been up and awake this morning, the newspaper would be lying disheveled around him.

I heard the sound of metal clattering on the parquet floor behind me. The undertaker had arrived. I turned and saw my grandmother trailing two men and a stretcher. The men went to work as I moved into the hall. My grandmother stayed behind to watch, paying her last respects.

"He's still in his pajamas," I heard her say. "I should give you something else to dress him in."

"Whatever makes you most comfortable, Mrs. Rothschild," said one of the undertakers. "Nobody will see him besides the funeral-home staff. Until the viewing, of course. You could take more time and pick out a suit then."

I kicked the runner on the hall floor and then looked up in time to see the most disconcerting sight of all: my grandfather, in profile, sliding off the sofa. His body moved slowly, seemingly of its own accord.

I could not look away. The men must have gathered his legs, because I didn't see hands on him until he was already slumped down. When they rolled my grandfather out of the room on the stretcher, he'd been placed in a black bag.

It's like a hanging bag, I thought, and tilted my head. I needed to wrap my mind around this. Not a sheet. Just a black bag, as if he were a suit. Only his head was exposed. The rest of him was zipped in place. And that's when I realized he was no longer my grandfather. He was a corpse.

My grandmother bent down and kissed the top of my grandfather's cold, bluish gray head. Her face was blank, but this was as much tenderness as I'd ever seen from her. Was she the one who'd wrapped the blankets around him? I imagined my grandmother sitting next to my dead grandfather in the twilight hours until Atse or Gloria came around to turn on all the lights at eight o'clock.

The undertakers strode purposefully down the hall, through the living room, out to the foyer, and into the elevator. My grandmother's cheeks ballooned as she watched them leave, and then she puffed out a mouthful of air. She patted me on the back.

"I think we need a drink," she said, and I knew she wasn't talking about coffee.

.   .   .   .

Hours later, after my grandmother had the fortitude to dress but not the strength to bathe, my Uncle James arrived. I didn't know who it was at first. It had been about three years since he'd brought his family to New York to visit, and I'd forgotten all the noise they made. I was sitting in the study, in the exact spot where my grandfather had been sitting in those blankets. My grandmother was standing at the window, looking onto Central Park. The apartment was silent, and we both glanced up at the terrific racket that exploded from the hall. The door slammed, and small children were whining. My grandmother and I locked eyes. She straightened up, steeling herself to greet her son and his family.

"Where is everyone?" I heard him say, too loudly. "I'm home!"

Atse came into the study, his head hung low. "You-know-who is here."

My grandmother rolled her eyes and walked toward the living room. I sat for a moment longer, willing myself to be nice, to be polite. I did not care for my uncle or his wife or their children, all for different reasons. To me, the children were competition, except we rarely saw them, and even I knew that it's hard to be jealous over people you see every couple years. My uncle was different, though. He was so greasy and brash. I could never see either of my grandparents in him. He had none of my grandmother's wit or my grandfather's demeanor. And then there was my uncle's wife, Cynthia. I didn't dislike her for any particular reason, but she was my uncle's wife, so that meant she was clearly lacking good sense.

Remember, I kept repeating to myself, *the man's just lost his father.* Still, I suspected that it was the anticipation of this moment, more than any other, that had inspired my grandmother to start drinking earlier. To her, my uncle was an all-around failure who called only when he wanted money. I remember asking her once why he didn't visit more, and she glanced at my grandfather before responding dryly, "I'd like to tell you, but it's a long story culminating in me being right—again." I understood that, much as with my mother, a lot had happened before I was born.

"Mawmaw, Mawmaw!" my cousins cried.

I shuddered. My grandmother hated that name, but still my uncle encouraged it.

"Isn't it great to see Mawmaw, kids?" he asked, and then they squealed some more. The elder, Gwendolyn, was eight years old. Jason was five. The last time I'd seen him, he was a toddler.

"Matthew," my grandmother called. I recognized that tone. It meant, *Get out here fast, or so help me I will drug you, pour honey on your body, and then stake you to an anthill.*

"Okay," my grandmother said, and when I peeked out into the hall, I saw her holding Jacob by the head, preventing the little boy from hugging her. "That's enough of that."

"He just wants to give you a hug, Mom," my uncle said. He tried to kiss my grandmother on the cheek, but she sidestepped them both and called my name again. For a moment I warmed toward my uncle's family; my grandmother's lack of physical affection was something we all had to deal with in some way.

"Hi," I said, lowering my voice and reaching out to shake my uncle's hand. I nodded at his wife and nodded again at their two children. "I hope you had a good—" I paused and smiled sheepishly. "A *safe* trip. I hope you had a safe trip."

We all stood in the hallway staring at one another in the awkward silence.

"I should go get some more glasses," my grandmother said, snapping around to leave.

I jumped after her. "I'll help you."

Once we were out of earshot, my grandmother hissed, "Well, this is a fine mess we're in now, goddamn it."

I didn't know what to say. What did she think was going to happen? Did she hope he'd skip the funeral? "It's not that bad," I started—which was, of course, the worst possible thing to say. If my grandfather were here, he'd already be cuddling with the grandkids and kissing his daughter-in-law. It wouldn't matter that my grandmother was hiding in the other room, because my grandfather made everyone feel welcome all on his own.

"Oh, not that bad, my foot," she said, storming into the kitchen. "You just wait and see how bad it gets. Soon your mother will be here, and they'll start playing off each other." She made a disgusted face and reached for two glasses from the cupboard and handed them to me. "I just know this isn't what I signed up for." She took a deep sigh. "Matthew, get the booze off the shelf. I can't reach." I found the large green bottle of Tanqueray gin and the bottle of tonic water, and we headed back to the living room.

While my uncle stood assessing the apartment for valuables to inherit, his children were jumping on an ottoman as Cynthia scolded them, "Sweet peas, don't jump up and down like that. Remember what we talked about? Showing Grandma how big we are?"

They ignored her.

My grandmother shot me a scornful look. *See?* she mouthed at me. She set the bottles down and quietly glared at the children. They froze.

"If you don't stop that noise, I'm going to zip you up in a trash bag just like they zipped up Grandpa." She did not shout, did not raise her voice at all—but what she said cut through the room.

The children shrieked and ducked behind their mother. Even I thought that was too harsh.

"*Mom!*" Cynthia gasped. She looked at my uncle, whose face had gone white with shock, silently pleading him to intercede.

"Tell them you were only kidding, Mom," my uncle said, trying to laugh. "They don't understand your sense of humor." I could tell he didn't, either.

"I wasn't kidding." She slammed down the bottles on the table. Cynthia jumped.

"They're little kids," my uncle said. "They don't know any better."

"That's why their parents should teach them," my grandmother said, studying the bottle. The kids peeked out from behind their mother's pant legs. My grandmother pointed a manicured finger at them. She smiled. "In my house," she said, and her voice softened, "there are rules. If you are going to stay here, rule one is no shouting. Rule two is don't jump on the furniture."

"They're just kids," my uncle repeated, smiling stupidly, and my grandmother fixed her icy stare on him until his smile disappeared. He sighed. "It is Mawmaw's house, kids," he said finally, and walked out of the room.

Cynthia shook her head. She gathered up the kids and went off to find my uncle, leaving my grandmother and me alone.

It occurred to me that nobody had mentioned my grandfather at all during that exchange, besides the garbage-bag reference. I felt as if we were already disrespecting the dead—though I didn't want to point that out. It would just make my grandmother angrier.

"Damn it," she said, and collapsed onto the sofa. I looked at her, thinking she was finally going to say something about this crazy morning, about my grandfather, something profound about our sadness and confusion and all the things we should have said to each other, even though we never did, while my grandfather was still alive.

She rested her head back on the cushions and sighed. "Matthew?"

I held my breath and waited.

"We forgot the ice."

.   .   .   .

If my uncle's failure to mention his missing father when he marched into our apartment earlier was just bad manners, it was downright creepy when he still said nothing at dinner. We sat through three courses of interminable silence—chewing, coughing, glasses clinking—before my grandmother rose and threw her linen napkin on the table.

"I've had enough of this day," she said, and left the room.

For a long moment, there was silence. My cousins looked worriedly at each other but wisely said nothing. Cynthia was staring at her plate. My uncle finally looked up at me, and I was momentarily fearful that I'd have to carry the conversation.

"So how're the ladies treating you?" he asked.

I had just swallowed some water. I almost choked. "Excuse me?"

"Girls," he said. He gestured to his wife, as if I had never heard the word before. "Girlfriends. Don't you have any of those up at school? I know I did. When I went there, they just loved me. Couldn't get enough." A goofy smile plastered itself across his face until he made eye contact with his scowling wife.

I needed to think about this one. How to answer his question and minimize the truth as much as possible. I did have a girlfriend, after all, even if I might never see her again.

I studied my uncle. Food was stuck to his shirt, his potbelly was overflowing from his pants below the table, and his plastic-framed glasses were ten years out of fashion. He was a slob with no taste. I'd seen pictures of my uncle when he was my age—back then he'd actually been a good-looking guy. Clean-cut, athletic, and apparently popular with the ladies. The pictures, however, failed to depict that he was a colossal, tragic bore.

Rising from my chair, I yawned. "I'm going to turn in, too. 'Night." I nodded to nobody in particular and left the room.

"Everyone goes to bed so early in this house," I heard my uncle say as I walked away. "I just don't understand it."

That night I dreamed about my grandfather. My grandmother and

I were sitting playing mah-jongg, a game I knew only from watching elderly Chinese people play in Chinatown. I was just about to shout "Mah-jongg!" when my grandfather came into the living room, at which point the game stopped abruptly. My grandmother looked up and sucked in a breath. I dropped my tiles.

I never really died, he said. *I've been in hiding, but I missed you two so much that . . . well, I'd like you to come into hiding with me.* My grandfather did not say whom he was hiding from, or why, but he did say we mustn't tell anyone he was alive and that our new home would be on the beach in Mexico. My grandmother and I stared at him. Then we looked at each other, and instantly we were lying on the beach, together again as a family, and then I was inside playing checkers on the Internet while they giggled together outside.

·   ·   ·   ·

By lunchtime the next day, my grandmother still hadn't left her room. My cousins sat quietly, coloring on the floor, while my uncle poked around my grandfather's study.

"I'm looking . . . for something," he said.

When I asked him, he wouldn't elaborate. He just kept looking through the books and shelves, opening and closing drawers. I tried giving him the benefit of the doubt. He was looking for memories— an old letter, pictures, his father's favorite book. But I knew he was really looking for the will. A few months earlier, I'd overheard my grandparents discussing the latest of my uncle's failed businesses. He was short on cash, as usual.

Cynthia was watching television, glancing every now and then at her kids. I sat in a chair behind them, off in the corner. I checked the clock every five seconds, wondering if I should be concerned about my grandmother. Now? No. Be patient. . . . Now? Should I go knock on her door? I was coaching myself for the task when I heard the front door click. Someone was unlocking it.

"Hello?"

My mother was home.

. . . .

I hadn't seen my mother in a few years—not since that trip to Italy when I was ten. We rarely spoke to each other over the phone, and we still hadn't discussed what went wrong in Rome. I didn't know exactly what to do. I had to go say hello, how are you, how was your trip, but then . . . A kiss on the cheek? A handshake? Ask her about her rotten husband whom she wasn't even living with anymore? Ask if she was seeing anyone new? What?

Her hair was long and dark now, not the blond I remembered. She was pulling off her coat and handing it to Atse when I met her in the hall.

"Hello!" she said enthusiastically, but when she removed her sunglasses, her eyes were puffy. I was taken aback—she'd been crying.

I said, "Hello." She moved closer, and I could smell her perfume, which I did not recognize. She kissed me on the nose and laughed, and *that* I remembered. My mother's laugh came easily, and its melodious effect lingered in the hall.

"My, look how handsome you've become. All grown up! Turn around."

"Turn around?" I asked.

She nodded and spun her hand like a top. "You've changed so much since I saw you last. It's amazing. Your grandparents sent me pictures, but they didn't do you justice. Where's all that baby fat?" She pinched my stomach, and I laughed, flattered.

I was thinking of a compliment to pay her back—she really looked stunning in her black suit—when my mother's expression changed. I turned to find my grandmother at the foot of the stairs.

"Mom," my mother said, and it came out in a whisper. My grandmother held out her arms ever so slightly, and my mother ran—*ran!*—to my grandmother's embrace. I hadn't ever seen my grandmother and mother embrace. I thought back to my uncle's arrival. I had always known that my grandmother didn't care for either of her children, but it never occurred to me that she might like one more than the other, and that the one she preferred was my mother.

"If you came home more often, you'd know how much he's changed." My grandmother winked at me.

"I'm so sorry," my mother said. Her face was buried in my grandmother's shoulder, but I could hear she was crying again.

"Little sis!" my uncle shouted as he charged in, breaking the mood. I wanted to hear what my mother could possibly be sorry about—my grandfather? me? what?—but now we'd have to listen to this man.

He studied his sister and their mother embracing. "Hey, what's the problem?"

"What's the problem?" my mother spit, and her face contorted in rage. She pulled away from my grandmother, and I took a step back to watch this play out fully. "What do you mean, what's the problem? This isn't a family reunion, brother dear."

"Did I say it was? I don't remember hearing that." He threw me a look of mock indignation and flung his hands up in surrender.

I watched the scene, feeling as if I were not a member of this family. My mother and uncle had lapsed into roles I did not understand, roles that obviously predated my existence in the home in which they grew up.

I pictured my grandmother forty years younger, standing over two wailing children. I saw my mother in a blue dress bordered with lace and bows, pointing savagely at my uncle, who, five years older, was throwing his adolescent Lacoste-clad arms up in surrender. They could have been fighting over anything; but something told me that all their fights eventually would play out in the same way. And the look on my grandmother's face puzzled me. This was a new expression, something I couldn't remember from all my years living with her: not quite resignation, but certainly something *undecided*. Almost as if she were an adult who had come upon two strange children in her apartment, and these children were arguing, and she felt obligated to step in—but wasn't quite sure how.

In that moment I started to understand how much my grandfather would be missed. If he were here, he'd lay his large hands on his children's respective shoulders. He'd talk to them, say, "You're both right," make them both feel important, calm them down, and then send them on their way. But he wasn't here now. And my grand-mother didn't know how to stop them.

"I had no idea how sick he was!" said my uncle.

"If you called more," said my mother, "or came to visit, you might have known."

My uncle smirked. "And you're any better?"

"Oh!" my mother gasped. "I live in Europe. Europe! It's not like I can fly back every weekend."

"Yeah, that's your answer for everything, isn't it? Move to Europe and hook up with Eurotrash. Mom knows I'm busy at work." He turned to my grandmother, his face pleading. "Don't you, Mom? It takes up a lot of time."

"Yes. Operating a car wash can be very time-consuming," said my grandmother, staring past him at the wall.

"A car wash?" my mother sneered. "You have a car wash? *You have a car wash, you have a car wash.*"

I felt myself physically recoil. Is this what my childhood would have been like living with my mother? "What," she would have said, "you have a boo-boo? *Matthew has a boo-boo, Matthew has a boo-boo.*"

"It's a *chain* of car washes." My uncle leaned forward and gritted his teeth on the word *chain*. "It's not like I'm running the goddamn hoses." Then, with a hint of pride, "It's actually the largest chain in the tristate area."

His wife, who had appeared at his side amid all the chaos, nod-ded. "At least his job isn't sitting around waiting for monthly al-imony checks," said Cynthia, glaring at my mother.

"You should try it," my mother said, "Then you wouldn't have to turn to my parents and ask for money."

I glanced over to my grandmother, who locked me with her "I told you so" look. I remembered Joe telling me to fill in for my grandfa-ther, but these people—my real family—were glorified strangers to me. And they weren't children anymore. How was I going to put my hands on their shoulders and take them out for ice cream?

"Seriously," my mother was saying. "When are you going to grow up?"

"Me?" Uncle James said. "When am *I* going to grow up? I'm not the one who gave up her kid to her parents"—he pointed at me triumphantly—"so *she* could go jet-setting around the world with her coked-out friends."

Ouch. In the silence that followed, I saw my mother's face. She looked angry and sad all at once—she had frozen. Even my grandmother was stunned. The insult was aimed at my mother, but I felt the sting, too. My grandmother and I both watched my mother. She put her hands flat on her hips and struck a pose like a model at the end of a runway, fierce and almost ludicrous. After years of distance and absence, my family was finally together, making up for the decades of missed fighting.

"Oh, I forgot," she said. "*You're* the responsible one. The one who got his girlfriend knocked up while his wife was at home raising his kids."

I turned to my uncle, waiting for him to deny the accusation. I didn't know if it were really true. After all, I had seen my mother exaggerate the facts more than once to get attention or to win a fight. But my uncle did not deny the accusation. He was silent and the next sound we heard was Cynthia breathing heavily and then running upstairs.

My mother ignored her. She stood, hands still on hips, daring my uncle to say anything more. He glared at her and sputtered but then rushed toward the stairs to follow his wife. As he thundered up after her, my mother turned to my cousins, who had witnessed the whole scene but obviously didn't understand what they had seen. She flashed them her biggest smile. "Guess whose favorite aunt has presents!" She turned to a small Louis Vuitton travel case and took it into the living room, where Gwendolyn and Jason danced around her feet.

When I could finally speak, I asked my grandmother, "What the hell was that?"

She shrugged. "That is the same old song and dance I've been watching for thirty-five years."

I felt like I was still reeling. "I've never seen it before."

"Well, no, of course not," she said. "You've never seen them together in the same room."

.   .   .   .

The funeral was two days later, and so many people showed up that the funeral home could barely accommodate the crowd. Looking around, I recognized some of the faces, but most were strangers. There must have been three hundred people in that dimly lit room, and it seemed as if they all knew me.

"Your grandfather talked about you all the time," said a woman I'd never met.

"Are you sure?" I asked, and she laughed.

"No, I'm serious," I said. "Are you sure? I'm not his only grandson." I pointed to my cousin Jason standing next to his sister.

"They're cute kids," the woman whispered, "but you were the one who really counted." She went to join her husband, who was speaking with my grandmother.

"She's right, you know," my mother said. She chortled, and for a moment I recognized my grandmother in her. "I don't know how you did it. Even when you had all those problems in school, neither of them would say anything against you." I was surprised to hear how much she knew about me. I wondered if she'd been asking all these years, or if my grandparents had volunteered the information. She looked at my grandmother. "I don't know if you'll ever understand what that really means. Especially from her."

"I must be charmed," I said, reverting back to sarcasm. It was easier than having a genuine conversation with her. There were still so many unresolved issues between us. Even as she was paying me a compliment, I couldn't relax in her presence.

My uncle came around on my other side, and I felt cartoonish with them both flanking me. Like I had a devil on one side and an angel on the other, except I couldn't tell which was which.

"Now that he's gone, nobody'll be able to do anything with her," my uncle said.

"I don't know about that," my mother said. "Matthew, maybe. She listens to him."

"Speaking of, did you ask him yet?"

My mother shook her head. "Haven't had a chance."

I hadn't seen the two of them say anything besides "Pass the salt" in the last two days since their blowout. It scared me to learn that, of all things, they'd been discussing me in secret. Perhaps I really was surrounded by two devils?

My mother touched my shoulder. "Matthew, your uncle and I were talking. What do you think about staying in New York for a while? Just until we see how she's going to do by herself."

That was it? I almost let out a sigh of relief. I would never have to go back to school, never have to face my roommate!

"I . . . I don't know," I said. "I guess that'd be fine, but how are you going to explain it to her?" I looked at my grandmother, who was talking with a friend.

"Leave that to me," my mother said. "I'll take care of everything. I would have your uncle do it"—she chuckled—"but that would just cause problems."

"What's that supposed to mean?" he asked.

"Come on, James. You know she hates you."

His mouth fell open. I felt a sudden twinge of sympathy for him. "Why would you say something like that today?" I asked my mother. "We're at a funeral for his father—and yours, too. You don't go around saying things like that at a funeral."

My uncle looked elated. I saw anger flash across my mother's face before she blinked back some tears.

"Matthew, you don't understand," she said.

"No, he's right."

We all turned. My grandmother was behind us.

"I don't know why you two feel like advertising our shame to all your grandfather's friends, but cut it out. Don't you have any re-spect?" She looked around, fake-smiling to onlookers before turning again to her family.

My mother and uncle looked like scolded children. My grandmother glared at them and continued. "I want you to stop this bickering. Do it for your father. It would destroy him to know you were doing this in front of people. It's the last thing you'll ever have to do for him. You can kill each other when we get home. Now, both of you. Go. Sit down. Now."

I waited for one of them to say the other had started it. But then we heard activity behind us. A man had ascended the platform above my grandfather's coffin.

"All right, Matthew," my grandmother said, "take me to my seat."

My uncle blinked and looked to my mother, who crossed her arms and smiled in what appeared to be triumph. Escorting my grandmother to her seat most certainly should have been my uncle's duty. He was the son. But my grandmother specifically asked me, and there was no way I could refuse. It was as if I had usurped his role—and, I realized, maybe I had.

"I want you to remember something, Matthew," my grandmother said as we walked up the aisle toward my grandfather's open casket.

"What's that?"

"He loved you very much. I know you've been wondering, but you have to let it go. Just because he didn't always agree with your decisions doesn't mean he didn't love you. In fact"—she patted my arm—"the last thing he said to me was that he felt like you were finally going to be all right."

It was as though my grandfather had given me one final message from the grave. *I know we've had problems, but I never stopped loving you.*

And then I felt it: an overwhelming sense of guilt rushing at me like a tidal wave, unstoppable. He had been so good to me. Without him I wouldn't even have been born! He was the one who'd made my mother have me. And then he'd raised me and loved me better than his own children. What had I given him in return?

We were already at our seats, and I closed my eyes. My grandmother clutched my hand, and I turned to her and saw a tear sliding down her cheek. I pressed her hand firmly and felt my own guilt start to dissipate, something else forming in its place. It took me a moment to realize what it was, but then I knew. It was obligation. Joe had been right. I would step into my grandfather's shoes and watch over my grandmother.

I would protect her.

I knew later that this was some kind of defining moment in my life—the kind of thing celebrities mention on *Oprah*. But I was lost in that moment. All I could do was stare at my grandfather in his dark suit and think that at any second we'd have to close the coffin lid. And then I would be the glue holding my family together.

Judaism for Dummies

I ' v e   h e a r d rabbis say that intermarriage is the cause of dwindling Jewish observance, but this was not the case in my family. The general rule was that my family was Jewish on holidays, when it might be acceptable to miss work or school, but we fell short of observing any actual Jewish tradition. As far as we were concerned, half the fun of Hanukkah was that it fell around the same time as Christmas, the day when you could have shrimp *and* pork at the local Chinese restaurant.

There were exceptions to this rule, however. My grandmother's nephew, Jordan, had refused to marry his Savannah-born Catholic wife, Peggy, until she converted to Judaism.

The year after my grandfather died, Jordan and Peggy invited my grandmother and me to a Passover seder at their place in Connecticut. This invitation surprised me; I could remember having celebrated Passover only once while my grandfather was alive, and it seemed odd to be doing it now that he was dead.

"They just want to make sure I'm still alive," said my grandmother as we drove out to Connecticut.

Since my grandfather's death, my grandmother rarely left the apartment that they had shared for more than fifty years. Without her husband my grandmother was content to roam around the rooms like a ghost. Most of her time during the day was spent watching the same old movies she had watched with my grandfather. If asked, my grandmother would say that she had spent sixty-odd years doing things and going places. She was now content to sit around and suck hard candy.

When Jordan and Peggy called, I was quick to accept their invitation, even though my grandmother was stepping on my foot as I did so. "That would be great," I said, wincing with pain. "I can't wait, and I'm sure Grandma would love to come."

Hanging up the phone, I saw that she was already pouting on the sofa. When I was a child, my grandmother would throw her hands on her hips and give you "the eye" when things did not go her way. Old age and cataracts made this difficult, and she now took to giving people the silent treatment instead. Age had not, however, dulled her reflexes, and I feared that if I got close enough, she might lunge at me.

"Come on, it's not that bad," I said.

"'I'm sure that Grandma would love to come,'" she mocked. "I don't know which grandma you were talking about, but the one I know thinks you're full of shit."

In the end we both knew she would go. It was whether or not she would behave that was in question. This would be her first family function since my grandfather's funeral, and it was anyone's guess what there would be for her to discuss with anyone. I'm sure that my grandmother must have thought about what her life would be like after my grandfather's death, but she probably didn't see herself as having to attend family functions. With no interest in my grandfather's family and minimal interest in her own, this was undoubtedly the most difficult part of being alive. Whenever my grandfather had voiced a desire for the two of them to spend time with family, my grandmother would say, "The deal is this: When I'm dead, you can spend as much time with them as you like, but not on my dime, buddy."

*   *   *   *

I was in my room dressing for Passover when I heard the sound of my grandmother's slippered feet sliding along the carpet.

"Do I look okay?" she said. She had chosen a tasteful red dress but had accessorized it with every necklace, brooch, bracelet, and ring she could fit on herself. Her earrings did not match, and she glistened like a showgirl at the Golden Nugget.

"Sure, if you want your insurance agent to have a heart attack."

"I don't want people to think I'm letting myself go. Now I have to take the ermine out of the freezer."

I knew she was only trying to cause trouble, as if bad behavior might get her out of the dinner. "Dress yourself like a sparkler," I said. "Go ahead. You're still going."

Maybe she finally figured there was no escaping it, but she'd taken off most of the jewelry by the time we left, leaving only a pearl necklace and some rings.

I had just received my learner's permit, so I gave Atse the day off and drove us myself. We didn't speak much in the car. My grandmother held on to the door in an attempt to stabilize herself, even though the car never sped past fifty miles per hour. Irritated by the quiet, she put on the CD changer and flipped until she found something offensive, Public Enemy, and we listened to it all the way to Connecticut.

Jordan and Peggy had only recently been married, and this was Peggy's first Passover. Plus, she had only recently finished the conversion to Judaism and was very serious that everything be done in strict Orthodox tradition. This meant we could potentially be sitting for hours before eating; traditionally, this dinner involved reading the entire story of the Exodus from a book called the Haggadah. Everyone takes turns reading from beginning to end, and as the reading rotates around the table, those who can read in Hebrew are encouraged to do so.

"I hope she doesn't have any geezers reading, or we'll be there all week," said my grandmother.

Driving through Jordan's neighborhood, I was reminded of the trend to purchase and renovate old farmhouses into country showplaces worthy of a Martha Stewart special. Jordan's house was no different. I was pulling in to the gravel driveway when Peggy came out of the house, wiping her hands on a checkered apron.

"Tell me she didn't cook a dinner for twenty people," said my grandmother, guessing at the number of guests. These dinners are a huge tradition for Jews, and they can be an elaborate production, but they are rarely home-cooked when there are twenty guests.

The car had barely come to a stop when Peggy flung open my grandmother's door. She pressed her face against my grandmother's cheek and wrapped her arms around my grandmother's shoulders.

"You must be my Aunt Sophie," she said.

My grandmother squeezed my arm. "Put the car in drive."

Peggy swatted my grandmother playfully. "Jordan said you were a joker." She looked at me. "And you must be Matthew."

I smiled and waved.

"Come inside, you two, so you can meet my family."

"Your family?" said my grandmother.

"Yes, I asked my parents and brothers and sisters and cousins to come up for the dinner. This is their first seder, too. Everyone got here last night from Savannah except my cousins, who live in Massachusetts; they came up today. We're all so excited to meet you."

If my grandmother didn't like her own family, she sure as hell wasn't going to like anybody else's. "I didn't know anything about any strange redneck—"

"I think it sounds great, Peggy," I jumped in. "It's nice when your *family* encourages something that you believe in."

Peggy let go of my grandmother and stood holding the car door. "Come on inside!"

Looking at me, my grandmother sighed. "You're dead to me."

As they were walking into the house, I heard my grandmother say to Peggy, "Because you're new and inexperienced, I'll help you out. The Russian Jews have a tradition of using vodka instead of wine to symbolize the plagues. . . ."

Peggy's gregarious southern family outnumbered my own stand-offish New York family, especially since the only members representing our side were my grandmother and me. Jordan explained that our relatives were "away for the holidays."

My grandmother grabbed his arm. "If your mother isn't here, why do I have to be?"

"We have lots of eccentrics in our family, too," said Peggy's mother, who was wearing a prairie skirt and knee-length leather boots, to Jordan.

Peggy led my grandmother away, and I spent some time catching up with Jordan's two children from his first marriage. Shortly before dinner I found my grandmother surrounded by a group of postdebutantes, each with teased-out hair. Two sisters in particular, one in a floral-print vest, the other wearing a puffy winter coat inside the house, took a particular interest in my grandmother.

"I just don't understand how you stay so small," said the first sister. "Look how small she is. Tell us your secret."

"They don't eat anything that rises, Marigold. I told you," said her sister. "It's all that Atkins."

"Actually," my grandmother said, "I don't eat at all. I just drink. I haven't had a real meal in over a year. You should try it."

I wrested her away from these women, saying that I had to make sure she used the bathroom before dinner.

"You wouldn't want me wetting my pants," said my grandmother, grinning at the two sisters.

Contrary to our initial observation, there were many caterers rushing through the kitchen preparing for the dinner; Peggy's apron must have been purely decorative. Apparently, having someone else cook your holiday meals is not a cultural tradition that applies only to Jewish women.

There were too many people to fit around the formal dining room table, so a smaller "kids' table" was brought into the room. Because I was under forty, I was assigned to this table. My grandmother was asked to sit at the formal table, but she would have none of it. She dug her fingers into my arm and said, "We suffer together, little man." Peggy objected, but my grandmother sat down, pretending not to hear.

There was a married couple at our table as well as some of Peggy's younger relatives and Jordan's two children. Looking around, I realized that my grandmother's original assumption as to why we had been invited was wrong: They weren't worried about whether she was still alive—Peggy and Jordan just needed bodies from his side of the family to fill up some chairs. Jordan's own mother had declined his invitation. She probably told her son to phone his Aunt Sophie and cousin Matthew, and Jordan probably sighed and said it was worth a try. It was my bright idea to accept, and there was no way I would be living it down anytime soon.

Jordan's own children had come home from college for this dinner.

"Not being home for Passover is like not being home for Christmas," Peggy told her family.

Reading from the Haggadah began smoothly, each of us doing a few paragraphs, rotating around the table for a few dozen pages. Then we reached the portion where the diners are meant to dip their fingers in their wineglass and touch their plate ten times to symbolize each of the ten plagues with which God punished the Egyptians.

"Let's use our pinkie fingers," Jordan suggested, "according to official tradition."

"Jordan!" my grandmother shouted. "Who raised you? That's not the way we do things."

"I think he's right, though, Aunt Sophie," Peggy said, flipping through the Haggadah. "I think I read somewhere that—"

"No. In our family, Peggy, you take a big gulp from the glass for each of the plagues. We must be authentic to our family traditions, too. That's what Judaism is all about. If she were here, Jordan's mother would back me up. My father was very strict. We did this for forty-some years, until the day his liver rotted and he died." She then smacked her ring against the wineglass; it was time for a refill. "Pinkie finger indeed. My father would roll over in his grave."

Finally the time came to put down our Haggadahs and eat. During the ceremony each guest is instructed to snack on symbolic foods, and the closer you get to the actual feast, the more stained the Haggadah's pages become. It would seem as if Jewish liturgical books serve a dual role: to be used for instruction and as a bib.

During dinner Peggy's family kept asking questions about why Jews do this or that. Peggy enjoyed answering most of the questions, and if she was unsure, she consulted her textbook, *Judaism for Dummies.* "An apt title if I ever heard one," my grandmother joked.

"Mama, why does Baby Jesus want us to eat these stale crackers?" asked Peggy's four-year-old niece. She was frowning at the piece of matzo her mother had just handed to her.

"Sweetheart," I heard Peggy's sister whisper in reply, "Baby Jesus says you can eat anything you want. It's the *Jews* who won't let you."

We tried to take our time through dinner because there was more reading to do after the meal, another ten pages or so. The food was good, but instead of our dining from the much-preferred buffet table, the caterers filled our plates for us.

"Goddamn, woman!" bellowed Peggy's father to one server. "This'd hardly be enough to feed a newborn, let alone a grown man. I am a growing man!"

"From side to side doesn't count," said my grandmother. I jabbed her with my elbow.

"So, Mrs. Rothschild," said Peggy's mother, turning to us with a polite smile, "what do you do in your spare time?"

My grandmother smiled back. "I'm a hooker," she responded, pouring another glass of wine.

And a hush fell over the crowd before Peggy began to laugh nervously, signaling the rest of her family to do the same. "Such . . . a pistol," she said, shooting angry looks at her husband.

The dining room was large, even with the two tables side by side. With most of the questions being directed from the big table to my grandmother at the small table, it was as if the tables were having a shouting match with each other.

"Aunt Sophie!" Peggy yelled. "Jordan said you're about to have a birthday. How old are you going to be?"

This, I believe, is the kind of question one is never supposed to ask. It would seem that two grown women might share this understanding more than anyone else, but maybe things are different in the South?

"Eighty-two," said my grandmother.

"But you don't look a day over sixty," said someone at the big table.

"I know," said my grandmother. "It really screws with my senior-citizen discount at Wendy's." She then looked at the server, who was standing by the door to the kitchen. "Sweetheart, either I need something stronger than wine or you're going to have to start bringing me two glasses at a time."

After that, the other guests seemed to wisely decide that silence was the way to go. We all said nothing, just stared at our plates while eating, until the young married couple at our table, cousins of Peggy's who lived in Massachusetts, began speaking to each other.

"Where's Mary?" said the man.

"She's at home," said his wife.

"She should be here."

"She didn't want to come."

"Neither did I, but I still came."

I had no real experience with married couples under the age of seventy, but if there was one thing I *could* recognize a mile away, it was an argument about to erupt.

"Just leave the bottle," my grandmother was saying, waving the server away.

"We had to come," the woman told her husband. Then, lowering her voice for the first time, "We live too close to say no."

"Then why isn't Mary here with us?"

"She doesn't need to be here. It would have bored her, and she would have caused problems. It's better that she stayed at home."

"I still think if I have to be here, she should be here, too."

"Amen," said my grandmother, lifting her glass and hiccupping.

The woman started. I suppose she hadn't realized that their argument had gained viewers. "You're right, Eddie!" she began to shout. "You are always fucking right! I should have drugged my twelve-year-old daughter and dumped her into the car to sit through this five-hour dinner!"

"That's what he did to me," said my grandmother, pointing to me. "And I'm still buzzed. It's probably all this booze, though." She tapped her glass. "Nothing like the kosher stuff."

"Stop it," I said under my breath, and from the bigger table

Peggy tapped her glass with her knife. "I think we're ready to continue," she called.

"You can tell she's not *really* Jewish," my grandmother said to me. "A real Jew would never break up an argument or take the food away."

"But why does Baby Jesus—"

The little girl's mother put her hand over her daughter's mouth.

Peggy was the last reader from the Haggadah, and the rest of us breathed a collective sigh of relief that it was over. I gently shoved my grandmother, who had missed her final turn in favor of a short nap. She looked up, temporarily disoriented before everything came into focus. She made a disgusted face. "I thought it was a dream," she said.

I was about to tell her we could go home soon when Peggy announced she had a final surprise. My grandmother looked at me, eyes narrowed.

Peggy had clasped her hands together. "We're all going out to the creek in the back of the house and reenact the Exodus!" She said this in the same tone in which one tells small children they're going out for ice cream or McDonald's; it's the kind of tone you use when you assume that your audience will be thrilled. But I was not thrilled, and if I was not thrilled, I couldn't even imagine what my grandmother was thinking. I was almost afraid to look at her.

"Peggy Sue, that sounds delightful!" said Peggy's mother.

The postdebutantes rose, all smiles and sunshine.

"Goddamn, woman! I am tired," said Peggy's father.

"Oh, Daddy," said Peggy, "it'll be fun. You'll see."

"Mama, what's the Exodus? Is that where Baby Jesus . . ."

As the guests all stood one by one, my grandmother grabbed me by the shirt. "Matthew," she hissed, "you better get me out of here, or I swear you are out of the will."

I told her not to be so melodramatic. "Please, just suck it up a few more minutes," I said. "Why are you being so difficult? You love to watch people make fools of themselves."

"I want to go home," she said, throwing her napkin onto the table. But she knew she was already outmatched. We all marched outside—it was still too cold—heading to the creek in the back of the farmhouse. This creek would now be the scene of the second parting of the Red Sea.

I heard Peggy telling her mother that she originally thought of writing out the parts and having us draw slips of paper from a big yarmulke. But Jordan advised against it. Instead she assigned the roles.

"So how about cranky Daddy plays the pharaoh?" Peggy said, handing everyone pages of a play she had written herself. Jordan would play Moses, Peggy would be Miriam, and the rest of us were the helpless Israelites chased across a footbridge by Peggy's father, the southern pharaoh.

"What the hell is the matter with you people?" said my grandmother, her patience finally exhausted. "This isn't a party—it's a religious dinner. You might as well have a piñata, for chrissake!" She threw her script on the ground with disgust. "I'm going to the car."

It really was too cold and too weird to be doing this, so I mouthed some conciliatory apologies to everyone and ran after her.

Six months later my grandmother's sister, Beatrice, called to say that Jordan had run off with his evangelical dental hygienist, a good Christian girl who did not mind having a married boyfriend but who would not give up her religion. Jordan didn't have a problem with this, and they were getting a new farmhouse together, where they could live in sin in peace. And the following spring, when Jordan called to invite my grandmother and me to Easter dinner, my grandmother was ready.

She snatched the phone from my hand when she heard who it was on the line. "Jordan, I'd love to, but the thing is, I just don't think I can handle a reenactment of the Crucifixion," she said, and hung up the phone.

Driving Miss Sophie

After my grandfather died, I had been living at home and attending the same school in the city for about two years when my grandmother suddenly announced I was going back to boarding school. The topic seemed to appear out of nowhere, and I was more surprised than hurt. One minute we were watching reruns of *Designing Women* in the living room, and the next she was telling me to vacate the premises. I waited for further explanation, but none came.

"Why?" I finally asked.

"You're cramping my style."

I was stumped. What was that supposed to mean?

"There are things I can't do with you around, Matthew."

I asked what these things were. She studied the carpet, as if the weave contained a list of hidden passions and she was taking her time to choose the most exciting item. "I don't know. Swing on the chandeliers. Slide down the banister. Lots of things."

I tried to imagine my eighty-two-year-old grandmother sliding down the banister, sailing past Gloria on the stairs. I touched her forehead to check for a fever. "Are you all right?"

"No, I'm fine. If you want to know the truth—"

I put my hand to my chest in mock surprise. "Oh, the truth? Hmm, what a novelty!"

She ignored me. "I want to be alone for a little while. I've never been alone, you know. I lived with your . . ." She waved her hand.

"Dog?" I offered, looking down at Static the dalmatian, who was still my grandmother's shadow.

"Howard," she said. She blew out a stream of air, exhausted.

"My grandfather?" I said, surprised. Had she actually forgotten his name?

"Yes. I lived with your grandfather for sixty years. I want to see what it's like to live alone. This doesn't have anything to do with you."

My grandmother was not the kind of woman who spared anyone's feelings, so I figured she meant it. The last time I was sent away, I was hurt, though I grew to appreciate my grandparents' position. I had been a terrible nuisance, always in trouble—but I wasn't anymore, at least not publicly.

And I had to admit I wasn't broken up about leaving this time. I'd never say this out loud, but I was growing restless in New York. Almost the only person whose company I shared was my grandmother, and while I enjoyed it, and loved her, I also wanted to be around kids my own age without feeling guilty. Occasionally people from school would invite me out to parties or movies or skating in the park, but did I go? No. Instead I sat around watching *The Nanny* with my grandmother, Atse, and Gloria. I knew that my grandmother wasn't technically alone with our staff all around, but I felt like I had to be there.

Of course, that was my fault, not my grandmother's, but since she hadn't objected, I assumed that things were going well. That she liked having me around. Maybe I'd misjudged the situation? Involuntarily my mind drifted back to my former roommate, Steve, and my face went all hot.

"I can't go back to the last school," I said.

"That's fine. You can pick this time. There are some nice schools up in New Hampshire, or Boston."

"Boston?"

Boston was four hours away. If I went to a school that far, I wouldn't be able to come home as often as when I was in Connecticut.

"Or New Hampshire," she repeated.

I threw my hands up. "Why don't you just send me to Switzerland?"

She actually considered this for a moment. "There *are* some nice schools in Switzerland."

I wondered when she became such an authority on boarding schools around the world, but I let it drop. Instead I imagined life at a new school, where nobody knew me. I could join the swim team again or play tennis. I had been using a personal trainer at the gym in our building, and I was in the best shape I'd ever been in. I had no love life and no idea how to fix this, but that was nothing new. At least away at school, I could finally have a social life. So, after winter break, I packed my bags and went off to a new school just outside Boston. I took new classes. I met a whole new group of kids. I actually made friends.

And if I wondered constantly about my grandmother, too—what she was doing with all her free time, her Matthew-free life—I didn't have to wait long to find out. She had been sneaking out of the house and driving. When my mother called me at school to report this, I had to laugh. "It's not funny," she said, but I ignored her. I had this vision of my grandmother dressed as a cross between a race-car driver and 1930s stunt pilot. I could see her in the classic convertible Jaguar my grandfather kept in the garage, flying down Fifth Avenue, weaving in and out of traffic with Static buckled into the passenger seat. Her scarf was blowing in the wind and maybe she even had on some goggles, too. Oh, yes, I thought it was mighty funny.

My grandmother's bad driving was notorious. It was so bad that the only living person who remembered her as a driver—her sister, my Great-Aunt Beatrice—would shudder whenever you asked her about it. We joked that if she hadn't been such a bad driver, she wouldn't have met my grandfather.

After my grandmother had totaled three cars by her sixteenth birthday, her father made her a deal: "You can always use the family chauffeur," he told her, "so long as you find a husband who can drive by your twenty-first birthday." At that point, my great-grandfather believed, her inability to drive would be her husband's problem. My grandmother admitted to me shortly before I went back to boarding school that this had put a serious crimp in her style. "I didn't want to get married. I thought married people were like wallpaper. Boring."

"But didn't you love Grandpa?" I asked.

"Oh, sure, but that's beside the point. My father was out there on the streets, pimping me out to anyone with a decent driving record!" She laughed. "Thank God for your grandfather."

My great-grandfather had noticed my grandfather's late-model Packard parked on (where else?) Park Avenue before he even learned his name—and when he found the owner in a nearby restaurant, he dragged the boy home and set him up with his daughter on a blind date. "Just don't take my car" was his only rule. Things must have gone well, because they were married a few months later—on my grandmother's twenty-first birthday—and she would not drive for another sixty years, until after my grandfather's death.

It was our maid, Gloria, who called my mother to tell her that my grandmother was sneaking out to drive, and my mother immediately made my grandmother promise she would stop. "She crossed her heart!" my mother told me over the phone. "What else could I ask for?"

"I don't know," I said. Sophie Rothschild crossing her heart? That was a promise less binding than Rabin and Arafat's handshake. "Maybe honesty? I once saw her promise a doctor that she'd go on a diet. To his face! Then she went outside and bought us extra-long chili cheese dogs from a street vendor. We ate them right in front of the doctor's window *and* waved at him."

"What about her promise?" My mother sounded genuinely shocked, as if she were talking through her hand.

"Well, I reminded her, and she looked at me like I was speaking Greek. Finally she said, 'Oh, that. He won't mind.'"

My grandmother was a pathological breaker of promises. She knew she wouldn't follow any diet just as surely as she knew she'd take the car keys again one day. So, not wanting to waste energy fighting, she made promises. Promises were easier than arguments. As I listened to my mother, I couldn't understand why I was the only one who understood this.

"I don't know how you let her talk you back into boarding school," my mother complained. "Now there's nobody to watch her." That wasn't true. Atse was there, and so was Gloria, who was almost as devoted to my grandmother as Static was. But my mother liked to have something to complain about, and besides, I liked it when she called. Since I had gone back to school, she called every week from her London town house. She updated me on my grandmother's antics from across the Atlantic, as if I weren't talking to my grandmother every night. I wasn't sure why my mother was doing all this. It wasn't like we ever spoke regularly before; why was she suddenly so chummy? When had my mother actually turned into . . . a mother?

Don't get me wrong, I was elated. Her phone calls made me feel special, like I was her confidant. She needed someone to talk to, and I was that someone. We were finally starting to have a real relationship. I just didn't know how it had started. And if I didn't know how she'd started to care about me, how could I stop her from getting bored with me again?

"It wasn't my choice to go away to school," I told her for the millionth time.

At least I didn't think it was. My grandmother didn't ask if I wanted to go back. She never *asked*. She *directed*. She told you what you were going to do, and if you refused . . . well, God help you.

"You think she'll really keep driving?" my mother asked.

"Have you ever known her to do anything someone else told her to?"

My mother sighed deeply. "Will you please talk to her?" she asked. "She listens to you, and I'm just so worried. I need you to do this for me."

And didn't I want my mother to need me?

After we hung up, I sat at my desk, staring at the wall. I heard some guys at the door, which was ajar. One of them opened his coat and revealed a bottle. He pointed down the hall, to his room. The other guys motioned for me to come and then hurried along, anxious to get the party started. I got up to join them, but then I thought about my grandmother at home, alone and bruised.

I sat back down.

I needed to call my grandmother. My mother was counting on me.

"I hear you've been lying to your children again," I said when she finally answered the phone.

She cackled on the other end. "I've been waiting for this call all day. Go ahead. Let's hear it."

" 'Let's hear it'?" I said. There were more guys walking down the hall. I was going to miss the fun again. I sighed. "I'm not the one with anything to tell. I haven't been out joyriding all night long like some people."

"What people? You know people who do that? Now, those are the friends I'd like to make."

"You don't even have a valid driver's license."

"So what?" she said. "What do you want from me, anyway? You want me to promise I won't do it again? Okay, I promise."

"I don't want any of your fake promises, old lady. I don't want to be sitting up here worrying about you all the time. That's what I want. I'll have you know I'm missing a perfectly good drinking party right now because of this."

She groaned. "Matthew, I really wish you'd reexamine your priorities." Then she hung up.

I knew this wouldn't be the last I heard about my grandmother driving, so I got up and went down the hall and played drinking games until I was buzzed and laughing and unable to worry about it anymore. I wasn't in New York. What could I do?

. . . .

A few days later, while I was in science class learning about diffusion, Gloria was once again calling my mother in London. My mother slammed the phone down as I was leaving class. She called my room and sat waiting. The phone rang and rang until I finally answered.

"She's been in an accident!" my mother wailed.

I felt as if someone had kicked me in the gut. "Is she . . . is she okay?"

"She's alive, if that's what you mean. Bruised everywhere, like an overripe banana. Banged her head on the steering wheel. I thought you were going to talk to her!"

"I did!" I said. "I'll talk to her again."

"Does she have to kill herself before you take this seriously? Matthew, I'm counting on you. I could do this myself, but you know how busy I am. If you can't reason with her, then I don't know what I'll do."

I said I would try again, and I called my grandmother.

"Well?" I said.

She was silent.

"Well!" I said, more aggressively than I should have.

"I couldn't remember how to get to the expressway, Matthew. I know there's a bridge involved. I was on the wrong street, and I tried to turn the car around." She sighed loudly. "Three-point turns have never been my specialty. I think I hit the brake when I should have accelerated. Or maybe it was the other way around."

"The other way around . . . !" I gripped the phone harder and squeezed my eyes shut. "You shouldn't be *driving* if you can't re-member which pedal is which!"

"Brake, accelerator—you expect me to remember everything?" she asked. "You're crazy."

I had her put Atse on the phone and told him to hide all the car keys. Then I called my mother back and bragged that I had finally solved the problem. "She won't be driving again anytime soon. I took care of it."

She seemed preoccupied. "Good. Finally. Now I have to go. I'm late. Some friends and I are going to this new club, where instead of tables and chairs you have beds and nightstands. Everyone's going," she said proudly, "and we have the Queen Bed."

I told myself that if she weren't so important, she would have thanked me, or even just sounded the tiniest bit appreciative. Still, at least she knew I could be counted on. We wouldn't have any more problems at home. I'd fixed that—and from all the way in Boston!

Until my grandmother set fire to the kitchen.

She had gotten hungry in the middle of the night and, not wanting to wake Atse or Gloria, decided to make herself some eggs. Unfortunately, she forgot what she was doing shortly after putting the eggs into the skillet. So she went back to bed. Atse and our dog, Static, woke her up when the smoke detectors could not.

"Oh, Matthew, I felt someone licking my face, and I thought it was your grandfather! Imagine my surprise."

The kitchen was engulfed in flames downstairs, smoke everywhere, smoke detectors wailing like air-raid sirens. None of this had surprised my grandmother. But the dog's kisses? That was another story.

She sighed. "It was an old kitchen, you know."

I asked if this was the same kitchen that she had just remodeled, but she had to get off the phone; there was some alarm sounding in the background.

"She can't stay by herself," my mother said the next time we spoke. "Someone needs to be there with her. I vote you."

"Me? Why me?"

"Because," my mother said, as if speaking to a five-year-old, "she *listens* to you."

I was on the phone in the dorm. I tried formulating a response, but I couldn't think of anything. My mother was right—I was the only one who could possibly handle my grandmother.

Still, I wasn't about to give up the new friends I'd made at this school to go back to New York and hang around baby-sitting. I wanted my mother to be happy with me, but I also wanted a life outside the house. "I don't want to leave here. I can't keep going from school to school," I said, hoping my mother wouldn't see the ridiculous irony of my statement. I certainly hadn't cared when I was *trying* to get kicked from school to school.

"Matthew?" My mother paused for a long moment. She wasn't used to this kind of situation—the kind she couldn't walk away from or hang up on. "Please. She *needs* you. I'm very tense right now."

The fight suddenly deflated out of me. My grandmother needed me, and I would go. It was as simple as that. I twisted the phone cord around my finger mutely.

"Unless," my mother said, her tone lightening, "she comes to Boston." When I didn't respond, she barreled on, her voice growing more animated. "Yes. I like that idea. I could get you two a house in Boston. She could bring Atse and Gloria. What do you think? That way you could stay with her and you wouldn't have to move back to New York."

I admitted I was excited at the prospect of staying at school.

"I'll take care of everything," she said. "Oh, I knew I could count on you."

Relieved, I said good-bye to her and caught up with my friends on the way to dinner. I'd have to leave the dorms and the parties and the doubtfully colored drinks—but at least I wouldn't be leaving school.

Only later, at dinner, did I stop in the middle of spaghetti and meatballs, the fork poised halfway between my plate and my mouth, and think it through. If my grandmother could so easily pick up and move with me in Boston, she could just as easily get on a plane and join my mother in London.

.   .   .   .

Ultimately I came around to my mother's idea without reservation. Atse's food was much better than dorm food, after all. But my grandmother had a different take on the situation.

"So much for my independence. All this from some lousy scorched eggs."

I reminded her about the driving, too.

"I hope you realize that you'll be the one driving me around now."

She was trying to get a rise out of me, to see if I'd object to carting her all over town. *Go inside,* I imagined her saying, *and see if they carry Depends undergarments. Extra absorbent.*

But I wasn't going to indulge her. "We can go wherever you want," I said. And if I was busy, Atse could double as my grandmother's chauffeur. We'd arrange something. "It'll be just like *Driving Miss Daisy.* You can be Jessica Tandy, and I can be Morgan Freeman."

"Why do I have to be the old woman?" she asked soberly.

"You *are* the old woman."

"Does that make you a black man?"

. . . .

We moved into a historic town house off the Boston Common in late summer, just before my senior year started. The house was beautiful—four floors decorated by the same designer who did our New York apartment's remodel shortly before my grandfather died. Gloria slept in the bedroom next to my grandmother's, and Atse slept up by me. When school started in September, I resolved to spend time with friends as well as my grandmother. Actually, my grandmother told me to get out of the house more. "Get out. Go be with kids your own age. Go do drugs and be promiscuous or whatever else Morley Safer says you children are doing."

One day, shortly after we'd moved in, we received an invitation to my Uncle James's second wedding. Just after my grandfather's funeral, Cynthia divorced my uncle. She took the house, took the kids, and he'd begun seeing this new woman almost immediately. I had not met his fiancée, but I assumed that she suffered from the same delusions his first wife had. As far as I was concerned, she was worthy of our pity, not our praise. Certainly not the crystal she had registered for at Tiffany's.

"Well, well, well," said my grandmother. "Howard is getting married again."

"No," I corrected. "Your *son* is getting married. Howard was your *husband*."

These little lapses in memory had become more common in the last few months, and my corrections became automatic. I'd stretch out the words for as long as I could, like someone speaking to a foreigner. I thought if I said them slowly, she would magically understand.

A confused expression spread across my grandmother's face. "That's right, he's my son. Not Howard."

I reasoned that at eighty-three years old my grandmother could justifiably forget a name once in a while. But this wasn't "once in a while" anymore. Atse had been working for my grandmother for al-most forty years, but some days she treated him like a stranger. She walked into the kitchen once, where Atse was putting the groceries away, and stopped short. "Excuse me? Who are you, and what are you doing in my kitchen?"

There were even times when my grandmother's own name es-caped her—I saw her signing a check one night, and she held her pen over the signature line, just staring at the paper, baffled. And something else: In the last few months, she had been lost seven times while out on walks, forgetting she now lived in Boston and not in New York City.

I kept chalking up these slips to her change in surroundings and her age. It wasn't until she began inventorying pantry items that I knew that something in her mind must be terribly broken.

"This box has only forty-nine packets, Howard!" My grand-mother waved a box of Sweet'N Low in my face. "Count them your-self if you don't believe me."

"I'm Matthew," I corrected her. I jerked my head away from the red and pink box. "I believe you. So what?"

"So what?" Eyebrows arched, she threw her hands onto her hips. "I'll tell you so what, mister. This box says there are fifty packets!"

She didn't even like Sweet'N Low. Only my grandfather had used them.

"I hope you're all happy." She flung the box down and marched out of the room. I picked it up and noticed that Gloria was at the door. She looked on the verge of tears.

"I think you should call your mother," she said. It was such an alien suggestion, *call your mother,* I thought I'd misheard her. I pic-tured my mother's reaction to this odd piece of news. "I don't know what to tell you, Matthew. Drug her?"

But Gloria was convinced. "She'll know what to do."

I looked at Gloria as if she'd lost her mind. I snorted. "Gloria, you don't call my mother for advice about people and"—I waved my arms around the room—"you know . . . reality. You call her to see if military jackets are in for fall."

Gloria insisted and handed me the cordless phone. "Call your mother."

I shrugged and dialed the number.

My mother breathed a heavy sigh before admitting, "I was afraid this would happen."

I understood immediately that I was about to learn a crucial secret. "What do you mean?" I asked, preparing myself for the worst.

"Matthew, Mom has Alzheimer's," she said carefully.

I almost dropped the phone. "Alzheimer's? How long have you known?" I could feel the bile rising in my throat.

"Before your grandfather died, he told me. She never would have."

"You've known about this for *two years?*"

Silence.

"And your brother knows also, right?"

Silence.

I remembered my grandfather's funeral when my mother and uncle had cornered me and asked me to move back to New York. Now it all made sense. They needed someone to keep an eye on their mother, and they were unwilling to do it themselves.

And my grandmother must have known, too. "That's why she sent me away, isn't it?" I asked. "Cramping her style," I said bitterly. "She made up all that business, didn't she?"

"She didn't want you to see her like this. I wanted to tell you, but she wouldn't let me. She said if you knew the truth, you'd never leave."

"And so you moved her here, anyway. Why?"

She paused. "After the kitchen fire, I flew to New York, and we went to the doctor. They also found evidence of a slight stroke. They weren't sure when, and it was small enough that Mom didn't even know herself it had happened."

My grandmother once nursed a broken wrist for two weeks because she couldn't stand the idea of waiting in a doctor's office. She never complained about aches and pains—or her feelings, for that matter. "So if my life isn't perfect," she once told me, "whose is?"

I was livid. "Didn't you think that *maybe* it would've a good idea to have told me about this first?"

"If I had," my mother said, "you wouldn't have done it. You wouldn't have let her move in with you."

I looked around to make sure I was alone. "Maybe that's because she needs a different kind of care. Like . . . a professional? A real doctor or a nurse!" I was practially hissing at my mother. "Not someone who doesn't know why the *hell* his grandmother looks at him like he's a *stranger*. And why isn't she with you or your brother?"

My mother laughed. "That's an awful idea. You know she hates him. Besides, you've got Gloria and Atse there, and they know all about this."

Now it made sense. *Call your mother.* "Of course they do!" I said. "Everyone in this family knows about everything, even the staff! Except—oh, yeah, me. But I'm the one who's supposed to take care of everything, right?"

And that's when I realized why she made all those calls from London while I was living at boarding school. She was still using me to keep an eye on my grandmother because she didn't want to. It all made sense now. That's why she called only when something was wrong. She was using me. She wanted me to feel appreciated, as if she finally cared, so I'd feel bad enough when she revealed she wanted my grandmother to live with me again. I wouldn't be able to argue—and of course she was right. I hadn't. And I'd played right into her plan.

She started to say something. "Matthew—"

I hung up, fuming.

"They didn't want me." It was my grandmother, suddenly standing behind me.

I spun around, feeling like a kid caught stealing candy. My grandmother moved carefully toward the sofa. "Everyone's too worried about themselves, except for you, Matthew, so you got stuck. But I'll try not to be too much trouble. You won't even know I'm here." She sat down and dug her fingers through a batch of M&M's in a candy dish. "I love the green ones."

It had never been my intention for her to overhear my conversation. I sat down beside her. "I . . ."

My grandmother stopped burrowing through the candy dish and looked up. "Listen, kid, I understand what you're going through. I don't know what the hell happened with them. I did everything everyone told me I was supposed to do: I had the best nannies, sent them to the best schools, made sure they had easy lives. If your grandfather's family hadn't been so goddamn pushy, I'd still have my children, and they wouldn't have been ruined like this."

What could I say to that?

"That's why with you," she said, "I thought, fuck them all. Forget it. I'll raise him my way. And now look at where we are." She chuckled. "They screwed us both this time."

I kept my eyes glued to the floor until I heard my grandmother hiccup.

I turned to her. She didn't have her face in her hands. She wasn't sobbing—that would be too gentle a term. Her chest was heaving, and waves of tears washed through her eyes, down her cheeks. They weren't graceful tears; they were monsters.

"It's okay, Grandma. Really." I was scared. I negotiated my arm around her shoulders awkwardly. Normally she responded to this kind of affection by pushing me away, but then again, normally she didn't cry. This person was not my grandmother. I didn't know who she was.

Suddenly she broke out of my half embrace. She grabbed my shoulders with ferocity, and her eyes, despite the tears, were open wide, staring at me.

"You're not like them. Do you understand? You're like me. Do you understand?"

Tears were sliding down her face, but her expression was so hopeful that I could only say, "I understand." But really, I didn't understand. If her children hadn't turned out like her, who *had* they grown up like? My grandfather? He never would have done this to his mother. In any other circumstances, my grandmother would be the one foisting an unwanted in-law onto an unsuspecting relative.

"It'll be okay if we're together and they can stay the hell away. Right?" She wiped at the tears with the back of her hand. "Right?"

"Yes, Grandma," I said nervously, but she wasn't satisfied.

"Promise me."

"I promise."

She nodded, as if confirming something she'd known all along. We sat together in the room silently, me staring straight ahead, her sniffling beside me. A few minutes later, eyes still moist, she blinked and looked at me. Her eyes were still glistening but her gaze had softened. "Matthew," she said, confused, "when did you come home?"

·   ·   ·   ·

Initially my grandmother refused to attend my uncle's second wedding. Obstinacy had become the clearest way to recognize her rare lucid moments, so I was oddly pleased as I explained that she had to attend. We were in the living room; once again I was watching television with her instead of going out with friends.

"Why should I go?" she asked. "He didn't come to my wedding."

I threw my hands up in the air. "How's it going to look if the mother of the groom boycotts her own son's wedding?"

"Like she's got some sense," she said, and turned up the television.

I wasn't sure if by "she" she meant herself or my uncle's new wife. But arguing was useless; at best, I knew I could ask her again in a few hours and hope she'd forgotten this conversation.

The wedding was to take place Thanksgiving weekend, and just as I hoped, when the time came to make travel plans, my grandmother's initial resolve had disappeared. Suddenly she was thrilled to be traveling. "It's been forever since I went on vacation, you know."

Attending a wedding wasn't really like going on vacation, I thought. She *hated* weddings, but I kept my mouth shut. Her moods were so erratic that I ruled out flying immediately. Driving from Boston to Georgetown wasn't ideal, but much better than enduring an "episode" on an airplane.

I had just loaded our suitcases into the trunk when my grandmother came striding out of the house, still buttoning her coat. I recognized that walk immediately and allowed myself to hope she'd be okay, at least for the weekend.

"You'd better not let my husband catch you out of uniform, Anthony. You know I don't care, but he'll be worried about what every goddamn bum on the street will think."

I smiled patiently at her. "I'm not the chauffeur. I'm your grandson. *Matthew.* Anthony hasn't worked for us in ten years." She blinked at me and stood by the rear car doors. So I opened one, and she climbed in.

A little while later, she called from the backseat, "You're driving too fast, Anthony." I ignored the name, but I slowed down. "You're driving too slow, Anthony." I sighed and sped up. "Did you forget to comb your hair, Anthony?"

We weren't even out of Massachusetts yet.

Thank God we weren't flying. Had we been on a plane, I imagined her screaming out every half hour, afraid that nobody was at the controls since the pilot was sitting beside her.

Hoping that some music would lull her to sleep, I found a Glenn Miller CD and played it. It worked, and the next time I heard from her was on the New Jersey Turnpike.

"Do you remember this song?" she asked. "Our second date. You brought me to the Stork Club, and Miller was playing this song."

I took some deep breaths to steady myself before answering. In the past, whenever there had been a problem, I'd always been able to fix it. But I was helpless now, and I was becoming more convinced that my grandmother needed serious help.

"No, Grandma, your husband brought you to the Stork Club. I wasn't born yet, because I'm your *grandson.*"

My grandmother sat quietly for a while, and the CD restarted.

"Read me the signs," she said.

"What?"

"Read me the signs," she repeated.

I looked at her through the rearview mirror. "Are you kidding?"

Her voice was growing sharper. "You always used to read me the signs."

"When did I ever read you the signs?" I asked, incredulous.

"Whenever we drive through the country!" She leaned forward and pounded the back of my seat. "You always, always read me the signs."

I don't know if it was the music, the highway speeding past, or my grandmother's shrill, hysterical insistence, but my patience burst. For months I had corrected her, I had led her down the right hallways when she went the wrong way, I reminded, I adjusted, I guided, I pulled for her and pushed for her, and I smiled and I spoke softly and I was patient.

But now my knuckles whitened against the steering wheel and venom pumped through my body. The highway was spinning in front of me, so I pulled the car onto the shoulder of the road. I unbuckled my seat belt, switched off the ignition, turned around in the front, and faced my grandmother in the backseat. "I am not your husband, woman!" I shouted, enraged, pounding the seat. "I. Am. Your. Grandson."

I saw my grandmother cringe in confusion and fear, but I couldn't stop. "Your husband read you the signs," I roared, "but he is dead. Dead. DEAD! Now, read the signs yourself!"

I suddenly realized how deranged I must have looked, and I flushed, feeling embarrassed. And then guilty. I turned back around and stared ahead at the road. The cars on the highway sped past us as we sat in the car together, silently. When I was a child, she'd always warned me to watch the things I said. "Once the words are out of your mouth, you can never take them back, and never is a long time." Interesting advice, coming from a woman who possessed no filter and said whatever the hell she wanted.

Finally I turned the ignition back on and continued the drive.

.   .   .   .

After my outburst on the New Jersey Turnpike, my grandmother stayed awake and silent for the rest of the drive, wordlessly spiting me.

When we finally reached my uncle's house, I pulled the car into the circular driveway, hoping he had hired a nurse to watch her. I walked around the car to open the back door. When I offered my grandmother my hand, she smacked it aside. "You rotten kid," she said. She glared and pursed her lips before lifting her brittle hand to slap me. "You rotten, rotten kid," she said, over and over, beating her fist on my chest.

She'd never hit me before, and all I could think was how painless it was. She was too weak to make a real impact. I turned away and walked toward the house. *Walk yourself up to the house, old lady,* I thought. *Better still, walk yourself back to Boston.* I don't know why, but I was furious with her. I knew it wasn't her, at least not the "her" I grew up with. She never would have hit me. Come to think of it, she never would have let me see her this way, either. I just wanted to be left alone.

I heard a thud behind me, like a sack of potatoes slipping off a shelf.

I spun around. My grandmother was lying facedown on the pavement, groaning. I froze. "Shit," I muttered. Weren't old people always breaking their bones over much smaller bumps? I looked around—as if someone else would help me—but I was alone. I rushed over and rolled her onto her back. There was a large cut across her forehead and cheek. Her hands were bleeding, too, and she lay there frightened, clearly in tremendous pain, and it was completely, entirely, utterly my fault.

"I'm scared," she said.

I had never heard my grandmother speak those words. *Get out of my way, you sack of shit*—that I would have expected. I couldn't admit it, but I was scared, too.

.   .   .   .   .

There had been some internal bleeding and a concussion, so after examining her the doctor we called recommended bed rest at my uncle's house. When he said that, I had to laugh. Ironically, this meant that while she was there at the house, where the wedding was to be held, she didn't actually have to attend the event. My mother, who was also there, got a nurse. I avoided speaking with my mother until my uncle confronted me outside my grandmother's bedroom.

"I don't understand how this could've happened," he said. "How could she just fall over?"

"James, she's . . ." My mother paused. She looked at me. "She's, like, eighty, right?"

"Eighty-three," I said.

"Oh," they both said.

"Well. There you have it," my mother said. "People are always falling over when they're that age. And they start needing walkers and wheelchairs. Their reflexes are . . ." She waved her hands, searching for the right word. ". . . weakened."

"She didn't sound weak when I talked to her," my uncle said, looking suspiciously at me.

"Knowing you," my mother said, "it's probably been a year since you last called. I call all the time. She's been going downhill for quite a while."

I looked up, surprised. A year—had it really been that long? I knew that living with someone day after day disguised the slightest changes, but how could my grandmother go from being so vibrant to being so fragile and in only a year?

I left them in the hall and went into my grandmother's room. She was hunched over in the bed, wearing a nightgown and staring at the television. I forced myself to take a good look at her for the first time in a while. I saw that my mother was right. My grandmother wasn't the same woman from last year. I knew she'd been losing weight steadily for months—she had told me as much—but I hadn't noticed this dramatic change until I saw her lying in a bed too big for her tiny body. Skin hung loosely on her small frame. Once a great beauty, and always admired by her friends for retaining her youthful appearance, she now looked every bit her age—and then some. It made me wonder where I'd been. We shared the same house. But had I been that . . . disengaged all this time?

"Grandma, sit up." I reached to adjust the pillows. "You're going to get a hump."

The nurse came in. "I was about to give her something so she can rest."

"Rest?" my grandmother said, looking from the television to the nurse. "What else am I doing?" I could tell she had difficulty focusing: Her speech was slurred, and her head wobbled. The nurse smiled sympathetically—at whom, I don't know—and said she'd return shortly, leaving my grandmother and me alone.

"What're you watching?" I asked.

She didn't answer.

Noticing a thick glob escaping from my grandmother's nose, I handed her a tissue. I wasn't comfortable seeing her like this; she was the most glamorous woman I knew, not some helpless old lady with a runny nose. When she didn't take the tissue, I held it for her, "Blow," I said. She blew her nose weakly and took the tissue in her hands. She tore it into pieces and started to cry.

I crouched down next to her and grasped her shoulders in my hands. "You can't give up."

"I'm all alone," she said, answering the unspoken question: Why?

"You're not alone. I'm here." I grabbed a new tissue, holding it to her nose again, instructing her to blow. I put the bits of discarded tissue into the new one, wrapping them up tightly. "Do you know who I am?" I asked.

She smirked, showing the first real trace of her former self that I'd seen in days. "You're the one who pushed me down and left me for dead." I was speechless, but then she filled the room with her cackling. "Oh, relax, Matthew. You always get so worked up."

I couldn't relax, though. *Wasn't* this my fault? I was the one who'd made a fuss for her to attend. It's not like she wanted to come in the first place. I was the one who'd lost my temper in the car, which caused her to get upset, which caused her to fall. And worst of all, though she routinely forgot most things, *this* she could remember clearly and was already making a joke out of it. I fought the urge to defend myself. I went to the dresser and retrieved a wooden brush.

"I should be mad at you, you know," I said, sitting on the bed. I ran the brush through her thin hair, gently, rhythmically, the way

I'd seen her do it many times before. "You didn't tell me about any of this. No warnings. Nothing."

She tilted her head back, making it easier for me to reach the hairline. "I really hoped I'd be gone by now. Euthanized like an old cat. Nothing too painful. Alas, here we are. You brushing my hair. Me like a rotting jack-o'-lantern." She opened and closed her mouth. "Where the hell *are* my teeth, anyway?"

The door pushed open, revealing my mother and uncle, both wearing smiles so exaggerated that I thought they were stoned.

"Great," my grandmother growled. "Now that the ship of fools is here, we can get the party started."

My uncle ignored the comment. That, or he was off in his own world. I could never be sure with him. "You missed the wedding, Mom."

"And it's not every day you get to see a real live circus," my mother said. "He married into a clan of bearded ladies." Her elbow grazed my uncle's ribs before she clapped her hands together.

It's interesting how things can suddenly click, how you can realize something so obvious, something that you should have known all along. Sitting on the bed, the brush in my hand, I realized that my mother and my uncle had no idea how to act around my grandmother. My mother fidgeted with her dress and jewelry. Hands stuffed in his pockets, my uncle rocked back and forth on his heels. In the absence of any conversation, which my grandfather would have supplied, my mother defaulted into mocking her brother, and my uncle, never a great wit in the first place, pouted and rocked even faster.

As a child, I knew we were different from other families, and I thought it was because of me. I was the extra variable in their equation, so whatever dysfunction existed was my fault. Now I realized I wasn't the one responsible for this terribly awkward moment. This . . . whatever this was, had been here long before me, and it was inextricably linked to my grandmother. Watching them now, I wanted to confess this realization. *We're so sad,* I wanted to say.

Instead I walked to the window as my mother prattled on about the wedding guests.

"And you should have seen the clothes, Mom. Tra-*gic*."

My uncle rocked. "I didn't see anything wrong with them."

Of course this left him wide open for my my mother's retort. "Look at yourself, brother dear. Did you fish that suit out of a Men's Wearhouse?"

I turned to them. Where would we be in a year? I wondered. Or two years? I looked at my grandmother and found myself calculating how much time she had left. She was eighty-three. Her mother had lived until she was eighty-five, so I reasoned that it wouldn't be long before the illness would take over completely. And then what would I do?

My mother, astonishingly, seemed to have read my mind. "Brother dear and I were talking," she said to my grandmother, but her eyes were fixed on me. "It's time for Matthew to start applying for college. Boston has so many colleges."

"Like forty, right?" my uncle said.

My grandmother looked at me. "I'd like for him to go somewhere else. Far away."

The three of them were looking at me now.

"She's right, Mom," my uncle said. "That way you can both stay in Boston."

I hadn't given much serious thought to college. I didn't have any schools in mind yet, and I bristled at being told where to go.

"No," my grandmother said. "I think that I'd like to live with my daughter now. I want Matthew to go far away, to see new things. On his own."

"You haven't thought this through, Mom," my mother said. She glanced back and forth anxiously, between me, her brother, and her mother. "You're tired."

Nodding, my grandmother said, "I am tired. But that doesn't change anything. I'll live with you. Your brother needs to devote himself to his new family now. Yours is already grown up."

I stayed by the window, waiting to see what would happen next. Would my mother bicker? Would my uncle agree? Would anyone consult *me* in deciding my future?

"Do you all understand what I want?" my grandmother said. "I don't want any confusion in case . . . something happens." I sensed that this kind of lucidity wouldn't occur many more times, and from the nature of my grandmother's remark, so did she.

My mother smiled tightly and kissed the top of my grandmother's head. My uncle did the same, but it was clear that he hadn't really understood what had just happened. They both left, and the nurse returned. My grandmother closed her eyes. The nurse signaled for me to leave and went to my grandmother, easing her down to rest.

.   .   .   .

By our last day in Georgetown—barely a week after we arrived—the lucidity my grandmother exhibited up in her room had all but vanished. Her speech was fine, but her thoughts were muddy again. As our bags were packed and loaded into the car, she sat in a chair by the window in her bedroom. This time when I needed to get her down the stairs and settle her in the car for the long ride, I wasn't taking any chances. I stood near her the entire time, and slowly we made our way down the dramatic staircase and out to the car.

"Watch your step," I said. I held my breath at every step she descended. "These bricks are tricky."

"It's a pretty house," she said, and smiled as if she'd never seen it before.

My mother and uncle were standing by the front door when we left. Pulling out of the driveway, I saw that my uncle was the first to go back into the house. My mother stood at the door watching the car until it turned out of sight. I never asked her what she was thinking that day as I drove away. I remember the look on her face, but my mother was still enough of a stranger to me that I couldn't tell what it meant. Defiance? Loss? Maybe she was remembering the days in the strawberry fields as a little girl, my grandmother standing over her, keeping watch. Maybe she was wondering what had happened between them in the years since then.

Hearing some noises from the backseat, I muted the stereo. At first I could barely make out what my grandmother was saying; it sounded like someone talking though a mouthful of marbles. Gradually it became clear. "Read me the signs," she was saying.

We were getting onto an overpass. I looked around until my eyes fell on the first available sign, on the opposite side of the road.

"Wrong way," I said. "It says we're going the wrong way."

100 Percent, Grade-A Hebrews

When it came right down to it, I decided to move to Winter Park, Florida, and attend Rollins College, not because it offered waterskiing as a major but because it pissed my mother off. "Who turns down Harvard?" she said after I rejected their acceptance offer. "But it's your life. Just as long as you take that dog with you."

My mother did not care for dogs, and while she was resigned to the fact that my grandmother would come to live with her, she flatly refused to take Static, too.

I first heard about Rollins through a college fair my senior year. When I learned that my only Jewish friend from boarding school, Dan Abramoff, was planning to go there, I applied and was accepted. So after I put my grandmother and Atse and Gloria on a plane bound for London, I packed my clothes, doped Static up with Benadryl, and hopped into my cobalt blue sports car to drive down from Boston to sunny Florida. At first I lived in a hotel close to campus, but about a week after I arrived, I was on a boat tour through the Winter Park chain of lakes, and I saw where I would live for the next six months.

The tour guide pointed out the house. It looked to be about one floor with at least one wall of floor-to-ceiling windows and sat perched on a small hill above a canal. "That's the Bachelor Pad," he said. "Everyone calls it that. It's smaller than its neighbors, and there's always some big party going on."

"Who lives there?" someone asked.

He squinted at the house. "It gets bought and sold every few years. Actually, looks like there's a For Sale sign on it right now."

I looked at the houses around it and saw he was right. The other houses were large white elephants, built by northern WASPs in the early 1900s before people had started moving to Palm Beach for the winter. Winter Park is the Old Money equivalent to a first wife.

It wasn't hard to get more information about the house. "Oh, yeah, the Bachelor Pad," said Kate, the upperclassman who'd been assigned to mentor me. "I've been to parties there. It's for sale again?" Since I still didn't know my way around, I asked her to drive me over to the house, and I copied down the real estate agent's number. A few days later, the agent showed me around, and I called my mother from the backyard.

"That's fine," she said, "do what you want. You have to live somewhere." I hadn't spoken to my mother since arriving in sunny Florida, and I wanted to ask about my grandmother, but she cut me off. "Matthew, I have to go now. There's a benefit at the Tate Modern. I'm late."

"I'll take it," I told the Realtor, and Static and I moved in later that month. It was September, and I was settling into the first semester of classes.

Because it fulfilled a general-education elective at Rollins, Dan and I signed up for the same Tuesday-morning class, Jewish Life and Thought. Dan's family was no more religious than my own, and although we couldn't know it from the course description, we were about to be exposed to a different view of Judaism than the ones held by our respective families: through the lens of a college professor who had converted to Judaism from Christianity.

Coming to his new religion late in life—he was probably in his sixties—Dr. Heidelberg embraced Judaism with a special kind of ferocity only converts can own. He fervently believed that it was his job to convert each one of his students—even his Jewish students—to Judaism, to help them see the light as he had. And while each class began differently—with discussion of a different aspect of Jewish life, either culturally or theologically—they all ended the same way: Dr. Heidelberg preaching against the evil of secular ways.

During a class discussion about keeping kosher and its theological implications, a bouncy blond sorority girl from Texas raised her hand. "Dr. Heidelberg, why can't you mix meat and dairy?" I thought it was a valid question. I was having trouble wrapping my mind around this, too: How did the biblical commandment not to boil a kid in the milk of its mother mean "Thou shalt not mix ice cream and steak"? It was especially troubling because this commandment applied to all meat, even meat that didn't produce milk. I didn't get it.

Dr. Heidelberg took his pen and found the sorority girl's name in the leather book he carried with him. In the beginning of the term, he had asked us all to share our religious affiliations, and then he cataloged that information in his book. Whenever anyone asked a question, he went back to the list. Clearly, their ignorance was a fault in their listed religion.

"Ah." He found her name. "Anne, I see that you're Baptist, so I know that you can't hope to understand this. Let's hear it explained by one of our Jewish students."

He took his pen and ran down the page until he found a victim.

"Dan Abramoff." He looked up. "Tell us please, why can't a grilled chicken with cheese be kosher?"

I gave Dan a sideways look, curious to hear his answer—and mostly relieved that it wasn't me whom Dr. Heidelberg had called upon to stand in for our entire religion. Dan scratched his head and finally admitted, "I have no idea why. One of my favorite home-cooked meals is my mom's chicken lasagna."

This was the wrong thing for Dan to say. Dr. Heidelberg almost choked, then launched into a thirty-minute lecture on how Judaism was falling through the cracks because of bad parents—which we had learned the previous week was also the reason Christianity was falling through the cracks—and how much work *he,* Dr. Heidelberg, had done to become a Jew and how people who were Jewish by birth were just throwing away their birthright over a pan of chicken lasagna. "And what," he said, stopping to catch his breath, "do you all think of *that*?"

The class was silent. We all looked nervously at each other. There were no more questions for the rest of class that day.

It wasn't until after class that I realized that the one subject the lecture *hadn't* addressed was Anne's original question. But the experience had left us all so raw that even the non-Jews momentarily gave up combining meat with dairy. After class Anne asked Dan, "Are all Jewish people like Dr. Heidelberg?" Dan scratched his head and admitted that he didn't know the answer to that question, either.

I was particularly moved by Heidelberg's assertion that part of my Jewish ignorance was my parents' fault, as it meant I could blame my mother, even though she wasn't the one who'd raised me. I decided that day to start keeping kosher as best as I could—and then I would call my mother and rub it in her face. I almost laughed as I imagined her introducing me as her Orthodox son. She had routinely rejected tradition and probably couldn't even spell "Hanukkah."

Later that afternoon I was standing at the counter of my favorite Italian hole-in-the-wall eatery, maybe ten minutes from the Bachelor Pad, the one owned by a Vietnamese lady with black teeth, when I ordered my first kosher meal: chicken parm without the parm.

"You want no parm?" she asked in heavily accented English. I said that that was exactly what I wanted, and she shrugged, then turned to scream something in Vietnamese in the general direction of the kitchen. This was a rather informal establishment, and she preferred not to write down the orders on paper for the cook.

After she took my order, though, I realized something else that even my secular upbringing had taught me. Kosher meat needs to be slaughtered in a certain way, and it's only kosher if it came from a kosher butcher, a *shochet*. I never doubted the cleanliness of the chickens that Ho Chi Minh kept in the alley behind the restaurant, but I hardly believed she doubled as both restaurateur and *shochet*. So I reminded myself that dropping the cheese was a start. Baby steps. It was still something I could rub in my mother's face later on.

You're powerless to stop God, I imagined myself telling her, like some Jewish martyr. *He gave us the commandments, and I have to keep them. You can go to hell if you want, but I'll be one of the righteous.*

I wouldn't know the first thing about hell or being righteous, but these sounded like the things a good Jewish boy should say to his sinning mother, and it made me smile.

I did not explain any of this to Ho Chi Minh. I knew she wasn't going to proselytize me into having cheese with my chicken. "We still charge you full price," she said when she brought it out. "Then we add some for more extra time."

What extra time? I might have put up a fight, but in the book on Judaism I had bought for Dr. Heidelberg's class, I'd read that kosher items were usually more expensive—with no explanation why—and so I scowled and let this go. If I couldn't have truly kosher chicken this meal, at least I could start paying for it. Years later, when I started eating only egg whites, I would have that same confusion. It may be less food to cook, but there is always an additional charge for pain and laziness.

That afternoon I called my mother and told her about going kosher. I tried to keep the glee out of my voice, but she laughed and said, "Oh, God, why would you do that?" I imagined her sitting around her London town house nibbling a shrimp cocktail. "That class has you brainwashed? You want to be Jewish all of a sudden?"

"I *am* Jewish," I said.

"What a drag. Now you'll have to find a nice Jewish girl to marry. Have some nice Jewish *babies* with fat thighs and bad noses. Yuck."

Conversations like these made me uncomfortable. If she was against my marrying a Jewish woman, I worried what she'd say if I ever told her I was gay.

"Well, we'll see," I said, changing the subject. "So how's Grandma doing?"

"Fine," my mother said, "no thanks to you. I'm the one who has to look after her, you know. It's not right. Isn't there something in your Bible that says you're supposed to honor me or something?"

I wondered whether you still had to honor your parents if they'd abandoned you when you were a baby, but I didn't say that. When I was younger, I didn't know how to verbalize any of the questions I had about her giving me up. As a nineteen-year-old, I felt as if too much time had passed for us to have that conversation in any meaningful way—so we just talked about other things most of the time.

Or as I did today, I preached.

.　.　.　.

I fit into Rollins well, since those in its population were just like the people I'd known at school in New England. As the first semester went on, Anne and I spent more and more time together outside class, talking about Heidelberg and Judaism; it was Anne who sat with me as I did research in our school's library, so I would have more clues as to what this religion was all about. My friendship with Anne was different from any other female friendship I'd ever had. She was pretty, but there was no sexual tension. She was smart, but there was no competition. There were no expectations, and when I was with her, I felt free to be myself, not the person I felt someone wanted or expected me to be.

Sometimes, late after a night of studying in the library, we'd walk around campus and talk. During one of these conversations, I first admitted out loud to being gay. I didn't feel I had much choice, since she'd asked me point-blank, "Matt, are you gay?"

What was I supposed to say? I was shocked by the bluntness of the question, but obviously she had sensed something. I realized that if I was going to come out of the closet, I should do it soon. Otherwise people would keep assuming I was straight, and that was turning into a complicated pain.

So I looked up from my books and faced Anne's curious gaze for a second before sheepishly nodding. "Yes," I said. I prayed this wouldn't affect our friendship.

"Good," she said, and laughed. "Now that's out of the way. There's this other boy who's in my Buddhism class, and I think you'd get along really well." And as she began telling me about this other guy, I couldn't help but think, *I'm free. I don't have to lie anymore.*

But then she brought me back to reality. "Does Dan know?"

Damn.

"No," I admitted. "I've never told him."

"Why?"

"I don't know that I was really sure myself before I got here. I have to tell him, I know, but I haven't figured out how yet."

She put her hand on mine. "Well, I think it's great, and I love you for you. If you need any help telling Dan, let me know. He has a big crush on me, and he'll do whatever I tell him to. No biggie."

"One step at a time," I said. "I need to work up to telling Dan. I'll tell him soon, though."

She nodded, and we went back to studying.

. . . .

As the semester continued, after every fact that I committed to memory, I called my mother to criticize her. "What are you doing shopping on the Sabbath? Don't you know that it's a sin to do work?"

"Since when is shopping work?" she asked. "Show me where it says that. Show me."

She hung up the phone when I offered to.

Two weeks later I learned that using the phone on the Sabbath was also technically a sin. In fact, I did so much reading that when called upon in class to explain deep theological questions like why the Jewish days started at sundown instead of sunrise, I earned a reputation as a fully knowledgeable and, since I'd started keeping my version of kosher, observant Jew. My understanding was based on rudimentary, vigorously canned sources such as *The Complete Idiot's Guide to Understanding Judaism* and *Kosher Sex.* But these were details that I kept to myself.

And Anne could always be counted on to keep Dr. Heidelberg on his toes. She asked questions the rest of us didn't have the courage to vocalize.

"Dr. Heidelberg, why do you need a ritual circumcision to convert when you're already circumcised?"

As always, it was a valid question. If someone had already been marked by a good surgeon, what was the point of being poked with another scalpel? Besides, this seemed like the type of thing that was best to do to babies or masochists, people who either wouldn't remember the event or didn't mind suffering. So maybe Dr. Heidelberg enjoyed pain?

"Because this is something that you love so much you can't imagine not being a part of it. The ritual *proves* your devotion. I would have walked over hot coals to become Jewish. How many people can really say that about their religion?"

"I couldn't," Anne admitted.

Dr. Heidelberg nodded proudly. "I'd never felt that kind of acceptance before I found Judaism," he said.

I'm not sure if it was his intention, but suddenly I felt horribly inadequate. I had been born with this wonderful gift—Judaism. Why hadn't I ever taken advantage of it on my own? As Dr. Heidelberg prattled on, discussing his close relationship with his rabbi, the rest of the class looked around the room. Who is this man? we wondered. Someone hired by our parents to make us feel guilty? My inbred sarcasm kicked in, and I shot Anne a look, hoping that this was something I could parlay into a joke later on, similar to cracking on Dr. Heidelberg's patchy sideburns or his Birkenstocks that were held together with rubber bands. But she was clearly entranced, which only made me feel worse.

I told Dan Abramoff about my guilt later that night at the Bachelor Pad. He admitted that he was feeling the same way. "At least you keep kosher," he said. "I can't stop eating bacon cheeseburgers for breakfast." We both sat silently, stewing in our shame. Then Dan looked up and smiled. "Hey, you've been spending a lot of time with Anne lately." He nudged me. "Anything going on there?"

I wanted to tell him the truth, but I couldn't form the words. So I changed the subject. I still didn't know how to reconcile my old life with whatever new life I would have at Rollins as . . . well, as a bona fide practicing homosexual. Dan was my best friend at Rollins, but he had also come with me from my old life at boarding school. What if he freaked out and told someone, and they told someone else? Before long, everyone from Boston would know. I wasn't ready for that yet.

"Let's call some people," I said, jumping up. "I haven't had a party yet, and that's what this place is famous for. I don't want to disappoint the neighbors."

So we started making calls. Over the next few hours, people trickled in, and Static walked around sniffing, enjoying the attention from new strangers. It seemed as if every guest brought beer. Sometime into the evening, Dan nudged me and pointed—Anne had arrived with some of her sorority sisters. Even from across the room, I could tell that her eyes were red. She looked like she'd been playing drinking games back at the sorority house. As they focused on me, her eyes grew wide, and she ran from her friends over to where Dan and I were standing. "Matt, I called my mother!" she said. "And I told her. I said, 'I know the truth, Mom.'"

"What truth?" I thought maybe she was talking about the truth of my sexuality. Had she and her mother spoken about me? I looked to Dan, afraid that Anne was about to blurt out my secret.

"That we're Jewish!" she said. "We're really just a bunch of Jews in Baptist clothing! With a last name like Singer, can we be anything else?"

I laughed, relieved. "I have no idea," I said. "What did she say?"

"She agreed! My father wasn't too convinced, but my mom and I definitely know the truth. We are one hundred percent, grade-A Hebrews!"

This only served to reinforce my growing suspicion that Dr. Heidelberg's class and my new friendship with Anne were both signs. I was supposed to start taking my religion more seriously, too. I was supposed to call my mother right this second and yell at her for discouraging me against learning anything about Judaism. After a couple of drinks, I went into my bedroom and reached for my phone, forgetting that it was only 7:00 A.M. in London.

When she picked up, I launched into a speech. "I just wanted to let you know that I don't appreciate the way you're always knocking what I want to do. If you were a little more religious, we would probably have a good rabbi, and then I wouldn't want to walk on hot coals right now."

There was a long silence. "Someone's been nipping at his Jewish wine again," said my mother. I heard a yawn. "Are you having a party? What's all that noise?"

"Never mind that. One day you're going to see that I'm trying to save your soul."

"Then I guess I should be thanking you," she said through another yawn.

I sighed. "A little more gratitude would be nice."

"Paying your tuition so you can wake me up and tell me I'm going to hell isn't enough? Now I have to thank you for the pleasure of these conversations? I'm going back to bed, Matthew. Call me later so I can make sure I don't have to call a Jewish undertaker to scrape you off the curb."

Jews needed their own undertakers? I hadn't gotten there yet in my amateur education. For someone so untutored in the ways of Judaism, my mother always had something appropriate to say nevertheless.

I went back out to the party and found Anne scratching Static's ears. "Matt, I love your dog!" she said. "I don't know why *you* don't love him more."

I often complained about Static's lack of affection toward me, but I still loved him. I looked down at him now, nuzzling himself up on Anne's jeans. He always did like girls best. "I do love him," I said. "He just doesn't love me back. You know, he's my grandmother's dog. I only have him because my mother would have sold him to a wallet factory."

Static trotted off and returned with his favorite toy, the rubber duck my grandmother gave him when he was a puppy. He dropped the toy in Anne's hand. "If I even get within a foot of that duck, he growls at me!" I said. I had long since accepted Static's quiet animosity toward me. Now it was just good for a joke.

She thanked him for the duck and put it back in his mouth. "I think it's sweet that you're taking care of your grandma's dog."

"He was supposed to be Matt's dog," said Dan, grinning and holding up a bottle to Anne. "His grandma tricked the dog into liking her best."

She laughed. "Did that really happen?" she asked me. I had to admit that it did.

Thinking about my grandmother in the middle of my crowded living room suddenly made me miss her more. My mother had said she was doing fine in London, but I wondered how true that was. I decided that when I called my mother later so she would know I was still alive, I would talk to Atse or Gloria, too, and get the real truth.

The morning after the party, the house was a wreck. I side-stepped cans and bottles on my way to the kitchen to make some coffee. While the coffee was brewing, I picked up the cordless phone and dialed the landline at my mother's town house instead of her cell; I wanted to intercept one of the servants and ask for Atse first—but he answered the phone himself.

"Atse!" I said.

"Look who it is! It's the rabbi. Your mother's told us all about you. I've been waiting for you to call and save my soul, too."

"Maybe I will. I'll have more luck with you, probably. But hey, I wanted to talk to you. Tell me how Grandma's doing. Mom won't give me a real answer."

"No?"

"You know how she is. She complains about having to watch her and never really tells me what's going on."

Atse was silent for a moment. "She's told you about the hospital, though, right?"

"What hospital?" I asked. My hangover started pounding hard. I reached for my coffee.

"The Alzheimer's hospital where your grandmother is staying."

When I didn't answer, he sighed and went on. My grandmother's condition had deteriorated to the point where her doctors recommended that she live in a special facility for Alzheimer's patients in Switzerland.

"How long ago was that?" I asked.

"Maybe three or four weeks? I can't believe that your mother didn't tell you."

But when I called my mother later, full of indignation and ready to yell, she said, "What was I going to do? If I told you, you would have wanted to leave school and come here. And what would that have solved? You're not here, so just let me handle it. That's the plan, right? I know I didn't ask for any of this!"

She did have a point. There was still another month left in the semester. I couldn't leave school and accept incompletes for all my grades. Wasn't that one of the main reasons for my coming out on my own, to have my own life?

"Okay," I said. "So what happens next? When does she come home?"

Pause. "She doesn't. She's going to stay there."

"What do you mean?" I shouted into the phone. "Why?"

"Matthew, she doesn't know any of us anymore. She needs full-time care with doctors and nurses, and it's too hard having her around here. I can't give up my own life anymore taking care of her. I still go and visit her."

"What are you talking about?" I said. "You sent her about as far away as you could. Switzerland! She might as well be in Japan for all the visits she's going to get. And when did you give up anything to take care of her? I'm the one who took care of her. You were never around."

"I don't intend to get into this now. I need to go."

I wasn't ready to stop. "No, I'm not—"

She hung up.

·   ·   ·   ·   ·

In the weeks that followed, the only relief from thinking I was to blame for my grandmother's situation was studying. I was more interested in Heidelberg's class than in any of my others, so I read all the textbooks, even the sections that weren't assigned. Through reading the Bible and commentaries on the Bible, I saw that not everything Heidelberg said was true. There were some commandments that weren't practiced by even observant Jews, and that led me to wonder: If some laws were ignored, then why weren't others? Like, say, the ones relating to homosexuality. Some denominations of Judaism were tolerant; others still wanted to stone the gays. And then there were the multiple interpretations of the Bible that confused me, too.

As we reviewed for the final, talking about the importance of the Sabbath, I raised my hand.

"Dr. Heidelberg, I don't understand how people can pick and choose what to follow. If people aren't supposed to do anything on the Sabbath but relax, then why have timers in their homes to turn the lights on and off? If they can't do it themselves, then why is it okay to have a machine do it?"

He nodded. "It's a good question, but there are a lot of things you have to do because you have faith that they're the right thing to do."

This was exactly the kind of answer I did not want to hear. "Getting a timer is the right thing to do?" I asked. "What am I having faith in? Electricity?"

"You have faith in the commandment. It's a commandment to keep the Sabbath."

"I understand that, but how can anyone tell you how to keep it? What's work to you might not be work to me."

He tried to counter this but couldn't adequately explain himself. He said something about the Bible's needing commentary and explanations and how most people couldn't understand its veracity, but nobody was having that.

"If one person can interpret it one way," said Anne, "then someone else could interpret it another way."

"And different levels of observation have multiple interpretations," said Dan.

"But they're not *real* Jews," Dr. Heidelberg sputtered—and that's where he lost us. It was all well and good for him to explain why *he* did things and even to tell us that we weren't taking advantage of our birthright. But to tell us that we weren't real Jews because we had a different interpretation from his? That wasn't going to fly.

Class ended around lunchtime, and I walked over to the Italian restaurant alone. When Ho Chi Minh saw me, she showed me her black-toothed grin.

"Hello again," I said.

"You want your chicken parm no parm?"

"Yes, please," I said. Then, as she turned around to scream the order in Vietnamese, "No, wait. Leave it on this time. Let's see what happens."

. . . .

When I got home from lunch, my answering machine was blinking. None of my friends from school had my home phone number—everyone used cell phones—and I was surprised to hear that the caller was my mother's first husband. "Hi, Matt, it's Tyler. Give me a call back?" Tyler called about once a week on Sundays, because I had no classes then, just to check in. It was strange for him to call on a Tuesday. I called him right back.

When he answered the phone, his voice sounded hollow. I asked, "What's wrong? You don't sound so good. Do you have a cold?"

"Why weren't you there?" he asked. "Of all people—you should have been there."

"What are you talking about?" I started to panic.

"The funeral," he said. "Why weren't you—"

Huh? "Who died? Mom?" I asked. I hadn't heard from her in about a week, and this would explain why.

"Matthew, what are you talking about? You missed your grand-mother's funeral."

I couldn't breathe.

I sat down. I stared at the phone. It had almost dropped from my hands. I heard Tyler calling my name. "Matthew? Hello?"

"Are you sure?" I asked. "You're sure she's gone?"

"Wait," he said, his voice growing louder, "you didn't know?"

"No, I didn't know," I mumbled. "Nobody told me."

"But your mother. She didn't call you? I spoke to her at the funeral today."

"Well, what did she say?"

"She said you couldn't come. That you were busy with school."

"She lied to you," I said, clutching the phone. "She never called me."

"I've known your mother for thirty years," he said. "I can't believe . . ." He paused. "Maybe she had Bridget call?" Bridget was my mother's secretary in London.

"Maybe she's a lying bitch!" I said, and hung up. I stood in the kitchen and gripped the counter. I tried to make sense of what had happened. My grandmother was gone. My grandmother was gone, and no one had told me. I didn't know what to feel. She was eighty-five. I'd known she wouldn't be around for much longer, and hadn't I come down here to Florida to escape watching her die slowly? But still, she was really gone now. So was my grandfather. Who was left? My mother?

My mother! How could she do this? How could she not tell me?

And if she told Tyler that I was too busy to come to the funeral, she'd told other people as well. But I wasn't too busy. What was I doing that was so important? Eating chicken parm without the parm? I would have come. How did she die? I wondered. Not around her family. She was in that expensive Swiss hospital. She had died alone.

I stood there in my kitchen, thinking of all this, repeating these questions in my head, mixing myself a cocktail of grief and fury. As nauseous as I felt, I knew had to call my mother. This wasn't going to be a conversation like any we'd had before, either. I cradled the phone for a long time before I could bring myself to punch the numbers.

"Hello?" she said, her voice full of sleep. I checked the time and figured it was past one in the morning in London.

"Hello?" she said again. I worked up the words to respond. What could I even say?

"Mother," I said.

"Oh, Matthew. What now? What time is it? Jesus!"

"Why didn't you tell me?" I asked. I was shaking, and my voice was pure aggression.

I could hear her breathing on the other end. I waited for her usual cat-and-mouse routine. *Tell you what?* she'd say, and then I'd have to tease it out of her, losing all my energy in the process. But she didn't. "I don't know," she said, and there was only sadness and maybe some loneliness in her tone. "I just don't know. You should have been here, I know. Okay? I know it. You had more right than anyone else, but I couldn't call you. I don't know why. I tried, I swear, but I didn't know what to say."

I thought she meant that she didn't know how to tell me the news, which I understood. There wouldn't have been any easy way to say it, but that didn't change the fact that she should have. My mother was crying by this point. I reminded myself that my grandmother had been gone mentally for a long time.

I felt my anger begin to melt as my mother sobbed. "Please don't hate me," she gasped. "I didn't know what to do. I wanted one day where I didn't have to share her."

"Share her? What are you talking about?"

"You were her favorite, Matthew. Everyone knew it. Everyone," she snapped at me. "And you could never do anything wrong in her eyes. I wanted one day when I could be the good child, when I didn't have to compete for approval."

I couldn't speak immediately, and when I finally did, the words were tentative. Surely I'd misunderstood something. "Are you telling me you didn't call me and tell me my grandmother had died because I'm competition?" I imagined the funeral I'd missed: my uncle rocking next to my grandmother's casket while my mother schmoozed with guests.

"You don't understand," she said.

"What don't I understand? You're telling me you're unhappy because you think she loved me more? Well, goddamn, maybe that's because she did! And can you blame her? What did you ever do to deserve her approval or love? Hell, you shipped her off to live with me when you knew she had Alzheimer's, and then you stuck her in a hospital so you wouldn't have to see her! You're a real model child."

"You are just like her! The two of you never tried to think of how hard all this was for me," she said.

"Mother, what is the matter with you? You go through life being as selfish as you can, and now you're surprised when people don't cut you a break?"

"I'm busy," she said. "I'm very busy."

"Doing what?" I shouted. "You don't do *anything*! You never have!"

"I don't think you should talk to me like that," she said. "I'm your mother."

I groaned. "No. No, you're not. You never were. You're not a mother. You weren't even a daughter."

She didn't say anything.

I tried to catch my breath. "I can't do this anymore," I said at last. "I can't continue like this, wondering why you are the way you are, waiting for you to wake up and see me for the first time, waiting for you to think of me as more than someone else on the payroll."

She still said nothing.

"I'm leaving. You can keep this house, Mother," I said. "I'm leaving tonight." I said this hoping she would begin to understand the damage she'd done—now and in the past. At the very least, maybe she would just *tell* me she understood, because it's what I wanted to hear. I don't know if that would have changed anything, but it didn't matter, because that's not what she did.

"And where will you go?" she asked, her voice stronger and dry now, all traces of sadness extinguished. "Who's going to pay your bills?" she said, stifling a laugh. "Or will you get a job to pay for that nice house and your nice car? Face it, Matthew, you need me. Without me what are you? There's no money for you right now. You won't see a penny from your trust fund until you're forty."

"I don't need you!" I shouted. "I don't need your money. I can get a job just like anyone else can."

Then, as if my life didn't already resemble a story line from a movie of the week based on a Barbara Taylor Bradford book, my mother let out a long, theatrical laugh.

"What job? You can't do anything! You can go if you want, but you'll be back. You'll come crawling back to me like everyone else does. I'll be here waiting when you do."

"You're wrong," I replied. "I don't need you. Now I don't even want you."

I hung up.

. . . .

It was beginning to storm outside, and raindrops slapped against the floor-to-ceiling windows in the living room, the ones that had first attracted me to this house. I put my palm against the window, feeling the chill of the glass, and breathed in deeply. "What am I going to do now?" I said out loud. But nobody was there to answer. Leaning forward, I put my forehead against the glass and thought of my grandmother. Can she see me? I wondered. What would she tell me to do?

I heard whimpering behind me, and I turned to see Static asleep on his bed, his eyes and paws twitching. He was all that was left of my grandparents. I walked to his bed and stood over him, watching him. They say that when dogs are asleep and moving their eyes and paws, they're dreaming. I couldn't imagine what he was dreaming of, but listening to his quiet whimpering, I wondered if he could hear someone banging a remote control against a sofa somewhere, yelling at the damn static.

Can I Call You Daddy?

"What am I going to do now?" I asked Dan.

"Why don't you stay here?" he said. Dan lived in a five-bedroom house close to Rollins with four other guys. They each had their own bedroom and bathroom and paid around five hundred dollars apiece. For the first time in my life, I had to figure out if this was something I could afford. "Derek is graduating early, and we'll need someone to take his place. It's only a couple of weeks from now. Nobody's going to mind if you and Static crash on the couch until then. That'll give you a chance to figure out . . ." He paused awkwardly. "You know, the money. With rent, cable, and utilities, it's like seven hundred."

"Money," I said absently. Making money would be my biggest problem. I had no real concept of how that was done. "What am I going to do?" I repeated.

"Sell your car?" he suggested.

It was a joke, but I realized he was right. My three-year-old Audi, a birthday present from my grandmother for my sixteenth birthday, would bring me enough profit to live on for a while—and even get a new, cheaper car. I marveled at how quickly I had started thinking about my life on a budget.

"Anyway," Dan said, "consider getting a job before you do anything drastic." He reminded me that there were job postings on the bulletin board in the religious department. I left Static with him and drove over to campus, where I found an ad from the Orlando

Jewish Community Center. Their youth department was hiring staff for an after-school program. The sign said they paid ten dollars an hour. So I drove over to the community center, filled out an application, and left my cell-phone number, hoping they'd call before my mother shut it off. *He can pay for his own phone now,* I imagined her saying. And then thinking of her made the fury rise up in my chest again, so I closed my eyes and focused on the weather.

In the meantime I still had money saved from the monthly allowance my mother had provided until then. It could propel me through the next couple of months, after which, if I didn't have a job, I'd have to seriously think about selling my Audi—which, aside from Static, was one of the last concrete reminders I had of my grandmother. But a few days later, Janet, the head of the Jewish Community Center's youth department, called to offer me a job.

"Now, you applied to assist the fifth-grade teacher," she said, and I heard her shuffling papers over the phone, "but we've had another position open up, and I'm wondering if you'd like that more."

"What is it?" I asked, eager for whatever she had to offer. I just wanted to start working.

"Teaching our little darlings, the kindergartners."

The what? I wondered if Janet might have had my application confused with someone else's. Couldn't she see that I had no experience with young children? She was calling me out of error, I thought. The real candidate, someone with several years of teaching experience, someone who had studied education and actually thrived on interacting with children—that person was going to end up scooping ice cream at Häagen-Dazs if I accepted his or her job. I had applied to assist the fifth-grade teacher because I thought that fifth-graders could be reasoned with. What do you say to a rowdy five-year-old? I sure as hell didn't know. The last thing I wanted was for a student to approach me twenty years later and blame me for his nervous twitch or for the failure of every relationship since the sandbox. "If that's the case," I would have to explain, "we should actually blame my mother. She's responsible for *my* nervous twitch and all of *my* failed relationships."

"Well?" Janet asked, snapping me back from my daydream.

I was sure I'd regret it later, but I did need a job, and if they gave me enough hours, I might not have to sell my car after all. "Okay. When can I start?"

"Tomorrow," she said. "And since you'll be teaching, you'll make twelve dollars an hour."

Twelve dollars an hour! I was so ecstatic that I almost hooted out loud.

. . . .

Teaching at this particular after-school program, an educational-enrichment series, was a transient position. During my first week, three teachers quit for the opportunity to travel cross-country as groupies for the band Matchbox Twenty. I, on the other hand, had no interest in pop rock and decided that a classroom full of slaves to get me endless refills of grape juice and Rice Krispies Treats would be more rewarding.

On my first day as Mr. Matt, a Friday afternoon in early December, I met Parker.

As he stood looking at me from the doorjamb, I caught sight of his kinky Jewish hair before I saw the dirty clothes. At first he didn't want to come into the classroom—I was a stranger—but gradually he moved closer to where two girls sat stacking dominoes. His clothes needed to be washed, I thought, but aside from that he wasn't very different from the other students. Then he jumped on the stack of dominoes, and I realized Parker would be a handful.

Standing there watching him dance all over the girls' dominoes, I had a sudden sensation of déjà vu. Didn't I do something like that once? Or something worse? I wasn't sure how to correct his behavior, but I couldn't focus on that now. I had been told to walk my students down to the auditorium for a mock Shabbat service conducted by the Judaica specialist, Marcy. So I had the kids form a line and march down to the auditorium, where I told them to sit in a circle and hum.

They all looked at me, waiting for further instruction. So I started humming one of the two Jewish songs I knew, "Hanukkah O Hanukkah," waiting for Marcy to arrive.

After five renditions of the Hanukkah song, I asked another teacher, a friendly young African-American woman named Keo, where this Marcy was.

She laughed. "Oh, she's on Jewish Standard Time."

"What's that?" I asked.

"That's where she gets to be somewhere between fifteen and thirty minutes late for everything and nobody bothers to ask her where she's been. It's a little cushion. Hispanics and black people have something like it, too."

"Really?" I considered this as my students kept humming. "I've been Jewish for almost twenty years, and nobody has ever told me that I could use my status as an excuse for being late." If I'd known that, maybe I wouldn't have been habitually early for everything.

I turned to the other Jewish song I knew, "The Dreidel Song," and started teaching it to my students, but it was clear they were growing restless. Most of the class made an effort, but Parker stood up with an angry face. "I'm not doing it anymore!" he shouted.

Apparently I hadn't spent any serious time thinking about my own experience as a child, because until that point it had never occurred to me that children this young could have such strong opinions. Truthfully—my own experiences aside—I wasn't interested in changing my perception. The other teachers, noticing Parker's behavior, watched me sympathetically. Parker marched across the floor and ducked behind the curtain of the auditorium stage, leaving me to sit and wonder, *Wait, can he even do that? I'm the teacher!*

I saw Parker's face poke out behind the curtain, mocking my authority.

"Mr. Matt, it's not fair how Parker gets to sit out of Shabbat," a little girl wearing a pink ribbon complained. "I want to sit out, too."

"So do I, pumpkin," I said, "but if we all didn't do what we're supposed to, then we'd have anarchy."

"What's a *anrocky?*" she asked.

"The word is *anarchy,* sweetheart, and it's what we're about to have if Parker doesn't get his little buns back over here."

"I think he's the main reason the other teachers left," Keo whispered. "He even drives off teachers from other grades; people would rather be unemployed than work anywhere near him." She began to laugh and said, "Good luck."

"He's the reason they couldn't find a teacher for this class, isn't he?" I asked. Janet had duped me. *These Jewish people are clever,* I thought.

She shook her head and apologized.

I didn't need apologies, I thought. I needed someone to call his mother and let her come and threaten to tell his father like any good mother on television would do.

I asked Keo to keep an eye on my students while I went after Parker, trying to figure out how to herd him back to the class. He sat against a wall behind the curtain, staring at the floor. I walked up to him and asked in the most sympathetic tone I could muster, "What's your problem, little boy? Do you want me to get in trouble?"

He waved me off with a gesture of finality, like a boy twice his age. "I just need some time alone," he said.

"Why?"

"Because I have a *migraine.*" He pointed to his temples.

I stood over him wondering if I should do something more. Should I threaten him? Yell? Remembering that none of those tactics worked on me as a child, and lacking anything more profound to say, I opted to do nothing.

"Okay, if you need anything, I'll be over there." I pointed to the rest of the group, who were banging their fists on the floor, screaming, "I hate Shabbat!"

"See what you're missing?" I said.

When Marcy finally arrived, toting an elementary-aged son and a toddler daughter, she apologized. "Sorry, everyone," she sighed into the microphone. "I had to drive my other daughter to work, and little Zev has a rash."

Normally every Friday night at sundown, the Sabbath candles are lit and the blessings are said over challah and wine. I'm not exactly sure why the Jewish Community Center felt they needed a mock Shabbat for the kids. After all, the children of observant families would do it later for real, and the children of nonobservant families wouldn't miss having a Shabbat. Anyway, we were all supposed to sing traditional Hebrew songs, do some coloring, and then light the candles. But Marcy spent much of Shabbat screaming at Zev, who took his sister's stroller hostage and ran in circles around the auditorium with it. For this reason we cut the singing short. Even so, Marcy's broken singing voice could be heard from all over the JCC as she galloped in hot pursuit of her son. Finally, out of breath, she sat down on an empty folding chair and shook her head in defeat.

As we watched Marcy's family drama unfold, I glanced back to the stage every so often. Parker yanked his face from view when he caught me looking. Eventually I gave up, almost forgetting he was there, and after half an hour, much to my relief, Marcy decided she'd had enough. "I don't think Zev's feeling well," she said. "Let's light the Shabbos candles and have the challah and ceremonial grape juice." I had not gotten this far in my Jewish studies at Rollins, so I was lost at the first shalom, lip-synching to blessings I'd never heard, hoping none of my students would catch on.

As the groups sang the prayer to welcome the Sabbath, Parker crept from his hiding place and plopped into my lap. "You're not supposed to cover your eyes while the candles are being lighted," he informed me.

"Why?"

He shrugged. "Just the women do."

As we left the auditorium Parker clutched my hand. "I'm sorry I ran away."

"Everyone needs time alone, I guess," I offered.

"Will you tell my mother? If you do, then I won't earn my sticker for today."

"I'll probably forget before she comes," I said.

. . . .

When it was time for dismissal, Parker pulled on my sleeve as I was helping a few other kids pack up. I looked down, and he asked, "Can I call you Daddy?"

I was surprised. "Why do you want to do that?"

"Because." He shrugged. "I want you to be my daddy."

"But I'm not your daddy."

"I don't have a daddy." He hugged me and then darted outside to meet his mother. On his way out, he bumped into Janet, the plump little woman with thick glasses who had hired me. She patted Parker on the head as he ran past. "How was your first day, Mr. Matt?"

"It was okay," I told her. "What's the story with Parker?"

She sat down and indicated a seat for me as well. "Mom has four kids, and she's raising them alone. They were living out of their van, but they're staying in a shelter now."

"A homeless shelter?" I asked.

She nodded.

"Do they need anything? Can I do anything for them?" I asked. I didn't know what I could do, but I figured that I could at least get him a pair of decent pants at the Gap.

"You probably could," she said, "but they get a lot from us— clothes and toys. People are supportive of their family despite how the children behave."

"What about the father?" I asked.

"Dad's not in the picture. He's not even supposed to know where they are; he was abusive. You have a very special bunch of darlings, Mr. Matt. I should probably tell you about some of the others."

"The others?" I asked.

"Let's see," she said, ticking off ailments on her fingers. "Eight kids with ADD who need meds in the afternoons, two epileptics with antiseizure meds you'll need to carry around, one girl with a fatal allergy to nuts—I probably should have told you that before snack time today—and Parker, the only student who lives in a homeless shelter."

"Why didn't you tell me about these kids?"

"If I had, you never would have taken the job."

I nodded. "You're probably right."

.   .   .   .

When I got home that night, I nearly collapsed. It had been just one day, and I was already weak from exhaustion. I spent the weekend wondering if I should go back the following Monday. Of course I was in over my head—I couldn't even keep straight in my mind which kid couldn't have peanuts—but then I thought about Parker. How none of the other teachers could handle him and how nobody liked him. Not even the other children in the class wanted to play with him. If I left, would anyone give him a chance to be better than the failure they expected him to be?

Something else nagged at me, too, but I couldn't put it into words until Tyler called that Sunday. While talking about my job and Parker, Tyler laughed. "He sounds exactly like how you were at his age."

"I hadn't really thought of that," I said, finally realizing why I'd been so drawn to this little boy. Parker was using my old strategies for getting attention. I had been just as difficult when I was his age, and since I couldn't verbalize my feelings, I often caused trouble. Didn't I refuse to pose in front of the Christmas tree? Didn't I scare off the other kids in my class with weird clothes? Hadn't I been the kid who tipped over the art-supplies table in kindergarten so I wouldn't have to talk about my mother for our Mother's Day celebration?

"No, I expect you hadn't. Maybe you're a much better person for the job than you thought."

"I guess that answers my question about whether to go back. Honestly, I was thinking about quitting."

Tyler paused, and I thought he was about to weave my mother into the conversation, like maybe I wouldn't have to have a job if I just called and worked things out with her. "Listen," he said, "I haven't told you this, but I respect what you're trying to do. I am very proud of you for getting this job and earning your own money. Now, I still think you should talk to your mother—when you're ready—but don't quit because it's difficult. And let me know if you need anything, really."

I thanked him and told him to have a nice week, that I'd talk to him again next Sunday. I was glad that these weekly calls hadn't stopped after my mother and I had fought.

"Oh, wait! I forgot. I'll be in New York in a couple of months for some meetings. How would you like a free trip? I'll get a couple of rooms at the Pierre for the weekend."

The prospect of going home excited me—I hadn't been to New York in almost two years, since I'd helped my grandmother move from Fifth Avenue to Boston—but I worried how it would feel to be home without going to the old apartment. And the Pierre was so close to the building. Still, it would be stupid to turn down a free trip.

"Sure, I'd love to go. Give me the dates, and I can fly out on a Friday and come back on Sunday. I can request days off from work, you know."

"How civilized," he said. He promised to call me the next week with actual dates.

· · · ·

The following Monday afternoon, after deciding that his first entrance into the classroom wasn't dramatic enough, Parker went back out into the hall so he could slam the door. I stood bracing myself in the middle of the classroom. Examining him more closely upon his return, I saw that his pants were stained, remnants of an accident he must have suffered earlier. He showed me a plant in a foam cup that he pulled out of his book bag and said, "His name is Herbert. He has to be close to me all the time."

Parker was already in a foul mood, so I gently explained that if he continued to carry Herbert around, the plant would be crushed. But Parker would hear none of that.

"*All* the time," he repeated. Again the hand gesture of finality. It occurred to me that he was giving me the bird; he just dropped the traditional middle finger to prevent punishment.

"Parker," I said, my smile vanishing, "you make it very hard for me to like you when you act this way. Why don't you tell me what you really need so I can help you?"

Silence.

"I could put the plant on the windowsill so that it gets light," I suggested. "You can pick it up before you leave."

"Someone might steal him," Parker said. "I want to give him to my baby brother. Do you have a plant, Daddy?"

I wanted to tell Parker that anyone could go out, pick weeds in a field, and put them in a cup. Presto, their very own Herbert! But I heard children laughing.

"And what are you laughing at, Sammy Joe?" I asked a little boy nearby.

"I'm Andrew," he said.

"What's wrong with Sammy Joe?" I asked, trying to deflect attention from a delicate situation.

"Are you Parker's father, Mr. Matt?" Andrew asked. A crowd was gathering. *This can't be good,* I thought.

"Well, no. It's just pretend, like a game," I told them.

Parker stared at the ground.

"Like when we play Daddy outside on the playground?" another little boy asked.

This was news to me. "How do you play Daddy?"

Andrew explained that Daddy was a variation on tag. I was only half listening, watching Parker for his reaction. He put the plant on the windowsill.

Later, when we were lining up to go out onto the playground, Parker shoved his way into first place. He grabbed my hand and looked up at me and smiled.

"You can't do that! You can't cut in line!" a boy screamed. "Mr. Matt, tell him he can't cut!"

I remembered telling my own kindergarten teacher how it was

okay to force people out of line, and I smiled. Not the reaction a teacher should have in this situation, but I couldn't help it. I laughed, remembering what I'd said back then: "My grandfather says it's okay to arm wrestle for a place in line. He said it's better than pushing people out of the way like my grandmother does in department stores."

"What are you laughing at, Mr. Matt?" another kid asked. I snapped back to reality, remembering where I was and what I was supposed to be doing.

"Nothing," I said. "Parker, get to the back of the line. You can't just push your way into any place you want."

When we got outside, the other grades were also out on the playground playing tag and shouting for a teacher to come push them on the swings. I quickly lost track of my individual students except for Parker. He went off by himself and sat in the middle of the field. I followed him and sat down.

"They don't like me," he said. "The other kids." He was snatching up tufts of grass, scattering them into the wind. I thought of how he'd destroyed a stack of dominoes on Friday and how he had just pushed his way into line. I didn't doubt it.

I picked up a blade of grass, held it between my thumbs, and blew. Parker watched. "Did you know that I played an instrument?" I asked, making the blade hum. Parker was already searching the field for a piece of grass to blow.

"It has to be perfect," he told me, and I wondered if I had been that anal at five. "What was your dad like?" he asked, not looking up from the ground.

"I don't know. I never met him."

He looked up. "Your mom had to raise you all alone?"

"No, she gave me to my grandparents," I said. Why was I telling this little boy my life story?

"Did you ever see *her* again?"

Sadly, I almost said no, but instead I said, "Yes."

Parker plucked a blade of the grass and crawled into my lap. I put the blade between his thumbs, pushing them together as tightly as I could without hurting him.

"Do you know how to whistle?" I asked.

He nodded.

"Same idea. Put your lips together and blow out."

He tried, but all that came out was the sound of him blowing air.

"You have to be patient," I told him. "Sometimes you have to work the hardest for the things you want the most." When in doubt, pull dime-store philosophy out of nowhere. But Parker didn't seem to care.

When it finally worked, and the blade of grass hummed with him, he settled back against my chest. "Do you miss your mom?" he asked.

"No." But even as I answered, I realized that it had come out too fast. In the middle of that field, all my hurt and disappointment flushed right back into my chest.

Parker looked upset.

"But I do miss my grandparents," I said. "It's hard to grow up without a dad or a mom, but my grandparents were like a mom and a dad to me. I miss them every day."

"I wish you were my daddy," he said.

"You like me, and I like you, too. And I can probably teach you a lot of things. But, Parker, I can't be your father."

"Why?"

"Because I'm nineteen years old. Because I can barely take care of a dog. Because I don't know what it's like to have a dad. Lots of reasons, pick one." I sat there in silence while Parker blew onto the piece of grass.

Having children had never crossed my mind, but that afternoon, sitting with Parker in my lap, I wondered what kind of father I would make. Did fathers and sons sit around in fields bonding over blades of grass? Was that all there was to it, or was there something more? I didn't often think about my own father—my mother had always taken up so much of my emotional energy.

Parker's mood picked up by the end of the day, and as he was walking out to meet his mother, he ran back into the classroom to hug me. "'Night, Daddy," he said. My shirt muffled the sound of his voice.

．　．　．　．

Months went by, and I didn't quit. Even more impressively, Janet didn't fire me. And Parker's behavior started to improve. The other children stopped teasing him and even invited him to play with them. He started saying please and thank you, but he didn't stop calling me Daddy, and I never asked him to. I liked the attention.

In early March, as I was leaving work, I reminded Janet about my upcoming trip to New York. In an effort to fit in, I hadn't told anyone at my job about my past. I was honest about where my mother lived and about not knowing my father, but I didn't divulge anything else. Fortunately, nobody asked for more information. So when I first told her about this trip, she nodded and said that it sounded nice. Not potentially traumatizing, as I was starting to fear it might be.

Janet flipped through her schedule and smiled at me. "I have you covered. If I don't remember before you leave, have a nice trip. Bring me back a key chain."

．　．　．　．

Because he was meeting with a client, Tyler wasn't at the hotel to meet me, but I saw him later for dinner in the hotel's dining room. "Remember to bring a suit," he'd told me earlier that week, and I'd packed my favorite, a black Armani with faint pinstripes. I walked into the dining room and saw Tyler—still tall and handsome— before he saw me. He was at the bar chatting easily with the bartender, and I could tell that the women in the restaurant were checking him out more than the menu.

Turning in his chair, Tyler saw me walking toward him and broke into a familiar smile. "Come here," he said with his slight British accent, and pulled me into an embrace. While we were locked in this bear hug, I could see that people were looking at us, probably thinking that we were father and son. And we could be father and son, too, were it not for my few stray red hairs and the occasional freckle, traces of my biological father's Irish family. Tyler truly was more of a father than my own.

Over dinner he politely steered the conversation away from my family and toward my new life in Orlando. After dessert he said, "There's a new exhibit at the Guggenheim I want to show you, if you don't mind?"

I didn't mind. I loved art and had made up my mind that I wanted to study art history at college. Of course, art in New York can be hit or miss, and I was glad this exhibit was at the Guggenheim and not the Met. I figured if it was a bust, then the loss would be negligible—maybe an hour or two—as opposed to the Met, which could take forever. And then there was the fact that the Met was right across the street from my old apartment.

"Now, tomorrow night," he said, "I have to have dinner with that client I came to meet. Will you be able to entertain yourself?"

"Sure," I said, but I didn't know how I would. I didn't know anyone I felt comfortable talking to in the city anymore. I had made some friends at Rollins who came from New York—people I knew indirectly from my prep-school days—but they were in Florida at school. And it was freezing outside. But I used to walk around New York in all kinds of weather.

So, for old times' sake, I walked down to the New York Public Library, where my grandfather had taught me to love books. I also walked down to FAO Schwarz and almost didn't go inside, because I was still scared the old manager who'd caught me shoplifting Barbies would be there, recognize me, and have me escorted from the premises. There's a great coffee shop around the corner from one of the dozen or so schools I got kicked out of, and I treated myself to some s'mores. I walked through the park down by Columbus Circle. But the one place I did not visit was our old Fifth Avenue apartment.

I promised myself I would not go back there. There was no reason to. Everyone was gone. I didn't even know if we still owned the apartment, so what was the point of walking past? To stir up some memories?

On Saturday morning after breakfast, Tyler asked if I was ready to go to the Guggenheim. "I'll call the car if you are," he said, and I breathed easier. I had worried that he would want to walk and we'd have to walk right past my old building, which would ruin the day. But driving wasn't bad at all. Fifth Avenue is a one-way street running south, so the car would have to go up Madison and loop around.

Tyler bought our tickets at the museum, and then we were walking toward the exhibit, up the large spiral ramp that climbs the endoskeleton of the beehive. Since I began packing for this trip, I'd been wondering if he would try to weave my mother into the general conversation, but so far he hadn't. It made me feel good to know that he respected my choice to maintain my distance from her, even though I knew he wanted us to make amends.

Tyler began talking about the floor art, and though I heard him, I wasn't fully paying attention. My gaze was drawn to a figure making its way down the spiral as we were making our way up. There were a lot of people on the spiral, but this figure was moving at mach speed and with familiar mannerisms. Tyler saw her, too, and stopped talking. This figure's cell phone was glued to her ear, and she was yapping away. Yapping so hard she didn't see the avant-garde floor art, Tyler, or me, though we were standing directly in her path.

I was transfixed, watching this woman. *There's something familiar about her,* I thought. *I must know her.* Her Chanel sunglasses were huge and obscured a third of her face, and I was trying to place her when she walked right into the floor art. Her heel pierced a foam ball meant to symbolize the commercialization of snowmen, and she teetered, rocking on this new addition to her shoe.

"Hang on," I heard her say into the phone, and somehow I knew that her eyes were rolling behind her sunglasses. "I stepped in some shit, and I have to get it off." She reached down to dislodge the ball and threw it over her shoulder. Without a word, she maneuvered through Tyler and me and kept walking down the ramp.

"For a minute I thought that was your mother," Tyler said.

"Oh, my God, you're right," I said, and realized that's why I thought I recognized her. The woman was just like my mother.

Tyler threw an arm around me. "It's the Upper East Side syndrome," he said, and in that moment I desperately missed my grandmother. The Upper East Side syndrome had been her joke. "I tell you, Matthew," she'd said to me many times, "this place is a sham all cooked up in some laboratory somewhere." She'd sigh dramatically before continuing. "Someday someone will discover it and see that I've been right all along." She must have told this to Tyler, too.

When he and I were done at the Guggenheim, it was time for lunch. "Remember you're on your own afterward," Tyler said. "But you get to choose where we go to eat."

I chose a French bistro in the East Eighties, and we had a nice couple of hours. "It's good to see you," he said again. "You look so grown up. I just wish your mother could see how well you've turned out."

"I hope so, but that's because of Grandma and Grandpa, and you know it. They gave me the freedom to make my own mistakes. Without them I don't know where I'd be."

"I know, but you should still think about calling your mother," he said.

"What do we have to talk about now?" I asked. "She was never a mother. She was like that girl at the museum, and I was the floor art stuck to her shoe. She never looked back."

He sighed. "That's not true. It may seem true now, but maybe one day—when you're finally able to talk—she can explain herself."

I didn't want to be rude or push the issue, so I let the subject drop, and the waiter brought the check.

On Park Avenue outside the restaurant, Tyler said he'd knock on my door later after his dinner. He turned north on Park, and I turned south, walking back toward the hotel. I was thinking about how it gets darker in New York earlier than in Orlando, when all of a sudden I turned onto Eighty-fourth and walked toward Fifth Avenue. Adrenaline was pumping through my body with every city block I passed, until there I was, looking at that green awning with my old address. It was freezing, and the wind was blowing as I stared at that awning. I wrapped my coat tighter and felt something in my pocket. It was my camera.

I pulled it out and snapped a picture of the American flag standing in front of the awning, then the address of the building itself. I wasn't sure what, if anything, I'd do with it, but it felt like I had to have that picture. It was strange to be there and not go inside, but I didn't feel scared or sad. I walked to the Central Park side of Fifth Avenue and took a picture of my old room's window. There was someone in there, someone looking out at the park. I wondered: Did whoever it was see me?

I took more pictures before the battery gave out and a menacing gust of wind told me it was time to leave. It was time to move on.

. . . .

I returned to work the Monday after I got back and gave Janet her key chain. She thanked me and gave me a hug, and I went off to get my classroom ready for the kids. Parker was absent that first day, and while I missed him, I was also thankful he wasn't there. The weekend had taken a lot of energy, and I was too tired to deal with whatever stunts he might pull.

But when he didn't show up to school by Wednesday, I walked down the hall to find his older brother. He wasn't in his class, either. I went to the office to see why they were absent.

"They're not coming anymore," said Janet. "Mom took the kids out. She has a sister down in Boca who said the family could stay with her."

"That's great," I said, trying to fake my enthusiasm.

"They'll be in a house now," she said. "Maybe it'll be more stable, too."

I nodded and turned around, walking back down to my classroom.

"Mr. Matt, Mr. Matt!" Andrew bounded over.

"Yeah, Sammy Joe?"

"Mr. Matt, can I water the plant?" he asked.

Parker had decided sometime before that Herbert should be the classroom pet, that he could find something else to give his brother.

"Sure, go grab some water. Then I'll tell you guys all about how plants grow."

Andrew took a cup and ran over to the water fountain, and I asked the other kids to sit in a circle so we could start a lesson. I grabbed Herbert, and as I rubbed my thumb across the surface of the cup, I wondered about Parker's new home and whose son he would be now.

m a t t r o t h s c h i l d currently lives on the cusp of gentrification in Orlando, Florida, with his adopted boxer, Baron—the first dog who's ever loved him. He teaches English and journalism at an inner-city high school. Visit him at www.mattrothschild.com.